DOMINION

Our Heavenly Mandate To Occupy Earth

By Paul Tubach, Jr.

DOMINION

"DOMINION" by Paul B. Tubach, Jr. is licensed under a Creative Commons Attribution-NonCommercial-NoDerivatives 4.0 International License

You are free to copy, share and redistribute the material in any medium, format or language as long as the text and content is not altered or misconstrued. Freely it was received… freely it is given. The licensor cannot revoke these freedoms as long as you follow these license terms:

- **Attribution** — You must give appropriate credit, provide a link to the website, and indicate if any changes were made. You may do so in any reasonable manner, but not in any way that suggests the author endorses you or your use. "Attribute this work" as: Paul Tubach, Jr., www.newearthministries.org.
- **NonCommercial** — You may not use the material for commercial purposes, i.e. not for any private, corporate, nonprofit or otherwise financial gain.
- **NoDerivatives** — If you remix, transform or build upon the material, you may not distribute the modified material. The creation or development of any derivatives, secondary workbooks or manuals from this book is reserved solely by the author.
- **No additional restrictions** — You may not apply legal terms or technological measures that legally restrict others from doing anything the license permits.

Paperback ISBN 978-1-949892-15-4
Library of Congress Number - pending
Produced in the United States of America
New Earth Ministries

Scriptures taken from the New King James Version. Copyright © 1982 by Thomas Nelson. Used by permission. All rights reserved.

Books and other materials are available online through www.newearthministries.org.

March 2018

Table of Contents

A. Introduction	xiii
1. The Plan	1
2. Why Are We Here	9
What Is Man?	12
3. Stewards and Caretakers	17
Why Are You Really Here?	18
Sojourners From Heaven	19
Men Are Like Houses	23
You Are A Soul	26
Living Tabernacles For The Divine	29
Glory Minded Stewards	32
The Born Identity	34
Stewards of Eternity	34
Continue To Live Eternally	39
The Kingdom Suffer Violence	47
Borrowers and Lenders	51
4. The Kingdom Of Heaven	53
Beginning Anew	62
Kingdom In Context	63
Lessons Learned	69
Two Kingdoms In Conflict	71
Spiritual Warfare	72
Principalities and powers	77
5. The Dominion	79
6. Dominion Defined	85
What Is Dominion	86
New Earth Dominion	89
The Domain	99
Heavy And Wordy	100

7. Places In The Kingdom	107
Places With Purpose	110
Temporary Nations and King	113
Vatican, The Nation	126
8. Have Dominion	131
Step One, Two	132
Step Three, Four	132
Step Five	135
Step Six	137
Step Seven, Eight	137
9. Christianity Is Not A Religion	141
10. The Kingdom of God	159
Mone and Meno	166
Transition Through Temporary	168
11. It Don't Come Easy	173
Jesus Our Conquering Redeemer	178
We Are At War!!!	188
Blessed Are The Peacemakers	194
12. End Times	199
13. The Father's Dominion	209
14. The Lord's Dominion	213
My Glory Will I Give	221
Tree Of Knowledge	227
Root Of Understanding	229
Glory Revealed In Man	233
15. Dominion Of Goodness	239
The Raptured Church	246
16. The Lord's Victorious Dominion	249

The Image Bearer Series

2. Listen – How To Hear God's Voice – better
3. Image – The Revelation Of God Himself
4. Dominion – Our Heavenly Mandate To Occupy Earth
5. Understand – What Jesus Wants You To Know – and Why
6. Commission – Created On Purpose For A Purpose
7. Gateways – Manifesting Heaven In The Midst Of Chaos
8. Here – The Kingdom Of Heaven Is

The Image Bearer Series is based upon Genesis 1:26-28: "Let us make man in Our image, according to Our likeness… and grant them dominion."

"Image" explains 'who' the Lord of Heaven and Earth is, "Understand" explains 'why' we are here, "Commission" explains 'what' man is and 'how' we were created by the Lord, "Dominion" explains 'what' we are supposed to be doing, "Gateways" explains 'how' we are to accomplish our earthly mission, and "Here" explains our eternal destination is actually – Earth.

Many tools were given to mankind that enables us to accomplish our mission objective to have dominion over the kingdom of darkness – and we need to comprehend this truth: earth is our 'Here' – and our 'when' is now! How God created us – and why – is directly related to our sanctification and accomplishing our multifaceted mission for being on earth.

Why are you here – and what's your purpose in life? These books will answer those questions.

When I began writing in August 2012, four drafts were completed within a year, then on Sept. 27, 2013, the Lord spoke to me and said: "You are My writer. Now write!" and then the Spirit directed me to finish draft #4 which became the initial book, "*Regenesis: A Sojourn To Remember Who We Are*," released in August 2014. Next, the Spirit directed me to work on draft #3 (in reverse order) and then, on October 24, the Spirit told me, "That is not one book with seven chapters – those are seven books." Thus, I have been writing the Image Bearer series under His anointing by hearing His voice and writing what I am directed to write.

Regenesis helped us discover man's true identity, as spiritual beings that are having a human experience, who were created good and upright by God "in His Own image according to His likeness" (Gen. 1:26-27), whereby we have been blessed with many wonderful grace attributes by the Lord to accomplish all that He purposed for man… since the beginning.

Yet for most of us, we've forgotten who we are… and we've forgotten what we are supposed to be doing. Regenesis reminds us who we are, and now, the Image Bearer series is reminding us what we are supposed to do, how we should do it – and more importantly "why" we are doing it.

The Image Bearer series builds upon that knowledge of truth that mankind was created good so as to become what we were created for: to bear His image and imitate Jesus in every respect according to His earthly example – and operate as His heavenly ambassadors for earth.

> ***The heavenly pattern for mankind is: imitate Jesus.***
> ***The earthly pattern for this world is: become like heaven.***

Who you are is not based upon what you do; "what you do" is based upon "who you are." We get our identity from Jesus. This realigned perspective regarding "who" we are … is to reorient the applecart of faith pointing in the right direction, to focus on Jesus, and to accomplish our primary mission: have dominion on earth – in the name of Jesus.

The numeric order in which the Spirit directed these books: 1,2,8,3,5,4,6,7 was not linear in the least. Let the Spirit guide you in the order He wants you to read them; however, learning how to "Hear God's Voice" is always mission critical to get started on His path for anyone.

On October 24, 2015, the Lord told me to put these books on the internet for free. This was unexpected, and then the Lord whispered to me, "Can you make money on My words? Freely you have received… freely give."

When the Lord tells you what to do, He will also give you His authority, with power and provision, to do all that He commands. We need to embrace this perspective regarding our life on earth in order to understand and comprehend who we are and what we are supposed to be doing. There is much joy and peace living in this manner, and yet… we all make this choice daily to live according to His purpose for His glory – or to live according to our best laid plans. If I can do it – so can you.

Jesus did it, and therefore – "As He is, so are we in this world" (1 John 4:17). I hope you enjoy the Image Bearer series. Grace and peace be yours in abundance.

It's all about Jesus – and God gets the glory!
!

Glossary of Terms and Definitions

These are some keys to help navigate and understand the scriptures.

Heaven – God's throne, God's home and the permanent place where God's glory dwells
heaven – the spiritual reality of God's kingdom and Christ's presence upon earth
Glory – the fullness of God's presence; the fullness of all God is
Shekinah Glory – the manifest presence of God's Spirit
Christ – the manifest expression of God in Jesus, and regenerate (born anew) men
Jesus – the manifested Living God; Lord of heaven and earth; Lord of Glory; Lord of Hosts
Host – army (a very important term omitted in the NIV and some other versions)
Host of heaven – angels; sons of God and our heavenly brethren (Rev. 19:10)
Host of earth – sons of men, becoming sons of God in the regeneration
Man – the generic term for male and female to connote mankind, humanity, etc.
Earth – the planet; one of three permanent places within the kingdom of God
Hell – the absence of God; one of three permanent places within the kingdom of God; the pit
World – temporary realm on earth under the dominion and operational control of Satan
Satan – Prince of "this world" (formerly known as Lucifer before he rebelled and fell to earth)
Sin – the operating system of this world in opposition to God's sovereignty; separation from God; things done that cause separation
Spirit – the operating system on earth under the Lord's dominion; the Holy Spirit; God's Spirit
Grace – attributes of God's character that are freely given to man

Light – a metaphor implying God's truth
Darkness – a metaphor implying evil – and sinful lies of "this world"
Wickedness – taking credit for what God has done
Evil – using God's glory and power to accomplish your personal agenda
Paradigm – the operating systems of sin or "by the Spirit" on earth
Paradise – the earthly realm in oneness with God apart from sin
Dwelling – a temporary place to live
Abode – a permanent place to live (of existence)
Rest – the permanent state of being where God's presence abides (in your heart and in heaven)
Kingdom of God – all places under the authority of Jesus
Kingdom of heaven – a term used exclusively in the gospel of Matthew to describe the kingdom of God as it pertains to earth under the Lordship of Jesus Christ

- Life – the source from which all creation exists, and is made alive, as coming from God through Christ Jesus, who is "the Life" and the "author and finisher" of faith (John 14:6; Heb. 12:2)
- Living – those persons spiritually alive with life, who no longer operate in the shadow of Death while sojourning in earthen vessels that will eventually perish for lack of life
- Alive – the spiritual state of being in existence from God's perspective, even apart from the body, and abiding eternally in communion with God's Presence and Spirit
- Dead – the spiritual state of being in existence from God's perspective, but temporarily separated from Him; the eventual disposition of the earthen body without life
- Death – the spiritual state of being permanently and eternally separated from God; the temporary holding place of unregenerate dead that wait there until the judgment

Introduction

Have you ever questioned how a loving God could allow tragic human suffering and death? Then you need to read this book. God allows it, but God does not cause it. God gave man dominion over earth, and if anyone is to blame, then blame the people that He entrusted to govern this planet – which is you and me.

Thirty years ago, I was ridiculed by someone unacquainted with God's truth about man having dominion over earth. Their bombastic rhetoric rejected any notion that God would entrust man with governance of earth. After all… look at how screwed up everything on earth is. Little did this person understand – God gave dominion to them as well.

Many false spiritual accusations came against the church and believers during the 70's and 80's to ridicule their faith as superstitious. Perhaps this is why I've never heard a sermon about man's dominion over earth – or perhaps the church does not know about man's primary mission on earth… to have dominion in the Lord's name.

We will contrast the term dominion from a Godly and worldly perspective to learn what it is… and what it's not. We will also understand how we, as believers in Christ Jesus, as His disciples and manifest representatives, are to implement the Lord's dominion for earth, and do His will.

As important as this book is to the church and to the saints of God, it is vital to understand the foundational principles within three books in the Image Bearer series before reading Dominion… in priority order: 3) Image; 8) Here; 5) Understand. Not knowing the fundamental basics of New Earth doctrine, which the first century apostles preached, will create some confusion that seems to conflict with many of our doctrines. It's akin to thinking with a Middle-Ages flat-world attitude within a Renaissance round-world mindset. Until we understand "why" man is on earth – from God's perspective – then it doesn't matter how many opinions we listen to.

You were created on purpose for a purpose… because the kingdom of heaven is now at hand!

1. The Plan

Why Fix The World...
When You Can Change It!

The church is about to experience something that it cannot understand, nor will it be able to fully comprehend – without knowledge of the truth provided by the Holy Spirit.

The times and seasons have come to fruition and now the times are being accelerated because, before a new age can begin, this current age must come to a close. The end of the age has been typecast many times over in an effort to help us understand the mystery of God's plan upon the earth; however, this plan has always been known, but the current church model has been unable (or perhaps unwilling) to understand and comprehend the signs and times. Signs are soon to become a thing of the past; times are now coming in order.

For most of us, we have forgotten who we are... and we have forgotten what we are supposed to be doing. Regenesis reminded us who we are, and now, the Image Bearer series is reminding us what we are supposed to do, how we should do it – and "why" we are doing it.

In order to fully comprehend the true reality, we need to go back to the basics of understanding three concepts: dominion, the nature of man, and the nature of heaven. When we understand these concepts, then and only then will we correctly interpret the signs and times that we are living in – as well as the end of the age that has already begun. The tribulation is set to begin, and all the elements are in place. Unless we understand who we are, and completely comprehend our mission, and understand the reality of heaven and earth within one bifurcated kingdom that is destined to operate in oneness again in the regeneration, then we will have no clue what events are about to transpire – and most importantly – why.

Dominion is the reason we are here; it is what we are supposed to do, as well as the reason why we are the way we are. This is our original command from God: have dominion over the earth. But do we understand what dominion means? By now, I'm sure you have heard the false definition by anti-religion individuals who scoff at Christian theology, so here is the definition from a Biblical perspective:

Dominion – is the delegated authority with power given to a subordinate to act on behalf of a sovereign.

"Have dominion" is God's first command to man. We were given the authority and the power to act, but so often is the case, man uses these God-given gifts to accomplish his own agenda, whereby the history of man on the earth has been a constant tug-of-war between dominion and domination. Unregenerate man seems chiefly concerned with his ability to promote himself, as well as peoples and nations upon the earth supporting his agenda. In contrast, the history of man's true nature, as a spiritual being residing upon the earth, has been a biblical history of God's commission to enlist the sons of men as agents of His redemption to usher in a regime change. These two dominions by two radically different people groups create two radically different kingdoms upon the earth, which has created a constant dynamic tension between true faith – and a counterfeit reality. One reality is based upon a lie, while the paradigm of Christ is based on truth: it's all about Jesus and Jesus is the Truth.

Dominion is often preached from man's perspective, but rarely understood from God's perspective. The best way to put the dominion of earth into context is this:

- "And Jesus came and spoke to them, saying, "All authority has been given to Me in heaven and on earth" (Matt. 28:18).
- Dominion of heaven and earth in God's kingdom belongs to the Lord Jesus Christ; "For by Him all things were created that are in heaven and that are on earth, visible and invisible, whether thrones or ***dominions*** or principalities or

powers. *All things were created through Him and for Him"* (Col. 1:16). "Then to Him was given dominion and glory and a kingdom, that all peoples, nations, and languages should serve Him. His dominion is an everlasting dominion, which shall not pass away, *and His kingdom the one which shall not be destroyed"* (Dan. 7:14).

- The Lord God gave the dominion of earth to the host of earth; "Then God said, "Let Us make man in Our image, according to Our likeness; **let them have dominion** over the fish of the sea, over the birds of the air, and over the cattle, ***over all the earth*** and over every creeping thing that creeps on the earth." (Gen. 1:26). "So God created man *in His own image"* (v.27) and we know our Creator's name is… Jesus Christ.

- Adam was put in the Garden of God with dominion given in order to be a caretaker for the earth, but Adam delivered man's dominion to Satan when he successfully tempted Adam in getting him to rebel against God. This is the same dominion that Satan tempted Jesus with: "Then the devil, taking Him (Jesus) up on a high mountain, showed Him all the kingdoms of the world in a moment of time. [6] And the devil said to Him, "***All this authority*** I will give You, and their glory; for ***this has been delivered to me***, and I give it to whomever I wish. [7] Therefore, if You will worship before me, all will be Yours" (Luke 4:5-7).

- Jesus accomplished perfectly the will of the Father and got this dominion and all authority back. "At that time Jesus answered and said, "I thank You, *Father, Lord of heaven and earth*, that You have hidden these things from the wise and prudent and have revealed them to babes. [26] Even so, Father, for so it seemed good in Your sight. [27] *All things have been delivered to Me* by My Father, and no one knows the Son except the Father" (Matt. 11:25-27).

- And now Jesus has given it back to us; "Behold, I give you the authority to trample on serpents and scorpions, and over all the power of the enemy, and nothing shall by any means hurt you" (Luke 10:19).

- And furthermore, Jesus said: "And I will give you the keys of the kingdom of heaven, and whatever you bind on earth will be bound in heaven, and whatever you loose on earth will be loosed in heaven" (Matt. 16:19).

This should help explain the complexity of man's reason upon the earth, as well as our positional relationship and subordinate dependence upon Jesus within a larger context. Our creeds and doctrines have correctly taught us "what" to believe, but they have not taught us the whole truth as to "why."

We were sent to earth to usher in a regime change – from darkness to light! We are world changers sent to manifest Christ's dominion, under His authority with His power manifested through us.

The significance and importance of this truth pertains to our high calling in Christ. For the first 3,775 years, men operated with a limited understanding of dominion, but since the advent of Christ and His resurrection, the dominion of Satan was overthrown, the power of sin and the penalty of death were conquered by His salvation and now we are being redeemed and sanctified in truth by the Holy Spirit. By grace, the dominion was restored to man according to faith in Jesus Christ and now, by grace, dominion is being released through man. For nearly 2,000 years, we have had the authority and the power to alter the course of human history and the destiny of this world in the name of Christ to the glory of the Father, but somehow… our teachings only taught us "what" but not "why" and certainly not "how."

Regardless of the reasons why, the truth was hidden for a season, but now is being revealed at this time by a multitude of revivalists for one reason: global revival. Revival has already begun! The "when" is happening now, but this is neither the end nor the beginning; this is the transition period at the beginning of the end before a new beginning occurs. This current age is coming to a close, a new age is about to begin, and the restoration of all things is coming soon – in which Christ's dominion over the earth with kingdom oneness under the Lordship of Jesus Christ is being manifested as a fresh outpouring of grace and glory through gateways of grace called: disciples of Jesus Christ.

We are living in the greatest time in human history, but it's about to get ugly – very ugly.

In order to understand the new age to come, it is essential to close out the old one. The close of this era of human history will be cataclysmic and tragic because this world is under the control of the Lord's enemies; and the tribulation should be nothing less than cataclysmic, as the birth pangs of a former condition releasing a birthing of this new age in the earth – so that we might do and become something "greater than" within this new paradigm with Christ.

In these present and future times, there will only be two types of people: those who understand – and those who *won't* (sheep and goats). The gospel message of Jesus Christ is very simplistic that borders on sublime magnificence: "You must be born again." There are hundreds if not thousands of implications woven within this kingdom concept, but herein constitutes the truth Jesus taught to initiate revival:

> "Unless a person is born anew from above, they cannot '*oida*' *understand* the kingdom of God." (John 3:3).

The entirety of Christian teaching and heartfelt application hinges upon this declaration by Jesus; man is simply incapable of comprehending spiritual matters unless they are born anew as a working of the Holy Spirit in them to bring spiritual truth with revelation understanding to them. The kingdom of heaven is all around us even now, but it cannot be perceived without spiritual understanding being given to us by the Spirit of Christ.

We were all created in the manner of men, as souls with spirit and flesh; however, Jesus is telling us His kingdom operates according to only one condition: "that which is spirit – operates according to the Spirit" (v.6). Flesh or spirit… the choice regarding which kingdom you chose to serve is yours – and yours alone.

If you live for the flesh, then you will want to gratify the desires of the flesh and give yourself all the credit for your works and accomplishments – but – if you desire to live according to your spirit by the Spirit, then you must thoroughly comprehend that you are a servant follower who hears and understands the Lord's voice and desires to do whatever He tells you to do. In this, it is no longer you doing it – it is Jesus doing it in you and through you – and God gets all the glory.

If you can say, "Jesus did it"… then God gets the glory. Everything else is just chaff and weeds in "the kingdom which shall be destroyed."

There is no longer any reason for Spirit-filled followers of Jesus to be standing in between two ways wondering WWJD; either you are able to give God glory in everything you do (that which is spirit) or you cannot (that which is flesh). Jesus does not judge you and nor does anyone else; you alone will judge yourself in the day of judgment by your thoughts and actions according to the Spirit of truth. There is no need to read further if you have not come to this principle understanding about the kingdom of God. Either you are born again – or you are not. Either you are all in – or you are not. If you do not know if you are born anew, then read Regenesis; by the time you arrive at the end of that book – you will know absolutely – then come back to this point to receive fresh new understanding about the Lord's dominion… and your purpose under heaven.

Have you been born again – or do you believe a theology that says you have been born again?

Being born again is not the same as salvation. Salvation comes by grace through faith after you have been thoroughly persuaded and convinced by the truth that Jesus is Lord of your life whereby you made a confident unretractable profession to live according to the way and teachings of Christ. Being born anew, however, is the

God given grace that enables us beyond basic faith to understand and comprehend the spiritual reality that surrounds us. If the Spirit has not birthed you, then understanding the mysteries of the kingdom and how the kingdom operates will remain a mystery to you. So now, look at the fruit of your life to find the answer, because Jesus only leads surrendered servant followers and disciples who have "entered into" a Divine personal relationship with Him and follow Him by the hearing of His voice! The sojourn you are on is magnificent – yet beyond comprehension – unless you have been born again!

Perilous times are ahead in which no man will be able to save himself; no amount of works, or prestige, or family connections, or religious affiliations, or overflowing bank accounts will be able to protect anyone from the calamity to come. Apart from the Spirit, there is no understanding, and without understanding, there is no hope, and without hope, there is nothing left. Love cannot prevail without hope in the truth! And Jesus is the Truth!

And in the end, three things remain: faith, hope and love – and the greatest of these is love.

Love conquers all! And Jesus is Love Incarnate!

This is not a fear-mongering book; it is a book of exhortation that comes with an eternal message of hope and love – and this glorious hope to which we are called is closer now than when we first believed. Jesus said He would never leave us or abandon us, and He sent His Spirit to guide us into all truth and to help us through difficult times to keep our eyes focused on Jesus, to hear His voice – and to follow Jesus only. There is no other way whereby we are saved.

Man relies upon God to help him, but ever since the beginning, God has been relying upon man to help Him. This is the key to understanding this book: God created man to partner with Him to have dominion and establish the kingdom of heaven upon the earth. We have been given a commission – with authority and power for conquest! This is why you are on the earth and it is your reason and purpose for being here. Who you are is incredibly magnificent! And yet…

It's all about Jesus – and God gets the glory!

"His dominion is an everlasting dominion, which shall not pass away,
and His kingdom the one which shall not be destroyed" (Dan. 7:14).

2. Why Are We Here?

Not long ago, I came across some of the best evangelical literature about the Gospel of Jesus Christ and what we, as Christians, believe as immutable truths and profess by faith. As I was getting ready to attend Sunday service at this church, the Spirit began to reveal something to me; this literature tells us "what" to believe, but it doesn't explain "why." Telling people "what" to believe without comprehending the reasons "why" makes for shallow doctrine – and lacks the spiritual understanding that man needs to be thoroughly convinced in the truth of the gospel.

Understanding the kingdom of God was a principal element of Christ's mission on earth.

This may be the most important of all truths that man needs to discover: why is man upon the earth? We seem to have all been born with an internal drive and motivation embedded within us to make this world a better place, but do we know why? And if our spiritual books teach us to look forward to our eternal reward elsewhere, then why do we still care about earth anyway?

What is earth that man should be mindful of it?

Our doctrines and creeds teach us all about Jesus Christ, His gospel, our faith in Christ and how we implement this faith in real, practical terms so we may live in harmony with one another, but it doesn't explain "why" we are here on earth in the first place. This is the big picture message that I write about – and the simple answer is this: this was God's plan since the beginning.

And His plan hasn't changed. We have been taught in our catechisms to know God, to love Him and serve Him as the reasons behind our faith, and this is great for small children to understand, but it does not answer the larger-than-cosmos question: why man and why the earth? Most of our Sunday sermons teach us Jesus came to save us from our sins so that we may live better lives that are pleasing to Him, to love one another, to edify one another and save others souls alive so that we can all inherit eternal life to be with Jesus in heaven; however, Jesus never promised us heaven… He only said some "shall enter *the kingdom of* heaven" (Matt. 7:21).

Besides, the kingdom of heaven that Jesus came to establish is already upon the earth. [1]

The big picture reason we are on earth is to have dominion over the earth. The Lord created us as "the host of earth" to inhabit earth and He commissioned mankind to have dominion over the earth before He ever formed Adam of the dust. This was His plan for *man and the earth* from day one – and this is still His plan today and tomorrow and forever.

Earth is man's rightful place, our *'oiketerion'* (3613 – *residence*) "principal place, proper domain"[2] and our eternal residence in the cosmos. This is why the sons of men were created by God in the beginning and our reason for existing has never changed. We are the eternal inhabitants of earth whereby we glorify God in the earth as we host His presence and live in communion with God our Creator, Jesus Christ. The complexity of our mission on earth was greatly compromised by Adam's fall from grace in the Garden; however, all men were restored once again in divine fellowship with the Father, by God's grace, through faith in Christ. Now, we can live as we were originally intended to live – as in the Garden, that is, if we choose to declare Jesus the Lord of our life.

Much has happened on earth in the past 5,775 years of the many generations of man since Adam, and much has transpired in the past 1,986 years since the resurrection of Jesus Christ, but during all this time – man's mission on the earth has not changed one iota. Mankind has gotten sidetracked by his tendency to create religious sounding doctrines to maintain a certain status quo upon the earth whereby men are more accountable to one another, but this was never God's intent; we are supposed to live in communion with

---

[1] Read "Here: The Kingdom of Heaven is."
[2] Strong's Concordance.

God and live "out of" His presence within us whereby we are accountable to Him and Him alone as servants of the Most High God.

Somehow, the doctrines of man have erased all mention of the dominion mandate given to him by God whereby his sense of purpose and eternal meaning for being upon the earth has been reinterpreted by theologians and philosophers ad nauseam. The evangelical literature I mentioned did not use the world dominion once as it relates to man; regrettably, this word was used in regard to Satan.

God created the earth for His glory, and He created man for His glory, and then He put man upon the earth to increase and multiply that glory in the earth as His image bearers. Many people may object to this puppeteer notion of God for man on the earth, but this is the truth regarding God's kingdom. And yet, He gave us free will to decide whether we want to participate in His kingdom or not, which is the most generous act of love and kindness any Sovereign has ever offered to anyone thus far on planet earth.

This is His plan for man and the earth whereby the earth was made for man and man was made for the earth; man and the earth were created by God for a purpose and they are inseparable from one another because they were both created as vessels for God's glory… and as vessels for one another.

> "And one cried to another and said: "Holy, holy, holy is the Lord of hosts; the whole earth is full of His glory!" (Isa. 6:3).

Mankind is the host of earth and mankind is inseparable from God and the purposes of God upon the earth – unless He chooses to live in rebellion against God and thereby refuses to believe that Jesus Christ is Lord, Savior, Redeemer and King of kings on earth. Man's eternal purpose in this life… and the life hereafter in the New Earth, is to have dominion over the earth. Man was created for a much higher purpose upon the earth than we can even imagine, but it seems mankind prefers to squabble over small-minded doctrines and small patches of dust despite the fact that the Lord told us we will inherit the Paradise of earth with the treasury of heaven made available to us wherein we shall live forever in His presence – and this, thankfully, will be apart from all the agonies that we experienced in this present life.

We have *all* been called through faith to live in hope, but we have been given a much greater hope to live for on this earth than we have been taught, and now the time has come to lay aside those elementary teachings of Christ and advance into maturity to establish the kingdom of Christ upon the earth that He purposed for us – ever since the beginning of time and creation.

This is the eternal hope whereby we hope: to abide in the Promised Land that we were promised.

Earth is the Promised Land! Man was created to have dominion – and dominion it will be. God's plan for the kingdom involves man, but it is not about man… it is all about Christ in us; and "Christ in us – our hope of glory" is being manifested in us and through us to the glory of God our Father for the everlasting glory of Christ's sovereign reign as Lord and King of heaven – and earth. Amen.

What Is Man?

Perhaps a better question is: Who is man? And where did he come from?

> "What is man that You are mindful of him, and the son of man that You visit him" (Psa. 8:4).

> "What is man, that You should exalt him, that You should set Your heart on him, [18] that You should visit him every morning, and test him every moment?" (Job 7:17, 18)

If man could comprehend what and who he is and where he came from, then our understanding would be enlightened wherein we might thoroughly comprehend our purpose on earth: to have dominion. Who man is and where he came from are two conjoined questions with one similar answer: ***because***… this is the plan of God.

This was not the answer you were expecting, I know, so allow this concept to wash over your mind: "***because***…As He [Jesus] is, so are we in the world" (1 John 4:17). Jesus created us and sent us to earth as His heavenly emissaries and ambassadors with a commission to govern the earth in His name… by hearing His voice and obediently following His example. We are His heavenly representatives sent to do His will on earth. Now, then, follow this train of thought:

- Jesus created us like Him, in *His Own* image according to His likeness (Gen. 1:26-28)
- Men are spiritual beings – a soul with spirit – and our soul is eternal (Eccl. 3:11)
- We existed "in Christ *before* the foundation of the world" (Eph. 1:4)
- God remembers us according to who we are, as being crowned with glory and honor, as existing in His presence even though we cannot remember those former days (Psalm 8; 82:1-8; 139:13-18; Prov. 8:22-31)
- Jesus is our heavenly Example who came to earth to teach us and remind us how we are to live in subordinate authority as servants by hearing His voice and doing His will (Luke 22:27; John 5:19; 10:27: 12:26)
- Jesus is the light of the world – and He commissioned us as "the light of the world" (Matt. 5:14)
- We are to become His disciples, imitate His example and continue to walk according to His truth to usher a regime change on earth (John 8:31, 32)
- We are His servants sent to earth, in His image, in a forward operating capacity, to operate under His authority

and power to have dominion in His name, to establish the kingdom of heaven upon earth – and to bring order to this chaotic and confused world that is under the domination of Satan (Luke 10:19)
- We are stewards and caretakers of His things, to produce glory in abundance and yield this glory unto God (Mark 4:8)
- Yet, we delivered our authority and our glory to Satan by entering into sin, so Jesus came to liberate us from our bondage to sin through sanctification by the Spirit of God (Luke 4:6; 10:22)
- Then Jesus sent a fresh release of His Spirit to teach us truth and empower us to continue our high calling in Christ to have dominion over His enemies in the earth (Acts 1:4)
- Our faithful obedience to Christ will be rewarded according to deeds of righteousness done in the name of Jesus – or punished through disobedience and unbelief (Prov. 11:8)
- Life does not end in death. Our future resurrection in Christ is the promise *with* the Spirit's guarantee of a better covenant wherein our hope of life eternal is guaranteed through faith, as well as our guarantee of greater glory in the New Earth (Heb. 7:22; 8:6)
- Our primary goal, then, as sojourners for one season of eternity on earth, is that we deliver our authority to Jesus as our Lord and Savior, that "should continue to live eternally" (Psa. 49:9) as an extension of our prior existence with God, through faithful obedience to Jesus so as not to forfeit the promise of life eternal or the glory to be revealed in us and through us in the regeneration
- We are sojourners sent from heaven to earth to accomplish a mission: have dominion – and to take back and redeem what the enemy stole from God – but we must also protect our soul and guard the seed of glory placed within us (the pearl of great price) from being corrupted by the cares of this world by the prince of darkness who rules the kingdom of darkness to entice, tempt and deceive spiritual beings (men) into doubt that leads to disobedience and unbelief. There is a heavenly battle between God and Satan; earth is

the battlefield and man's soul is the prize; man is the agent of the Lord's salvation and redemption for the earth, and mankind must trust and serve Jesus, our Lord and Savior. We are servant soldiers sent for conquest and earthly dominion… in the name of Jesus.
- Thy kingdom come, Thy will be done – on earth as it is in heaven!!!

The truth of this message is found within the scriptures, yet it seems few have comprehended the mystery of man upon the earth. The Holy Spirit (aka the Spirit of Truth) is guiding me through this process to write nearly one thousand pages for the Image Bearer series in order to help us understand and comprehend why we are on earth in the first place. This condensed bullet-point synopsis is the result of hearing the Voice of Truth over four years and meditating on His truth to write a New Earth Doctrine that reorients the applecart of faith to point in the right direction… to focus our attention and affections on Jesus only.

The mind of man is the battlefield for earthly supremacy and dominion, which is why the Spirit was sent to sanctify us in the truth, that we may "Not be conformed to this world, but be transformed by the renewing of your mind, that you may prove what is that good and acceptable and perfect will of God" (Rom. 12:2).

Newness, through truth, change and oneness is what our mission on earth is all about.

What is man that God is mindful of him? We are regime changers for the earth – in the likeness of Jesus Christ – and we get our identity and purpose under heaven by being in relationship with our Lord and Redeemer, Jesus Christ, as we host His Presence and Spirit.

> "Not by might nor by power, but by My Spirit,'
> says the Lord of hosts" (Zech. 4:6).

As I often say, It's not about me… it's about He who dwells in me!

It's all about Jesus – and God gets the glory! Amen.

3. Stewards and Caretakers

We were sent to earth as spiritual beings to dwell within earthen vessels: A) to contain something of value; B) to produce an increase; and C) to establish the kingdom of heaven upon the earth. We are heavenly ambassadors and servants that must give an account unto God for those things we were entrusted with to complete our dominion mandate for the earth – whereby we will be judged according to what we did – or didn't do.

> "For if I do this willingly, I have a reward; but if against my will, I have been entrusted with a stewardship" (1 Cor. 9:17).

Are you using your gifts, talents, time, treasure and resources to build your kingdom – or His? In the judgment, we may be asked only one thing: did you properly steward those things entrusted to your care? We are stewards of His blessing, stewards of His favor, stewards of His provision, stewards of His love and grace, and stewards of His glory – and heavenly caretakers of the earth – for the praise of His glory. Were you a good steward of His things?

*We are stewards and caretakers who were sent to tend His garden, and we are being tested to see if we are **taking care of** His things... or **taking credit for** His things.*

What is the biblical perspective of stewardship? Stewardship is translated: *'epitropos'* (2012) "a manager" into whose care "something is committed" in the sense of being given authority and power to operate under a commission (as a manager, guardian, tutor, commissioner); and *'oikonomia'* (3622) "administration" of a household or estate, especially in regards to economy or affairs (*oikos*-house + *nomos*-to parcel out), to operate as an "overseer" who arranges for the proper management of an estate that was entrusted into their care.[3]

---

[3] Definition and terms from Strong's Concordance.

Within this larger context, mankind was commissioned (let, granted, leased, apportioned) a share of the Master's estate and commanded (with delegated authority and power) to have dominion to: A) steward it; B) *'tereo'* – "keep, take care of, and protect from loss or injury;" and C) produce an increase that yields (gives) God all glory in the thing produced. We are not here to produce anything for our personal kingdom; we are here to delight ourselves in the Lord and to "have joy" in service to God by establishing and expanding His kingdom on earth.

It seems many of our doctrines teach us material wealth and possessions are outward indicators of God's blessing and favor being manifested toward us, which is partially true; however, "rain falls upon the just and the unjust alike." Material blessings have more to do with expanding the kingdom of God through us rather than selfishly enjoying the fruit of our labor to build our kingdom while neglecting our purpose under heaven for dwelling on earth in the first place.

Why Are You Really Here?

We are not on earth to live, die and populate heaven, as some of our doctrines seem to indicate; if God wanted spirit-babies, then there are easier ways of creating them other than sending them to earth and putting souls into earth suits. One day, I encountered two LDS missionaries and began asking them this question: why are you on earth? They replied, "We are here to receive a body because God has a body, and when we die we will return home to heaven in resurrection bodies."[4] So I pressed the issue: why are you on earth? And then their doctrines started coming out, so I asked them again in order to help them understand the core reason why we are here. Then they asked me for my opinion (and thus, their minds were open for a moment to receive truth they were seeking): God is in heaven and Satan opposes the kingdom of God on earth, so he wages war in the heavens and on earth for

---

[4] God is Spirit, is invisible and without a body. I proceeded to show them eight scriptures to validate this point and to debunk their false theology. See p. 11-12 in "Image" book #2.

worldwide domination… wherein man is the battleground; we are the conquest *and* the prize! We were sent to have dominion over Satan's domination and redeem the earth.

"But man forgot who he was and what his purpose on earth is. We need to remember!

"We are being tested by the Lord to determine which kingdom we prefer. This body is our life support vehicle *and* the means whereby we are being tested and sanctified – either to walk in the truth and live… or to walk in rebellion and disobedience to die in death. Saints… you are being tested to prove your allegiance to the Lord – either you are training your body to walk in obedience and righteousness as a consecrated holy vessel unto the Lord Jesus – or you are using your body to walk in sin and gratify the carnal cravings of the flesh. The flesh was created with weakness to be subject to the Lord – or to sin. The flesh is merely a vehicle to test our resolve and to choose His Way or any other. So I ask you… where have you placed your trust?

"We are here for a reason – we are here for God's good pleasure and it has everything to do with our eternal purpose: have dominion on earth. We are in a spiritual fight: light against darkness, good against evil, order against chaos, and truth against the lie of "this world" that is in opposition to (anti) Christ."[5]

Therefore, we must remember who we are, who the Lord is who calls us, and why we are on earth. Jesus knew these answers at the age of twelve: "Did you not know that I must be about My Father's business?" (Luke 2:49) Perhaps it's time we come to know this truth as well.

Sojourners From Heaven

As I mentioned in the previous chapter, if we knew why we are here – and understood our reason for being on earth and God's

---

[5] Excerpt copied from "Understand" section titled: "Why Do You Strive?"

purpose under heaven for us, then our perception would become dramatically changed and realigned to embrace a New Earth dominion mindset. The answer to this question, "why are we here" is woven within the pages of this book, but let me ask you another question: how did you get here? If you believe the message thus far that your soul is eternal and you are a spiritual being having a human experience, then how did you get here?

The simplest way to explain how you got here is: **you were inserted into the fabric of time**.

Think about this for a moment. You are an eternal soul that is having a human experience for one season of eternity on earth. Your soul existed in God's presence, then you were inserted into the fabric of time, and following this life you "enter into... the resurrection of life" where the life you had *in* Christ "before the foundation of the world" continues *with* Christ into life eternal.

How were you inserted? If this mystery could be proved beyond the shadow of any doubt, then perhaps the darkness has been pierced. The answer is: we were inserted into the fabric of time, in the fullness of time, according to the predetermination of God, to fulfill our designated purpose under heaven... in the similitude of Christ Jesus. We got here the same way Jesus did!

> "The Holy Spirit will come upon you, and the power of the Highest will overshadow you" (Luke 1:35).

The Holy Spirit overshadowed Mary and she conceived. Even though she was a virgin and man's seed was not involved, she conceived a Child and named Him: Jesus.

This conception was miraculous and supernatural, yet within the realm of the Holy Spirit's activities to advance the kingdom of God upon the earth, this was... spirit normal. As spiritual beings, we have lost this connection with the miraculous and the supernatural – even though all of us got here in the exact same manner – by the overshadowing of the Holy Spirit.[6] In this regard, your parents are the instruments the Lord used to insert you into the fabric of time on earth within that miraculous instantaneous moment we call: conception. This is why we must honor our parents because they are the means which God used to insert you as a created being into His creation – at just the right time! And this is why we must also reverence conception!!!

You were inserted into the fabric of time – and you are here on earth for a specific purpose. The elements of your physical being that were given to you (eye, hair and skin color; body type, intellect, character and spirit) are all heavenly grace gifts from God to help you accomplish your earthly objectives; and you were inserted into a geographic location within a certain culture to usher in a regime change within this culture at this specific time. And yet… your purpose on earth is even more profound than this! Jesus created you to become like Him and manifest His Presence and Spirit within you – within everything you think, say and do! Your *reason* for being here is very intentional, and yet – your *purpose* remains somewhat of a mystery until you enter into a divine relationship with Jesus and ask Him: who am I?

    Lord Jesus, what is Your will and purpose for me?

We get our true identity from Christ by abiding "in" Christ. "Who" you are really doesn't matter; who you are with "Christ in you" is all that ever matters.

As I often say… "It's not about me – it's about He who dwells in me."

---

[6] Some people may reject this concept as something attributed solely to Jesus, so read "Image" in the Image Bearer series to understand and comprehend how and why our reality on earth was manifested *and* exemplified by Jesus. Everything He said and did serves as our heaven-sent example regarding: who we are, why we are here, how we got here, how to live and – more importantly – what we should be doing while we are here on earth.

To discover our true identity, we must "enter into" Christ and abide "in" Him to understand who we are – and comprehend our mission and purpose in life as we dwell upon a planet spinning 1,000 miles per hour orbiting 67,000 miles per hour through the cosmos just 90 million miles away from a nuclear fireball. The supernatural is happening all around us – and, by grace, the miraculous is happening within us as well.

Who you are within the kingdom of God is phenomenal and fantastic! The problem, it seems, is we have believed a great many lies from the enemy about who we are, who the Lord God is – and why we are here. If the enemy can keep the focus of our attention and affection on anything other than Jesus and the kingdom, then our purpose under heaven has become misguided.

Perhaps the easiest distraction by the enemy is to focus our attention on: self. We seem to be obsessed with outward appearance as our primary indicator of personal self-worth wherein we judge and denigrate other people based upon how we perceive them physically – and yet God dwells in them the same as He dwells in you. The enemy will deceive us and cause us to judge others by tearing one another apart in bigoted ignorance for this reason alone: God dwells in everyone.

> "There is one body and one Spirit, just as you were called in one hope of your calling; [5] one Lord, one faith, one baptism; [6] one God and Father of all, who is above all, and through all, ***and in you all***" (Eph. 4:4-6).

The enemy will deceive us with many false narratives in an attempt to destroy the earthen vessel God placed us in – as well as the earthen vessels of others within whom God dwells. For this reason, then, I transition our discussion from the eternal glory that resides within man, to being a good steward and caretaker of the earthen vessel He formed around each one of us… for which we must also give an account.

Men Are Like Houses

> "What house will you build for Me? says the Lord,
> or what is the place of My rest?" (Acts 7:49).

Consider your life (in the abstract) as a spiritual house that you are building for God's glory. Do you build it so large that you are unable to finish construction because you didn't calculate the cost? Or has it become so large you cannot manage it whereby it falls into disrepair? Or do you build it so small that it cannot grow and expand to accommodate an increase in provision through faith? Your house may stay small because you do not want to look like a foolish builder who did not have vision and big dreams – yet failed, however, to plan for miraculous increase.

The structure of your house represents the plans you have for your life. You can do whatever you want with this life, but your life is not your own. The materials you are building with and the very substance of your life itself all belong to the One who owns the earth and the land and the fullness thereof. You are just a steward of "the house." You are a steward and caretaker of His things. It is yours (theoretically) for as long as you inhabit it, and then it shall belong, once again, to the One who gave it to you. "The earth is the Lord's." "You are not your own."

> "Or do you not know that your body is the temple of the Holy Spirit who is in you, whom you have from God, and *you are not your own*? [20] For you were bought at a price; therefore glorify God in your body and in your spirit, which are God's" (1 Cor. 6:19, 20).

If we could perceive our reality as temporary, and mankind as sojourners on earth… and as renters and caretakers of God's things, then life on earth would make more sense.

Regardless of what you do or where you live, it costs you something in order to stay where you live and survive on a daily basis. You may be a subsistence person who is able to get by on a modicum of resources; you may be a meager person with a simple shelter that protects you from the elements and weather as you tend a small garden to trade resources with others; you may be a modest person with a nice house and furnishings, or a professional person with a generous income to live very comfortably, or you may be an extravagant person with an outrageously large mansion and luxurious lifestyle. Regardless of where or how you live, it will always cost you something. Therefore, calculate the cost before you begin building your house of faith.

It seems the Lord is very interested in what we build, how we build – and why! The Lord is a nation builder… and we are builders of houses… and He wants us to be good stewards and caretakers of His things. You may think your things belong to you, but in reality (i.e. the reality of God's kingdom) everything in heaven and on earth belongs to God, as well as the fullness thereof. Nothing you have or own belongs to you; you are only using it for a short period of time while you sojourn on this earth – and then it will belong to another – or it turns back into dust.

> Jesus said: "Take heed and beware of covetousness, for one's life does not consist in the abundance of the things he possesses" (Luke 12:15).

You are a house that belongs to God. The kind of a dwelling you build to host the Presence of the Divine is predicated upon "who" the Lord predestined you to be. A wise builder always calculates beforehand what to build based upon the intended use by the occupants and the purpose designated by the Architect, but if you don't know who you are or what you are supposed to be doing, then how can you be classified as a wise builder?

Is your house too large? If it is, then reduce it and make it smaller, or invite others under your roof to share the bounty. Is your house maintained poorly? If it is, then start caretaking it. Is your house overly maintained? Then spend more time loving others – and less time window-dressing and painting to impress others. Are you worried about robbers, rust and moths? Then pray often, live in peace, and accumulate only what is necessary to live a good moral life. Do you love your house to satisfy every whim and fancy, or do you hate your house and could care less if it burns down or is washed away in a flood? Is your house built for vacation, or recreation, or is it a non-stop workshop?

If you think *we* are still talking about *buildings*, then you need a paradigm shift.

We are talking about the "domain" the Lord has entrusted into your care that you are responsible for – which also includes your physical house: i.e. your body. We need to see ourselves as shareholders, tenders, caretakers, stewards and managers of God's things in His dominion who are creating, tending and taking care of designated places, persons and communities through whom we accomplish God's will to establish the kingdom of heaven upon the earth. Your house is one component of your "domain" the Lord entrusted to you as a gateway through whom God is releasing heavenly things upon the earth – for the praise of His glory.

Managers knowingly understand they do not own what they manage; however, they expect to receive a return of the proceeds (as recompense) for their successful and prosperous management of those resources on behalf of the owner. They get a reward for their efforts, both good and bad, depending on whether they were faithful and diligent, or corrupt and lawless with their master's resources. And our life on earth is built around this Divine principle.

Can you see yourself in a different light? Everything you are making and saving and striving for will last only a few moments and then you will be rewarded in eternity for your faithfulness as a steward, manager and "shareholder" of His things. It doesn't matter what you did or what you made according to the flesh that glorifies self; what matters is: what heavenly good did you do with the Lord's things He entrusted to you while you were on earth? Did you work to establish His kingdom – and give Him all glory – or did you produce an increase to build your kingdom?

Who you are dictates what you do – which pertains to Whose you are. You can do all the right religious stuff in an attempt to be pleasing to God, but if you don't acknowledge God as your Source of everything you are – and as your Provider for everything you possess, then you are just a clanging cymbal. ***Either you are a faithful steward or a worthless servant***! Are you doing your Master's business or are you building your own kingdom… having forgotten what the true kingdom of heaven on earth – *and within you* – is all about?

Ask the Lord to open your eyes and to speak to you regarding which type of house He wants you to build and steward for Him? Your tabernacle (soul) is primary; the outer house is secondary.

> "Unless the Lord builds the house, they labor in vain who build it; unless the Lord guards the city, the watchman stays awake in vain" (Psa. 127:1).

If you do not see yourself in these examples, then you are probably a faithful steward. Hooray! You perceive your house as something that you can move away from and leave behind without grieving over it – or any stuff related to it. It is neither too large nor too ornately furnished that if you had to move, you could get up and go tomorrow. Large or small is irrelevant; having and possessing is an illusion; everything belongs to the Lord. Build the house the Lord wants you to build – and then be a good steward and caretaker of His things.

And yet…

You Are A Soul

… and your eternal soul belongs to you (Psa. 49:9).

Think of all the detrimental things you do to your house. Do you overfeed it, starve it, pump it full of chemicals, deprive it of healthy nutrients, sit around all day, ignore preventative maintenance visits to the doctor, disregard early warning signs of serious illness, cut it, smoke it, drown it, jack it up or dumb it down? Do you take quick-fix pills rather than change your lifestyle or behaviors? Listen, we all have pain and illnesses and we deal with it differently, but how you deal with it has a direct bearing on how you perceive the Lord... who gave your earth suit to you.

Some illnesses[7] happening to your body may be indicators of what is spiritually going on inside your house according to the manner in which you care for and tend your soul.

What kind of things are you putting in your house? Are you filling it with good and noble and trustworthy things, or are you filling it with garbage and unright things? As they say: you not only become what you eat, you become an outward manifestation of the things you consume – physically *and* spiritually.

We are still talking about man as being a house, not just the outside organic carbon-based shell, but as a complete building with rooms and furnishings with the atmosphere of God dwelling within our soul as well. What kinds of things are you putting into your house? Are you watching graphically violent TV shows, perhaps occult shows with vampires, zombies, witches or other grim things? Are you listening to nightly "negative fear-based news" about murder and mayhem in the streets? Let's compare this with a cooking analogy: would you put gasoline in pudding or dirt in your desert? What is it that you are doing, day after day, to either sanctify or pollute your soul?

You are a spiritual being having a human experience, but some of us are contaminating our vessels with every ungodly, vile and filthy thing. Your soul is in distress and this is evidenced by the

---

[7] Illnesses represent issues effecting man, including feelings caused by diseases which are pathological conditions negatively affecting the body and organs, and also includes feelings caused by spiritual conditions of the soul.

manner of drugs we take in order to combat self-inflicted diseases[8] like depression, anxiety, fear and rage. Prescription medicines cannot fix these problems; they just mask the symptoms or minimize them. For example: I was erringly diagnosed with sleep disturbance and prescribed medicines that (secondarily) created insomnia, but I foolishly keep taking them at higher doses for 15 years and became addicted to them... and then the side effects began to appear, which became worse than the original problem I started with. Rather than take another med to counteract that side effect and another one to counteract those side effects, what do you suppose was my next proper course of action? For me, it required transitioning off the meds to return my body to a previous state of balance and then address the original problem. My issue, like many of us, was this: I had manifestations of problems in the body that were not physical; they were spiritual. My soul was in angst with anxiety! My soul was not at rest!

We are spiritual beings and our physical issues may be soul related. In this case, who would you go see for a proper diagnosis: a medical doctor for the body or a spiritual physician for the soul? Let me encourage you to pray and seek the Lord for guidance because He created you and He is the Great Physician. Trust Him. He can put all your broken and unbroken pieces together again and He can heal whatever needs to be healed, so ask Him what He thinks you should do. He really does love you and cares for you and wants you to seek His counsel in these matters.

Perhaps we should inspect our attic before we replace the furnace.

> "Be transformed by the renewing of your mind,
> that you may prove what is that good and
> acceptable and perfect will of God" (Rom. 12:2).

---

[8] "Disease refers to the medical establishment's perspective; sickness refers to society's perspective; illness is the way a patient perceives their condition;" University of Ottawa (SIM) curriculum.

We are renters living in leased houses, and we are vinedressers granted vineyards to manage for the owner while He is away.

> "Hear another parable: There was a certain landowner who planted a vineyard and set a hedge around it, dug a winepress in it and built a tower. And he leased it to vinedressers and went into a far country" (Matt. 21:33).

Our body is temporary. Everything of "this world" is temporary. Our soul is all we possess in this life and the next. We can do whatever we want to these houses, and we will be held accountable for our stewardship of them, but what you do with your soul determines where it will abide eternally!

Living Tabernacles for the Divine

These bodies are houses with an inner tabernacle (the most holy place). These bodies do not belong to us; we are borrowing them in order for God to see what we put in them (our storehouse), what we produce through them (for His glory) and, most importantly… if we will establish a permanent inner room for the Lord to abide within us. If a permanent dwelling place (abode) for the Lord has not been established by us, then our godless house is expendable.

As stewards of these bodies – we can dishonor them; we can disrespect them; we can abuse them; we can abuse others with them; we can control and manipulate others with them; we can defraud and cheat others with them; we can compromise the health and vitality of others; we can starve them; we can freeze them; we can leave them exposed and naked; we can dress them ornately and fatten them with delicacies; we can festoon them with jewels, precious gems, paints, perfumes, glitter, braids and whatnots. We have been given earthen bodies for a season and can do whatever we want to them – and this is one way we show our heavenly Father what we think of Him in regards to the way we steward this body – which belongs to Him.

Death merchants have an interesting spin on the manner in which we take care of and honor the human body after we die. We purchase expensive coffins with all the finest ornamentation for your body which you don't even get to enjoy – and then they use your money to do this to you. They dress you up in a suit or dress that probably doesn't fit – or else they bought one (with your money) to make you look presentable. They gave you shoes – for whatever reasons I fail to comprehend, since no one ever sees the bottom half of the casket and I doubt you will use them. They purchase lots of fresh cut flowers (with your money) that die alongside your dead corpse. Add to this the music, candles, incense, the celebration of life programs with your picture on the cover and a brief description of who you were and what you did. In all this, God is not impressed; He knows "who" you are from the inside out and "what" you did for Him. Then you are driven in a special vehicle to a permitted cemetery where you are placed in a concrete bathtub with a concrete lid six feet down with a monument overhead that reads: rest in peace. Then we memorialize this moment with a large, engraved granite tombstone that tells others all the particulars so ancestry buffs can find out their lineage 100 years from now. Yup, this is the spot of your eternal rest. Before the dirt has settled over you, the stewardship of your former house by others becomes just as controlled and meticulous in the afterlife as it was managed in life. But where do you see your life in this specific instant of time? Right now, where do you see yourself in this picture – apart from the body? If you are reading this, then your afterlife has not yet happened, so, where do you see yourself? If you do not know where you are… while all this is taking place, then perhaps you should go find out before you read another word.

We spend more time, money and effort taking care of the house… with little regard for our soul.

We all need to take time and reassess who we are in order to consider and reprioritize what we are doing that matters most. Is what you are doing now going to last for all eternity? Since you cannot send it ahead, then it all stays behind; however, works of righteousness done in the Lord's name that give glory to Him will be carried forward into eternity and placed into your eternal account as your treasure and true riches in heaven's storehouse.

Will any your worldly works survive the test of time? No! Therefore, I challenge everyone – be who you were preordained to be and do what you were predestined to do.

Have you ever heard those eulogies that say, "their time was cut short" or "too soon" or "there was never enough time" or "there was so much to look forward to before this happened" or other laments about life being too short? What is time anyway? Can eternity define it? Yes, eternity has constrained it, and God created time so that we could keep track of what we did and when, but in the end, we are often too rushed to enjoy life and yet somehow blame time for our failure to experience the joy and fullness of it? What are we focusing our attention on?

It was never my intention to make a mockery of life by denigrating the dignity of death, "for the end of a thing is better than its beginning" (Eccl. 7:8), but my point of this is: we pour all our effort into this life with little regard for life eternal. We are poor caretakers of our soul!

The Parable of the Unjust Steward was the Lord's way of teaching us to consider where we are going after this life… and to plan ahead! Jesus "praised" the unjust wicked servant who had more sense than sons of light to plan ahead – because he store-housed goods of unrighteous mammon in the place where he was going (which wasn't a good place; see p. 68). If you do not know where you will spend eternity… and you do not know what you will be doing when you get there, then how on earth are you planning your steps according to faith if you do not know what you need to plan for? We oftentimes like to think we are being faithful, but if we do not know what we are supposed to be doing… then how can our works be considered faithful, let alone righteous?

> "He who is faithful in what is least is faithful also in much; and he who is unjust in what is least is unjust also in much" (Luke 16:10).

We care more about satisfying our cares in this life than planning ahead for life eternal.

You did not come into this world with anything in your pockets. We exist as a compound of various elements which all came from someone or something else.

Our earthen vessels were loaned to us and we are simply borrowing His earthly elements (hydrogen, oxygen, carbon, potassium, etc) for this short season on earth in order to do His business for the limited days we are alive in the flesh. But another life will be lived after this one ends. Meditate on this... because that life will be experienced eternally.

Glory Minded Stewards

> "The Father loves the Son, and has given all things into His hand" (John 3:35).

Jesus glorified the Father and the Father is glorified in the Son (John 13:31; 14:13; 17:1, 5).

This is the heavenly example that we are to follow: love God, glorify God and He will glorify Himself in you and through you – and will give all things into your hands. So, now, what manner of men ought you to be? What manner of spirit ought you to be? What manner of life ought you to live so as to dignify this moment in human history with your devotion to Christ as you host God's presence within you? *What* you are and *what* you do is oftentimes window-dressing; *who* you are "in Christ" is what matters most!

The glory of the Lord will be revealed in you and through you, through faith, to the praise of His glory! However, God is not impressed by all the things we make and do, but God is glorified by your acknowledgement that He did it to you, for you, in you, with you and through you. Amen!

Before power is released through you, glory must be revealed in you – that gives glory to God.

The *"who"* within you desires life eternal, but the worldly man clutters their existence with the multitude of many cares cramped into small calendars – with a box around each day. We have relegated our precious time to lifeless clocks and boxes. We have vigorous schedules to keep, but we rarely take time to breathe the fresh anointing of the Spirit. We have become more concerned with "doing" than "being" which is the trick of the enemy… to keep us so busy that we lose focus of our mission parameters and, thus, prevail against his kingdom. Your presence in this life will be held accountable to one thing: stewardship. In that day, we must all give an account of what we did (faithful or unfaithful) in the execution of our assigned duties and responsibilities. Did you know Jesus? Did He know you? Did you learn to love as you were commanded to? Did you live according to His will – or yours?

In that day, when we pass from this life to the next, there will not be a long eulogy or a list of accomplishments on the other side. The only deeds that matter to Jesus are those with His glory attached to it. ***If His glory isn't in it, then I don't want it***!

All of our moments and experiences on earth may be reduced to just one phrase: what did you do with the things I entrusted to you? Or perhaps: did you learn to love? Do not love this world, which teaches us irreverent definitions of love; therefore, walk in the love of God. God is love, but if you do not know God, then how can you possibly know what love is? How do we know what anything is apart from wisdom and understanding that comes to us by the Spirit of God? God loves you, and yet… you doubt... so how is it possible you know anything about love apart from Jesus who is Love Incarnate? If you need to take a couple moments to meditate on this truth, go ahead. This book will still be here when you get back. If you need to take the rest of the afternoon to go for a walk outside in order to contemplate this truth, go ahead. Most employers understand what a mental-health break is. If you need to take the rest of the week or the remainder of the month or perhaps an entire year to spend time with God to restore your relationship with Him, don't you think this eternal relationship is worth it? Indeed, it is. God says that His thoughts toward you are precious and more numerous than the grains of sand on the beach. He loves you and wants to spend quality time with you. Fifty minutes on Sunday is disingenuous to the One who loves you and gave His life for you. God is not impressed.

The Born Identity

We were all born into this world – but if you want to live eternally, then you must be born again into the kingdom of heaven by the Spirit of God.[9]

We do not get our identity from what we do, things we have or institutions we belong to. Who you are – is found in Christ alone. We discover our true identity "in Christ" by hosting His presence and being in communion (oneness) with Him. Half the battle we face on earth is remembering who we are; the other half is remembering who Jesus is. Once we remember who we are from God's perspective, we can get back "to doing our Father's business."

Stewards of Eternity

> "God placed eternity in our heart" (Eccl. 3:11)…
> "that your soul should continue to live eternally"
> (Psa. 49:9).

We are spiritual beings that are having a human experience for once season of eternity on earth.

---

[9] Born again (or anew) was said by Jesus as the means whereby we are birthed by the Spirit of God to comprehend spiritual matters and understand how the kingdom of God operates (John 3:3-8).

It seems being a good steward and caretaker also involves making preparations for life eternal – through deeds of righteousness. But – what is life eternal – and where do we wait before "the Day of Christ" when we must stand before the judgment seat of Christ to give an account of what we did and didn't do? Our doctrines teach us we go to heaven when we die, but this is a false heaven theology. Heaven is not a courtroom used in the Day of Judgment; Heaven is God's throne. Hades (not to be confused with Hell) is the place where the resurrection of life occurs.

> "… those who have done good, to the resurrection of life, and those who have done evil, to the resurrection of condemnation" (John 5:29).

> "I am He who lives, and was dead, and behold, I am alive forevermore. Amen. And I have the keys of Hades and of Death" (Rev. 1:18).

Hades is the temporary holding place for those who professed faith (believed) in Jesus and are waiting for the resurrection of life, and then the judgment of all stewards will commence by separating sheep from goats… where obedient sheep are rewarded according to deeds of righteousness… and disobedient goats are sent into outer darkness. If this contradicts what your tradition teaches, then read Chapter 6: "Where Do We Go From Here" in book #7: "Here: The Kingdom of Heaven Is" to learn about fourteen places within the kingdom of God where people go based upon their deeds done on earth. Our eternal destination can be complicated, but… to keep it simple… simply do what Jesus said:

> "My sheep hear My voice, and I know them, and they follow Me" (John 10:27).

Herein is the greatest difference between the modern church and the first century church: they listened to the voice of the Lord. They ~~wanted~~ desired to follow Jesus and risked everything to become like Him… as one of His disciples… as authentic obedient sheep, but today… we have a great many goats strutting around in sheep's clothing saying they believe things about Jesus and claim salvation without truly believing "into" Christ and becoming a true follower and disciple.

When you follow Jesus and do what He tells you by hearing His voice, then you will be rewarded for righteous deeds in faithful obedience to Jesus. Righteous deeds, in this respect, gives glory to God in everything you think, say and do. We do not follow traditions, denominations, sacraments, religious doctrines or anything else; we must follow Jesus only!

> "O Death, where is your sting? O Hades, where is your victory?" (1 Cor. 15:55).

This life is just a shadow and foretaste of life eternal on earth, but our doctrines do not even teach us how to prepare for life beyond our initial salvation from Death to life (into Hades) – or our just reward from Hades into life eternal in Paradise. If you are not preparing for life eternal in Paradise right here and now, then what on earth are you doing?

> "… by so much more Jesus has become a surety of a better covenant" (Heb. 7:22).

"Once saved always saved" through faith in Christ is the initial promise (step one: our surety) of salvation *from Death* (the place for those unworthy of judgment) *to life* (the place for those worthy to receive judgment and recompense); however, if you refuse to "hear His voice" and the sanctification of your faith (which constitutes a full faith conversion to turn away from this world to obediently follow Christ) is compromised by disobedience, then life eternal (step two: the guarantee by the Spirit) can be forfeited by you and your eternity now resides in outer darkness (which will be explained in Chapter 7). Life eternal is the Paradise of God for good and faithful stewards, not lukewarm complacent unsanctified mediocre goats.

The Old Covenant existed with many promises, yet Jesus instituted a New Covenant with better promises that are guaranteed by Him as the surety (initial earnest payment and redemption) of this better covenant... *and*... He sent forth His Spirit to also serve as a guarantee for this covenant for those who profess allegiance and discipleship obedience to Christ whereby they will receive the promise of resurrection into life eternal... by the Spirit. The word "surety" (*egguos*-1450) represents something a bondsman (in this case, Christ) pledges as "bail who personally answers for anyone, whether with his life or with his property."[10] Jesus offered Himself as a living sacrifice to post bail on your behalf to save you from Death, but now we must "work out our salvation with fear and trembling" under the guidance and tutoring of the Holy Spirit to sanctify us and prepare us for works of righteousness... in the name of Jesus Christ.

The most important thing you will ever do in this life and the life to come – is to gain the assurance of life eternal! This blessed assurance and certainty comes only through faith, though not as the faith of your fathers in obedience to any religion, but rather... with fullness of understanding, having been thoroughly persuaded and convinced by the truth of the Gospel that results in having a personal relationship with Jesus. Faith is *not* something that you believe, have or profess; faith is *not* teachings or doctrines of any particular denomination; faith *is* "entering into oneness" with Jesus as your Lord, Master and Savior to live according to His way as He instructs you by hearing His voice. ***Faith is not what you believe – but doing what you believe is the truth.*** If you have not entered into oneness "with" Christ that allows Jesus to live in communion with you – and to Sovereignly rule and reign through you, then by faith... you believe things about Christ that are worthy of (step one) salvation... yet may not understand that life eternal ***abides "in" Christ***.

By faith, we claim Jesus dwells in us – but are you established "in Christ"?

---

[10] Strong's Concordance.

Faith is not what you believe... faith is living obediently according to what you believe is true!

The world's system has turned the reality of salvation upside down to create confusion in our mind. When you "enter into" faith with Jesus as your Lord and Master, it is imperative that you follow Him! In order to make sure there is no turning back, the scriptures teach us to crucify the old man (your former self) that yearns for the things of this world that keeps you held captive in bondage to sin, lawlessness, and those sinful passions that are hostile to Christ and the kingdom of God. You cannot keep living two lives – with one foot in the world and one foot in the kingdom. If you claim salvation by faith, yet continue to live as a slave to sin – then the salvation message has been compromised and life eternal may be forfeited by your disobedience.

What does the Bible, our book of faith, teach us? Through faith, we become a new creation (2 Cor. 5:17); the old man has passed away when we have been born anew. When we believe this truth to live by faith (which may take time to fully grasp and implement), then we have passed from Death to life. The old man is rendered obsolete and no longer exists to crave the cares of this world, so what happened to it? It was crucified with Christ on the cross.

> "I have been crucified with Christ; it is no longer I who live, but Christ lives in me; and the *life* which I now live in the flesh I live by faith in the Son of God, who loved me and gave Himself for me" (Gal. 2:20).

The old man that lived in hostility toward Jesus in the flesh according to sin must die before life can begin anew in spiritual newness according to the Spirit. Why? Unless the old man dies and turns away from sin, it will continue to crave sin and the cares of this world. It is unscriptural and spiritually impossible to live in lukewarm mediocrity *and* claim eternal salvation by living in sin. The operating system of this world (sin) is diametrically opposed to the operating system of the kingdom of heaven (Spirit). You cannot live in both kingdoms, so "Choose this day whom you will serve... but as for me and my house, we will serve the Lord" (Joshua 24:15).

> "That which is born of the flesh is flesh, and that which is born of the Spirit is spirit" (John 3:6).

You MUST be born of the Spirit to understand the kingdom of heaven and enter life eternal.

The new man raised in baptism through repentance is raised in resurrection newness with Christ Jesus. Your new life in Christ (which resides with your soul and spirit) converted (turned away) from the operating system of sin in this world and now seeks to live according to the operating system of heaven by the Spirit of God dwelling in you.

The old man focused on deeds of the flesh to glorify sin, but the new man born of the Spirit must focus on Jesus and glorify God.

Your born identity in this world is temporary – but your born anew identity in Christ to live according to new covenant truth... will transform you by the renewing of your mind by the Spirit of God to operate according to the kingdom of God whereby He establishes you as a new creation "in" Christ. The new man in Christ walks in liberty and freedom in the Spirit and must not forfeit life eternal by returning to disobedience in sin, in order that "you should continue to live eternally" (Psa. 49:9).

Continue to Live Eternally

Through faith in Christ – your beginning anew is when eternity begins anew – for you. Eternity doesn't happen after you die. Eternity has been happening around you and within you since before you were even born. This worldly system has turned the reality of eternity inside out and wants you to believe your hope in the eternal is far away in the outer cosmos, but in reality, eternity has already been hidden in your heart (Eccl. 3:11).

The worldly system has also turned the reality of salvation upside down.

Salvation through faith in Christ is our surety (Heb. 7:22)[11] and *initial down payment* (with the promise of the Spirit to follow as a guarantee; Eph. 1:13, 14) as we continue in faithful obedience to Christ as His disciple. If we do not honor our covenant agreement with Jesus to satisfy the promissory note, then our covenant reward is forfeited. If we refuse the sanctification of the Spirit, then we forfeit our precious guarantee. Salvation, in this regard, is conditional "if-then" based upon our continued obedience to follow Jesus, hear His voice and walk in the truth.

We have Christ's surety (the certainty of salvation from death to life) as the initial payment, yet we must continue in faith to fulfill our promissory obligation, with the Spirit of Promise dwelling within us to change us and transform us into the image of Christ – which is our covenant agreement with Him. Jesus calls to us and says, "Follow Me!" This is not an invitation… this is a command! We have been given a promissory note (a redemption coupon) to redeem our soul out of Hades; however, even though you may have the redemption coupon in hand, goats dressed in sheep clothing are easily recognized by Jesus for who they are, as hypocrites, pretending to look like sheep. Test your faith and ask Jesus to show you the truth about what you believe, what you must do to be restored to Him, and what you must do to continue "in" Christ.

> "If you abide in My word, you are My disciples indeed" (John 8:31).

Through faith in Jesus, we are saved by grace. This is our initial salvation and guarantee of escape from Death to life; however, we

---

[11] Surety defined as: 1.) security against loss or damage or for the fulfillment of an obligation, the payment of a debt, etc.; a pledge, guaranty, or bond. 2.) a person who has made himself or herself responsible for another, as a sponsor, godparent, or bondsman. Source: Dictionary.com.

"must continue to live eternally" (Psa. 49:9) by "entering into" life eternal "in" Christ Jesus by surrendering the old man. What does this mean? You can only live one life at a time; you cannot enter life eternal with an old man that merely believes through faith, as if believing in Jesus is all you need and now you can return to business as usual.

Eternity begins anew once you have been born anew by the Spirit and comprehended the meaning of life is about loving and serving Jesus. Jesus is the Life. Jesus is the Resurrection and the Life. Jesus is life eternal– and through faith "in" Christ, the resurrection is already within you (it just hasn't happened yet). Everything within this world is nothing, nor is it anything, apart from Jesus.

In order to enter into life eternal, your old man must die; you cannot drag it into a covenant relationship with Christ because – it is dead – and Jesus is the life.

Eternity operates according to an entirely separate set of ordinances.

Our soul is eternal – and it will spend eternity somewhere after the Judgment, so it is technically "wrong" to say that we gain eternity through faith, but to keep it simple… eternity begins *anew* (for you) the moment you have declared yourself dead to this worldly life and are born *anew* in the kingdom of God by the Spirit of God. What happens after this – is up to you! Continue, then, to "work out your own salvation with fear and trembling" (Phil. 2:12). This world will try to tell you that you must physically die before eternity happens, but this is a lie straight from the pit of hell – by Satan who wants you to remain separated from God for *all* eternity. Eternity begins anew the moment you have passed from death to life – according to faith, through the Spirit – whereby your old man is dead to the cares of this world and now your new man, the inner man, has been raised to newness of life. This is a type and shadow of your future resurrection – and it happens the moment faith has been firmly rooted and established in you by the Spirit of truth operating within you to sanctify you. This is merely salvation from Death to life (in Hades) at this point, but as yet... you must continue to press forward and strive (*agonizomai*) to enter the narrow gate to attain the prize of life eternal.

> "For many are called, but few are chosen" (Matt. 22:14).

The old man living in darkness was already rendered dead through trespasses and sin... and now you need to walk away from it and start walking in a new way as a new creation in Christ. Being alive in the flesh yet apart from (hostile to) Christ, you were accounted as dead in Death, but eternity is a place of life through the Spirit. Through faith, you must surrender your old life to be crucified with Christ to become one with Christ... "in" Christ. Death and life have nothing in common. Your corpse was left hanging on the cross, so leave it up there. Turn away from it! Disregard it! Move on... and follow Jesus!

You must be born anew by the Spirit (John 3:3-8) and given a new life.

If you are not walking in His Way, then you are not living with the light of eternity within you.

If the old man has already been rendered dead, then why are you still promoting it and gratifying it? This is the ten million dollar question! If your old body that was given to you as a loaner/rental unit was reckoned dead and obsolete, then get rid of it so you can freely live as you were intended to live. You have been set free. You are no longer a slave to this former life in the flesh on earth because now you are a resident of heaven. You are a legal resident of heaven – now! Heaven is not a place you ascend to after you die; you have already descended into heaven which resides in your heart. This world would have your believe otherwise, so let me prove it.

Where is the kingdom of heaven? Wherever the King is! (John 3:13) How do we know where the kingdom of heaven is? Jesus came proclaiming, "Repent, for the kingdom of heaven is at hand"

(Matt. 4:17). Jesus told us... where He is... the kingdom of heaven is. How did He know this? Because Jesus is the King of heaven and He brought heaven down to us. We cannot go to heaven, so Jesus brought heaven down to us!

> "The kingdom of God is in you" (Luke 17:21).

Consider this seemingly obscure but vitally important scripture:

> "And from the days of John the Baptist until now the kingdom of heaven suffers violence, and the violent take it by force" (Matt. 11:12).

Jesus is telling us that "from days of John the Baptist – *until now*" (even today) the kingdom of heaven (on earth) suffers violence. Jesus is the King of heaven and He established the kingdom of heaven on earth and manifested it through His disciples, yet violent men in opposition to the kingdom of heaven will violently try to prevent the kingdom from happening – with violence.

Jesus is the King of heaven – and if Jesus abides in our hearts through faith – now, then, where is the kingdom of heaven? Yup! It is in your heart (Eph. 3:17) and you are building and stewarding one kingdom or "any other" in your heart (read Regensis, Chapter 7).

Is heaven out there in the cosmos somewhere? Well, the prince of this world (Satan) wants you to believe this so you spend more time seeking heaven rather than seeking Jesus. If you think and believe that heaven is somewhere far away, then you might rationalize living however you want to live here on earth. All the devil has – are lies, trickery and deceit, which he uses quite effectively. He starts by telling us 90% truth with a 10% lie, which over time becomes 10% truth and 90% lie.

Know the truth and the truth shall set you free.

Doctrinal disassociation has assented to heaven residing high above the clouds in the cosmos. After all, isn't God high and lifted up and exalted? Do you really think God needs a special place in order for Him to be exalted and worshipped and magnified? "The kingdom of God is in you" and "you must worship Him in spirit and in truth" (John 4:23-24). In this instance, the word "spirit" in not capitalized as is done when referencing the Holy Spirit (i.e. the Spirit of God). This spirit is the spirit within you; it resides as a partner with your soul and constitutes the other half (in oneness) of who you are. For all intents and purposes, let's locate this special place somewhere within you, such as your heart. If you believe in Jesus and Jesus is in your heart, then you are able to worship Him in Presence and Spirit wherever you go because your heart is a tabernacle for the Lord of heaven – on earth. The glory of God is not a special place or moment that can only be found at conferences and revivals or in churches. God is having a conference with you in your heart and a revival is happening in this very moment within you, but you have been taught to run to and fro seeking the glory cloud and inspirational speeches to get all excited in your faith and be challenged to live vigorously for Christ. Humm. Well, doesn't this sound silly now that you know the truth? The enemy wants you to believe you have to go to places and events where God will show up, when all the while, the presence of the Lord resides within you. The glory cloud is within you. Signs and wonders are within you. The resurrection is within you. Wait… repeat that last part one more time… the resurrection is within me? Indeed. Let's add up the truth of the scriptures like this:

Jesus said, "I am the Resurrection and the Life" (John 11:25).

Through faith, you offered your old man as a living sacrifice (Rom. 12:1), you have been crucified with Christ (Gal. 2:20), now you have been raised up "in Christ" as a new creation (2 Cor. 5:17; Eph. 2:6). Jesus is the Resurrection and the Life. Since Christ is in you, then the resurrection is also in you. The old you is completely dead and the real you has passed from death to life. You have already been resurrected through faith, but you have been taught to wait for it. You are already operating in eternity right now, but as long as the enemy makes you think about waiting and waiting, then he has conquered the truth of eternity with his lies and deception.

The death of the body is merely a transitional time as we wait in-between performances before changing into New Earth clothing.

Jesus said, "I am the Resurrection and the Life" (John 11:25). The old you no longer exists; who you are now is a new creation "in" Christ. You are an entirely new person who entered into faith and now Christ (life eternal) abides in you as you abide "in" Him. Life eternal abides in you!!! Do you see this circle of faith in action now? Jesus abides with/in you, and you abide in Jesus.

> "Abide in Me, and I in you. As the branch cannot bear fruit of itself, unless it abides in the vine, neither can you, unless you abide in Me. [5] "I am the vine, you *are* the branches. He who abides in Me, and I in him, bears much fruit; <u>for without Me you can do nothing</u>. [6] ***If*** anyone does not abide in Me, he is cast out as a branch and is withered; and *they* gather them and throw *them* into the fire, and they are burned" (John 15:4-6).

> Jesus said to him, "***If*** anyone loves Me, he will keep My word; and My Father will love him, and **We** will come to him and make **Our** home with him. [24] He who does not love Me does not keep My words; and the word which you hear is not Mine but the Father's who sent Me" (John 14:23, 24).

Jesus is telling us that "We" (i.e. the Father, Son and Holy Spirit) will "make Our abode with him." The Father and Son sit upon thrones in heaven – and they also abide in your heart through faith where They sit Sovereignly upon the throne of your heart, ***IF*** you have yielded your kingdom to Jesus and have laid aside your crown at His feet. This is the truth straight from the mouth of Jesus. If you love Jesus, then you will keep His word! If you do not keep His word, then you do not love Him. This truth is plain – and simple.

By grace, through faith, the kingdom of heaven is wherever the King is – which resides in your new man (not the old man that you were born with, which is still hanging upon the cross). It was for this reason that you needed to be born again (anew) and were promised a new heart and a new spirit when you came to the knowledge of the truth through faith in Christ (Ezek. 36:26, 27). There is not supposed to be one shred of old man remaining within you if you have died to self and are alive in Christ. The old heart and spirit, which were corrupted by sin, were replaced the moment you were born anew. Now, it is the Holy Spirit within you to transform you by the renewing of your mind (Rom. 12:2) to thoroughly and completely regenerate the mind of your soul so as to create a holy habitation for the Divine. The Godhead *dwells* temporarily within all men, but it cannot *abide* permanently within your tabernacle (heart, mind, soul and spirit) unless it has been washed, renewed and sanctified by the Holy Spirit.

The old man prior to your Spirit-filled life of faith was dead to God, which must be rendered thoroughly and completely dead by you… which requires an act of your will to accomplish this. You must do this! The message of the gospel is not to make you a better person with upgrades; the message is for you to surrender that life in order to receive a new one so that you can live this new life according to the Spirit through faith, in harmony and communion with God, not as a new and improved version of your old self, but as a new creation in Christ who walks and talks and operates like Christ in resurrected power because Christ is now Lord and Master within this "resurrection life" you are now living.

At some point, you will realize that your former life was never real to begin with. It was just a shadow of the true life you were meant to live – in obedience to Christ – in word and deed.

One final point! Eternity has two destinations – and only two: Life Eternal and Hell. If you are born anew and Jesus abides in you, then the kingdom of heaven is in you and, therefore, you are already operating in eternity. "I have put eternity in their hearts" (Eccl. 3:11).

If you do not want to believe the kingdom of heaven is within you, well… that is your choice. You do not have to believe Jesus is in you. No one is forcing you to accept this teaching; however, if you do accept it, then live like you mean it. The kingdom of heaven is within you; now go, and tell others that the kingdom of heaven is at hand (in their midst). What you say is the gospel truth. The time for more of heaven to invade earth – in one regenerated soul at a time – is at hand!

It's all about Jesus and God gets the glory!

The Kingdom Suffers Violence

Jesus is the king of heaven. Jesus told His followers that the kingdom of heaven is at hand; truly, it is within arms' reach. Sometimes we take the scriptures to mean more than what was intended rather than accept it on face value: what Jesus said is what Jesus meant. Heaven is at hand. Heaven is in your midst! Reach out! Grab hold of it! Embrace it! Live it!

We are sojourners sent from heaven to live upon the earth with one purpose: to invade earth with the atmosphere of heaven. You are an earth invader. There is a world of darkness upon the earth and you have been sent as a light of truth into the world. "You are the light of the world" (Matt. 5:14). You are sons of light" (1 Thess. 5:5) and "children of light" (Eph. 5:8) and since you are an adopted child of God, then you are "heirs" of the kingdom (Rom. 8:17).

Now that you know who you are, perhaps it is time we start living according to the way in which we were created: as conquerors, priests, prophets, liberators, watchmen, worshippers, as messengers of truth, and as faithful witnesses (martyrs). Yes, the word "witness" comes from the Greek word *'martur'* (3144; martyr). Consider this: you are residing in enemy territory and this world of darkness is being exposed to the light of Christ Jesus within you. There is nothing in this world that wants you here and will 'martyr' you any chance it gets. This world of darkness will do everything possible to silence the light of truth within you because the kingdom of God is in you and you are a minister of God's truth. The kingdom of darkness will stop at nothing to silence you, your testimony and your faithful witness. If doubt and despair will not work, then the darkness will rob you of your health and wealth. If these will not work, then the darkness will inflict you with spiritual diseases like depression and anxiety. If these will not hinder you, then you can expect to come under spiritual attack by unclean spirits. If this does not work, you can expect to be persecuted. This begins as mild sufferings to compromise the integrity of the message and the witness within you. Next, principalities and powers will begin to work against you through other people around you, including family members and people in your place of work. The darkness cannot kill you (Job x:x; Job's life could not be touched), but it can surely influence the minds of unsanctified hearts around you to harm you, crush your spirit, kill God's vision for your life and utterly destroy you to prevent the truth from coming out. How do I know this happens? Because it is happening to me even as I write. I do not bring a message that I have not experienced. In all this suffering and persecution, the scriptures tell us to do one thing: Endure. Persist! Remain standing! Fight the good fight – and keep the faith!

Endure!

Remain faithful regardless of what happens. You are already dead, yet alive in Christ, so what more can they do to you? Eternity happened the very instant you were born anew and now you are already living in eternity, so, what are you afraid of? What can they possibly do that hasn't already been done? Consider death in this life… as a promotion into life eternal.

Think on things above!

If the kingdom of heaven in within you, then you are a threat to the kingdom of darkness and you will come under attack in the face of suffering and persecution. Remember the first Bible verse you were taught: "I can do *all things* through Christ who strengthens me" (Phil. 4:13). "And we know that *all things* work together for good to those who love God, to those who are the called according to His purpose" (Rom. 8:28). "All things" is talking about suffering and persecution, so read it within this context, beginning in verse 18 through verse 39.

In like manner, the kingdom of darkness persecuted Christ, so expect to be persecuted, even to the point of death. Jesus did not promise you health, wealth and abundance; on the contrary – if the kingdom of heaven is within you, then you are a member of an invading army, along with the host of heaven, who have been sent to take back this planet from the prince of darkness. The enemy is more than happy to prosper you and bless you and keep you comfortably compromised in your kingdom, as long as you leave them alone. Test both kingdoms in this: start living like Jesus by giving your abundance away to build the kingdom of heaven in the hearts of men. When you do, you will experience a purity of truth – in holiness – unlike any time in your life as you are filled with God's grace, mercy and truth… and then watch the darkness begin to vigorously attack you and chip away at your earthly life… and, especially, your integrity!

If you are not a threat to the darkness, even the darkness will bless your life.

If you are perceived as an enemy of this world, then you vulnerable to attack!

We do not wage war against flesh and bone, but against principalities and powers – where – in heavenly places. Where are the heavenly places? Yup. They are within your heart and mind, if you will. If the kingdom of heaven is within you, then "you have been seated in heavenly places in Christ Jesus" whereby principalities and powers will come against you and wage war against your heart and mind; in your mind for the knowledge of the truth; and in your heart because that is where the kingdom of heaven is being built. You are a veritable battlefield. Is it any wonder why we seem to suffer strange ailments, tribulations, sufferings, woes, calamities, uncertain futures, anxiety, despair, depression and desperation? You are under attack because you have been deemed a high-valued target. These are words of consolation and encouragement to help you endure, to continue on – and to press onward to attain the prize: life eternal.

> "My brethren, count it all joy when you fall into various trials" (James 1:2).

It takes much spiritual wisdom in order to discern whether the Lord is blessing you – or the enemy. The enemy wants to bless you and enjoy yourself here; to remain as long as you want and to boldly teach others how wonderfully blessed illuminated-darkness is. It takes much spiritual wisdom in order to discern if you are experiencing tribulation as a result of the Lord's hand of correction upon your life to move you into deeper waters of faith and truth in order to sanctify you for divine service – or the enemy is doing it to distract you and get you off mission (which is to come against darkness). Everything that is happening to you may appear circumstantial, so how do you know if it is the Lord or the enemy at work? It is impossible to know apart from the Spirit, who partners with your spirit, Who was sent by the Lord Jesus to help you, guide you, strengthen you, comfort you and counsel you in all truth and righteousness. Only the Spirit can tell you which is which, but here is a simple litmus test: if there is peace, and it is drawing you into a closer relationship with the Lord, then it is ordained by God. Sometimes it is God doing it; sometimes it is God allowing it to happen through the enemy; either way, it should draw you into a closer faith-walk in Christ. If you are backsliding and falling away, then this is the hand of the enemy because God does not want anyone to perish, but for all to come to faith in Jesus Christ. If you are operating in status quo to maintain a modest decorum of dignified religious piety, then this is the hand of the enemy. If heaven is in you, then darkness hates you. Darkness is not worried about people with false truth, doubt and unbelief; all darkness has to do is keep them comfortable and prevent them from knowing the truth. Darkness will not challenge them or rock their boat; darkness will keep them complacent and titillate their minds with new teachings to keep them interested up to a point; darkness must maintain the status quo and keep you apart from the Spirit of truth – at all cost. The kingdom of heaven has commissioned the Holy Spirit to reside in you and lead you into all truth. Darkness is afraid of the Holy Spirit – and so are many of our congregations today. The kingdom of heaven is at hand. Do not despair! Press onward. Press in. Exercise dominion over the darkness. Endure! Redeem and take back what the enemy has stolen from the Lord, your God and King. Why do you continue to live like hell on earth if the kingdom of heaven is in you? Heaven has been invading the darkness since Genesis 1:3? You were sent as an ambassador of light to invade the darkness, so, what have you done today to advance the kingdom of heaven?

It is all about Jesus and God gets the glory! Amen.

Borrowers and Lenders

We own nothing in this life. We are borrowers and lenders; we are stewards of what already belongs to God. It is His kingdom, but the deceiver would have you believe otherwise, to believe the illusion in which you can acquire and own things, never knowing which day the Lord will call your spirit back home and you breathe your last breath.

This is why there are specific guidelines regarding Jewish borrowing and lending. It was never really yours to begin with. Take title to it, but do not own it. Take possession of the land, but do not own it.

He who is faithful with much will be given more in the kingdom to come.

4. The Kingdom – of Heaven

Much has been written over time about Heaven and the kingdom of heaven. Many things that were written came from information gathered from the scriptures, some writings came from personal experiences of people that "entered into" a heavenly place while still a resident of earth, but in a previous book, I wrote about Heaven and the kingdom of heaven as two distinctly different places, one which we cannot enter into – and the other which resides upon the same place as this book: the earth. We are the host of earth, sojourners from Heaven and eternal residents of earth, who were sent to establish the kingdom of heaven upon the earth.

We were sent here on a mission to perform various tasks according to the will of God. Our first commandment came from God on the sixth day: "have dominion… over the earth." The second commandment came from Jesus: "Love one another as I have loved you." This book will explain what "the dominion" is – and what it is not. But first, some basic understanding:

One major key to understand the scriptures in regard to the kingdom of heaven is: man does not enter into Heaven… heaven enters into man. Heaven (capital H) is God's throne and eternal "home" – and heaven is the presence of God that we are to host within our heart-home.

> "Heaven is My throne, and earth is My footstool. What house will you build for Me? says the Lord, or what is the place of My rest?" (Acts 7:49)

> "Repent. The kingdom of heaven is at hand" (Matt. 4:17).

When Jesus said this, He was making several very significant statements. 1) I Am the King of Heaven; 2) I have authority to bring the tangible reality of heaven to earth; 3) the presence of God is in your midst; 4) you must repent and turn away from the kingdom you are living in.

This last point is highly significant! Jesus did not specifically tell us we were living in an alternate reality that is under the control of Satan who operates as "the ruler of this world" (John 12:31) within the dominion of darkness to sow seeds of doubt in order to keep us in bondage to the operating system of sin – and thus – keep us separated from God. The scriptures seem to approach this point as if those living at that time understood they were living within the kingdom of darkness; however, fast forward two thousand years and it seems this world has little if any understanding of this demonic reality that surrounds us which constantly bombards us with deceptive lies to keep us from abiding with the Lord our God.

If you have been born of water and you are living upon the earth, then you have been born into the counterfeit kingdom of darkness where sin predominates. Some of our doctrines say "we are born in sin" but I would tweak this slightly… "we are born into sin," i.e. born into this sinful world that is under Satan's domination. Perhaps the greatest deception by the enemy is simply: keeping us from perceiving the kingdom of darkness exists. If we remain unaware this kingdom exists, then we are also easily persuaded the devil does not exist either.

So, now, in order to enter into the kingdom of heaven, you must – first – be set free from the kingdom you are living in. Fortunately for us, the Holy Spirit is always alongside us to guide us in the truth so that we may live according to the way Jesus predestined for us to walk within.

> "No one has ascended to heaven but He who came down from heaven, *that is,* the Son of Man who is in heaven" (John 3:13)

How can Jesus, who is the King of Heaven, be standing upon the earth and tell us that He is "in heaven." Once again, I point out the subtle distinction between Heaven and heaven… and this, then, is one of the main keys to comprehending the scriptures. Heaven on earth is the presence of Jesus, and... if Christ is in you, then heaven is within you. This is what Jesus said:

> "The kingdom of God is within you" (Luke 17:21).[12]

Many of us would like to think in this manner, but sadly, this is impossible unless a person is born again. Why?" Because our minds have been using the operating system of this world (sin) for so long that we do not even know about the operating system of God's kingdom (Spirit). We cannot understand how the kingdom of God operates unless we have been '*geneo anothen*' – born anew from above.

> "Jesus answered and said to him, "Most assuredly, I say to you, unless one is born again, he cannot *understand* the kingdom of God" (John 3:3; *oida-*G1492).

Everyone on earth has been born of flesh as one passing through the waters of birth, but unless you have been born of the Spirit whereby you are converted through repentance to become a new creature, then it is impossible to understand and comprehend how the kingdom of God operates. You must be born into the kingdom of God before you will be taught the operating principles of the kingdom... and many mysteries as well. However, many spiritual leaders today attempt to teach sheep without being born again by the Spirit of truth; worse yet, some even profess a theology that says they are born again without ever having been born again.

---

[12] The term "kingdom of heaven" is found only in the gospel of Matthew. He was writing to Jewish people who regard the name of God with such religious zeal that they often substitute the word "heaven" for God. This subtle difference allows us to understand the kingdom of God better, especially in light of who Jesus is: Lord of heaven and earth! The kingdom of heaven and the kingdom of God represent the same reality of Christ's presence on earth.

Therefore… it is imperative to be born anew from above by the Spirit of truth.

You cannot understand the kingdom of heaven apart from the Spirit, nor can you live according to the truth… nor can you live as a citizen of heaven… nor can you possess life eternal apart from the Spirit because the Holy Spirit is our tutor and guide to reveal Christ to us so that we may know the truth, walk in the truth and abide in the Truth, i.e. Jesus Christ.

Jesus spent His entire life teaching everyone two things: remember… and understand. Nearly all, if not all, of the parables and teachings of Jesus were instructional platforms to teach us about the kingdom of God and how it operates. Mankind had been behind enemy lines for so long that they had thoroughly forgotten three things: 1) Who the Lord God is; 2) remember who they are; and 3) understand what they are supposed to be doing on earth. If you are on a similar journey to understand spiritual things, then read the following books that correspond to the three forgotten things: 1) Image; 2) Regenesis; 3) Understand.

Once you know the truth of God, then your life will be inextricably changed… and thus, your mind will begin to think differently (under the tutoring of the Spirit) and your manner of living will be dramatically changed – all for the better – so that you may be an authentic member of God's kingdom and a true citizen of heaven. This is the incredibly awesome Good News. Jesus ushered in a regime change and now you are a representative of His Kingdom to hear His voice and do all that He commands.

Step #1: Repent… and be converted! Know the truth… and more so… live according to the truth and the truth will make you free. Faith is not "what you believe" but rather… living according to what you believe!

If, however, you continue to live according to the manner of your unregenerate self, then the new birth did not take root. Your life must be inextricably altered by the Spirit who continues to convert us over and over with truth in order to be changed by the truth so as to be conformed to the image of Christ dwelling within you. If you are not becoming more like the Lord who is dwelling within you, then the seed of truth did not produce the essential root of understanding whereby you can grow to become like Jesus to produce the fruit of the Spirit.

Ask the Lord and find out from Him where you stand. Do not run to pastors, priests or rabbi's to seek their opinion! Seek the Lord and hear His voice for yourself. Why settle for second-hand truth when you can get pure truth from the Lord through the Holy Spirit.

> "But seek first the kingdom of God and His righteousness, and all these things shall be added to you" (Matt. 6:33).

This is highly significant. Jesus wants us to seek the kingdom of God in order to escape the kingdom of darkness – and He wants us to seek *His Righteousness*! Jesus is "the Righteousness of God" and also *Jehovah Tsidkenu*: The Lord our Righteousness (Jer. 23:6; 33:16). Mankind has been offered two things – and it is a package deal! You cannot "enter" the kingdom of heaven unless you have also declared your sovereign allegiance to Jesus. And you cannot seek and find the kingdom of God apart from the guidance of the Holy Spirit.

Indeed, our spiritual sojourn on earth to enter into the Lord's salvation begins with and continues on "in the Spirit." Secondly, you do not have a righteousness of your own according to your own works (John 1:13); however, once you have been born again and Christ "our Righteousness" is abiding within you, then all your works on account of faithful obedience to Jesus – by the hearing of His Voice – will be credited into your account as "righteousness" which will pass through (and survive) the judgment fire. Righteousness, in this regard, represents our spiritual currency which is deposited into our heavenly account which we will use to exchange for true riches in heaven – once we get to the other side of the judgment fire. Is this all making sense now?

> "That which is born of the flesh is flesh; that which is born of the Spirit is spirit" (John 3:3).

You are a spiritual being that is having a human experience. If you continue to live according to the flesh in the kingdom of darkness, you cannot live according to the Spirit in God's kingdom! The Spirit of God will hold you in contempt!!!

> "For what profit is it to a man if he gains the whole world, and loses his own soul? Or what will a man give in exchange for his soul?" (Matt. 16:26).

Therefore, it is imperative to make sure you are born anew from above by the Spirit of God before you read one more word. What benefit will you derive from reading more words about the kingdom of God and having dominion if you have already forfeited your soul to the flames of hell – apart from the Spirit's conversion? Unless this matter has been resolved, and you have been thoroughly persuaded and convinced by the truth to trust in Jesus completely – and thus, you have surrendered your heart-throne to the Sovereignty of Jesus and have declared total allegiance to Jesus as your Lord and your God... then put this book down and settle this with Him right now!

The dominion that Jesus offers His disciples in His kingdom includes His authority and His power to perform His will – not yours. If you think, erringly, that you can learn the principles of the kingdom and operate with dominion authority and dominion power apart from being born anew... then you have deceived yourself and are not living according to the truth.

> "And do not be conformed to this world, but be transformed by the renewing of your mind, that you may prove what *is* that good and acceptable and perfect will of God" (Rom. 12:2).

Step #2: become His disciple. It is not enough to be a believer of Jesus, for even demons believe – and tremble (James 2:19). Jesus is seeking disciples that are seeking Him who desire to hear His voice and do what He says to advance His kingdom upon the earth and usher in a regime change – in the presence of His enemies! Passive spectators, casual admirers and make-believers are merely hypocrites in sheep clothing thinking they may inherit something by claiming to know Jesus; however, what you know is irrelevant! What matters is: does Jesus know you?

> "Not everyone who says to Me, 'Lord, Lord,' shall enter the kingdom of heaven, but he who does the will of My Father in heaven. ^{22} Many will say to Me in that day, 'Lord, Lord, have we not prophesied in Your name, cast out demons in Your name, and done many wonders in Your name?' ^{23} And then I will declare to them, 'I never knew you; depart from Me, you who practice lawlessness!" (Matt. 7:21-23)

Do you believe in a doctrine that says you have a personal relationship with Jesus – or do you "have" a personal relationship with Him by hearing His voice?

> "My sheep hear My voice, and I know them, and they follow Me" (John 10:27).

Do you claim Jesus dwells in you? How wonderful. Yet Jesus wants to abide in you – and you in Him – because in Him we have life eternal by the Spirit He has given (John14:20; 15:5-8; 1 John 3:24; 4:13; 5:11, 12, 20). If His Spirit is dwelling within you, then your desire is keep His word, be His disciple and live according to the truth in righteousness.

> "Now he who keeps His commandments abides in Him, and He in him. And by this we know that He abides in us, by the Spirit whom He has given us" (1 John 3:24).

> "You are My friends *IF* you do whatever I command you" (John 15:14).

Settle this right here and now before you read another word! If you have not heard His voice, then you are not in a love-and-trust personal relationship with Jesus. This is the message that the Lord has been declaring ever since the beginning: hear Him and believe!

Entering into the kingdom of heaven is not man's ascension in Heaven… but rather, man's conversion to live according to the truth within a personal relationship with Jesus Christ!

There are two kingdoms upon the earth – and man has an eternal choice to either live as an unwitting accomplice in the kingdom of darkness and be judged unworthy of salvation – or live as a citizen of the kingdom of heaven that is upon the earth. There is a spiritual door that allows us to leave the darkness, and this Door is called Jesus Christ Himself (John 10:7, 9). We have a choice to make! Either walk through the Door and leave all the cares of "this world" behind you and be obedient to Jesus to establish the kingdom of heaven upon the earth… or continue to live on your side of the door as a slave to sin in the kingdom of darkness. The choice is yours. There is no middle ground of faith – and lukewarm faith is merely an illusion. You cannot keep standing in between two ways because you are standing in the middle of an enormous spiritual war upon the earth.

> "And Elijah came to all the people, and said, "How long will you falter between two opinions? If the Lord *is* God, follow Him; but if Baal, follow him." But the people answered him not a word" (1 Kings 18:21).

There are four problems within the church today: Christian atheism, Christian agnosticism, denominational Christianity and lukewarm Christianity.

- Christian atheism does not believe the truth
- Christian agnosticism say they believe in some of the truth but don't live it

- Denominational Christianity determines what the sheep are to believe
- Lukewarm Christianity believes half-heartedly, but chooses to do whatever they want

The difference between truly believing Jesus at His word to become His disciple versus believing what you want to believe can be likened to an astronaut believing the earth is flat by refusing to acknowledge the third dimension; it can be likened to an adult continuing to believe the Santa Claus myth or babies are delivered by storks; it can be likened to a song playing within your mind that you refuse to sing. This is the realm of knowing, but not understanding! This is the paradox of Hades within men: "the place of not understanding" within the reality of all knowing.

If you truly understand the truth that Jesus taught, then His truth will compel you to live much differently than the world that surrounds you… which is all based on an irreverent lie. If you claim to know Christ and have a personal relationship with Him, how wonderful… that Christ is in you, but… are you in Christ? This is the other half of the spiritual transaction whereby your temporary dwelling becomes a *permanent abode* that can never be forfeited on account of entering into "His rest." In this place, your divine relationship in Christ is eternally redeemed. It is no longer the place of wondering or standing in two ways, but rather, you are now abiding in… "the place of understanding." You are now… ALL IN!!!

> "And if it seems evil to you to serve the Lord, choose for yourselves this day whom you will serve, whether the gods which your fathers served that *were* on the other side of the River, or the gods of the Amorites, in whose land you dwell. But as for me and my house, we will serve the Lord" (Joshua 24:15).

Repent. Convert. Be transformed by the renewing of your mind. The mystery of man upon the earth is sanctification! Our thought processes must be converted by the truth through sanctification by the Spirit to thoroughly "believe and become" a disciple of Jesus!

You cannot claim Jesus as your friend… unless you are His disciple (John 15:14, 15).

Beginning Anew

The Lord said, "Heaven is My throne," and yet the scriptures never say that "man goes to heaven." Not even once. Some men have gone into heaven, like Elijah and Moses, as have many saints who have been martyred for the sake of Christ, as will two future witnesses in Revelation, and also the great multitude that comes out of the great tribulation (which hasn't happened yet), but as for the rest of us, we are the host of earth and we are the eternal residents of earth. And now we will find out the reason why we were sent here to have dominion.

Jesus came and dwelt upon earth to teach us (mankind) how to live as children of God within the kingdom of heaven – that is upon the earth right now! To be sure, man has no problem living upon the earth in the manner of his choice according to his strength, will and determination, but Jesus came to teach us and to show us how to live as children of God, as spiritual beings upon the earth, so as to establish His dominion called the kingdom of heaven upon the earth. This is not a new idea; Jesus has been teaching mankind how to live this way since day eight.

Thousands of kingdoms and dynasties, great and small, have already been built upon the earth over the past 5,775 years by many leaders of nations, both great and small, but we never stopped to ask ourselves: why do we desire to live this way? Why? Because this is who we are: people created within the context of inhabitants living within a kingdom – as kingdom builders.

The kingdom of heaven upon the earth is supposed to be an exact copy of the Heavenly kingdom. It exists today as a type and shadow in its present condition, but when the "veil" is taken away and the kingdom of God is revealed, the glory which the earth had before the great rebellion in heaven spilled over onto earth will be restored in oneness. This oneness condition became deformed by Satan which temporarily took captive the earth and its glory, yet it will – once again – be made anew again from above. In the regeneration, God is not going to make all new things ... He is going to make all things new – again. And this includes you!

Jesus came as "the Way" to show us the way. We forgot who we are and how we were supposed to live as sojourners of Heaven upon the earth, so He came to teach us, remind us and to show us how to live. Jesus came as the Messiah to accomplish many things in order to fulfill the Law, but His primary mission was to show us "the way," and His second mission parameter was to testify to the truth against the rulers of the darkness upon the earth (Eph. 6:12). Armed with His truth and the indwelling Spirit, we are now able to understand how the kingdom of God operates.

Jesus has the authority to teach us in a manner as no other person has – or ever could – or ever will, because He is the Archetype of a better way. The Father gave Jesus all authority and power and dominion as the Divine Creator of Heaven and Earth, and He has come to us at least 30 times[13] prior to His incarnation to teach us the way and manner of living in God's kingdom. Him we must hear; Him we must serve; Him we must follow obediently. Jesus did not come as just a good and righteous teacher who lived a perfectly sinless life, nor did He come as just a prophet who could accurately quote and interpret the scriptures; Jesus came as God Incarnate to repeat the words that He spoke to prophets long ago, but this time, He demonstrated it as a living example, as Immanuel: God with us.

Kingdom in Context

The stories and parables that Jesus taught were intended to teach us several things:

---

[13] Read about the 30 Theophanies in "Image."

- Who the Lord our God is
- Who we are
- What we are to do
- How the kingdom of God operates
- How to live according to God's righteousness (the way)
- How to walk in the truth according to the Spirit of life
- How to comprehend and perceive the kingdom of heaven (on earth) as the place wherein men function as gateways and conduits for heavenly things to pass through – in order for us to restore the earth to its pre-Adamic condition as Paradise, the Garden of Eden

Many times, Jesus taught us by saying, "The kingdom of heaven is like…" and many people have written extensively about the inherent meanings in these phrases to describe what heaven is like, which is partially true, yet we must now also learn from these phrases how we, as earthen vessels, are to transform earth into the likeness of heaven.

Jesus did not give us glimpses into Heaven to know what it would be like when we return (which is now regarded as a false heaven theology), Jesus was teaching us how to convert, transform and return earth to a pre-regenerative condition of heaven that existed before the cataclysm in Heaven altered earth.

The restoration of all things has always been the Father's plan of regeneration since day one. And now it is up to the sons of men to live according to the manner in which we were called, to live like sons of God, in order to restore earth once more into heaven's likeness as a kingdom "of" heaven within God's kingdom under Christ's dominion upon the earth. This is the big picture gospel, so read it again.

Jesus made man in His image according to His likeness to be His representative image bearers upon the earth. The Father is pure good, pure light, pure love, pure truth, in whom there is only pure goodness, in whom there is no variation or shifting of shadows, so

Jesus became the avenging arm as the Sovereign Lord in Whom justice and judgment is accomplished. Jesus was sent, as the only begotten Son, as our Creator who created us in "His Own" image, to be Lord and Master over all His representatives (men) to reclaim from Satan what he stole from God – and to redeem the inheritance that was promised to His faithful obedient followers. Jesus is also the hand of mercy and grace through Whom we may attain mercy and forgiveness because He accomplished perfectly all the requirements needed to pay the redemption price for our penalty (as a substitutiary sacrifice for our sin that leads to death) which we were unable to pay.

Mankind was sent to earth, into hostile territory, and put in harm's way to take back what the enemy stole from God, but when Adam stumbled over the threshold of offense into sin, this operation… which began as a recovery and cleanup mission then became a hostage rescue mission as well.

> "The kingdom of heaven suffers violence and violent men *take it by force*" (Matt. 11:12; *are pressing in forcefully*)

The violent nature of the kingdom of darkness has been forcefully advancing against the kingdom of heaven upon the earth since Satan's fall from Heaven; and it is within this context that man was placed within an arena dominated by sin to win a battle he cannot achieve apart from the Spirit! If he tries to live apart from the Divine relationship that God instituted that resides in Christ – and Christ alone, then his redemption is forfeited by him; however, when man chooses to walk with the Lord in spirit and in truth, then he can live with the empowering of the Spirit of God dwelling within him to accomplish more than he ever thought or imagined possible. We are the bride, the wedding gift is earth – and we have been invited to the table of conquest at the wedding feast in the presence of our enemies! We are to prepare ourselves and the earth for our bridegroom, Jesus Christ, who will return again with justice and judgment against His enemies, and with a loving embrace for all who considered the things of this earth worthless in comparison to the surpassing glory that awaits for those who live obediently to accomplish His perfect will.

"Man was created and sent to have dominion over this world in which Satan rules as a prince of rebellion, but man was deceived into delivering over to Satan the glory and the authority that God had given them. What began as man's dominion mandate in the Garden to take back and redeem the world from Satan's dominion became a rescue and recovery mission for the Lord Jesus. The plan also involved recovering that with was stolen from God in Heaven by Satan which resulted in his expulsion from Heaven; Satan received God's glory (worship) and then kept it for Himself whereby iniquity was found in him. And then he instigated a rebellion in Heaven against God with the glory that he stole from God. Christ's mission was manifold and predetermined, and it didn't just include saving man and restoring the glory of God in man; it also included taking away the sin of the world, triumphing over Satan, recovering what was stolen by him, saving mankind and restoring the glory of God in Heaven and the earth as well."[14]

This is the big picture gospel – and we are at war!!! Now is the time for sons of God (not the unregenerate sons of men) to push back, not against flesh and blood, nor by might or power, but by God's Spirit against principalities and powers raised up against the knowledge of God and His Christ because this is a spiritual battle that can only be won by the Holy Spirit who dwells within us through faith in Jesus Christ – being armed with only one weapon: truth. And this is the good news: no weapon formed against us will prosper. And, again, more good news: nothing can separate us from the love of God. *If you are on His side, then He has got your back – and He will be victorious in you and through you!*

The institutional church has taken a very passive, complacent and non-combative position toward evil, filling the heavens with many pious prayers asking God to do something and save us from our own handiwork, but alas, it is not we who are waiting upon God… rather, it is God who is waiting on us! We are partnered with

---

[14] Excerpt from "Image," section titled "Once Upon A Cross."

Christ in this mission and He is waiting on us to make our move. All authority and power belongs to Jesus, and then Jesus gave this authority and power to His disciples to have dominion in His name (Luke 10:19); and this is why Jesus is seeking disciples, so they may manifest His authority and power over the enemy and have dominion in His name! Jesus also sent the Holy Spirit to dwell within us so that we may be endued with *'dunamis'* power – whereby we serve the Lord of glory in newness as gateways of grace through whom heavenly resources pass through to strengthen and encourage the brethren… and to overcome evil in this world with good.

We are living in the last days when miraculous events and "greater works" will begin taking place with such regularity that the events themselves will be the sign for – or against – this faithless generation, much like Jesus and His miracles were a sign against the faithless generation in His parousia, as was the flood a sign against the faithless generation in Noah's day.

> Jesus said, "My kingdom is not of this world. If My kingdom were of this world, My servants would fight" (John 18:36).

Let's pay close attention to what Jesus is saying. If Jesus told us that this earth is not in His possession, then it would be an inaccurate statement. If Jesus said My kingdom is not of this earth, then that would be inaccurate as well. Jesus told us His kingdom "is not of this world" because this worldly kingdom in its current capacity is under the domination of Satan at the hands of unregenerate sinful men, who handed over their dominion authority to govern earth under Satan's influence – in sin. But when we yield our lives according Galatians 2:20 so that Christ dwells in us as our Lord and Sovereign King to operate through us by the Spirit of the Lord, then this earthly placed called "this world" will become transformed, by grace and glory, into the eternal place within "the kingdom of heaven" called "the Paradise of God" which operates *in* oneness within the kingdom of God.

What is the kingdom of heaven like? This is perhaps the most important thing Jesus came to teach us: how the kingdom of heaven operates. Why? So that we can re-establish heaven upon the earth – (where the permanent presence of God resides– and abides) firstly, within our heart as His disciples, and secondly, upon the new earth as sons of God.

> "Therefore He [Jesus] said: "A certain nobleman **went into** a far country to receive for himself a kingdom and to return" (Luke 19:12). "Then He began to tell the people this parable: "A certain man planted a vineyard, leased it to vinedressers, and **went into** a far country for a long time'" (Luke 20:9).

Jesus used this teaching to convey many kingdom truths regarding man as vinedressers put on earth to tend His garden, whereby He leased it to us and granted us dominion to have authority over this earth on His behalf. And Jesus also taught we will be judged – either to be rewarded as faithful servants that are fruitful in obedience in doing His will or punished as unjust stewards. It is interesting, however, that the far country Jesus went to was Heaven's throne, and yet… Jesus has been dwelling within us the entire time as well.

> "Then the King will say to those on His right hand, 'Come, you blessed of My Father, inherit the kingdom prepared for you from the foundation of the world" (Matt. 25:34)

King Jesus does not offer us eternal bliss in His throne-room place called Heaven. Rather, we inherit "the kingdom that He prepared for us" which He purposed since before the foundation of the world to give those according to faithfulness. It becomes vitally important, therefore, to thoroughly understand and comprehend what the Lord Jesus means by dominion and kingdom in this present age, as well as the kingdom that Jesus went to prepare for us that He purposed for us – in the beginning (John 14:3).

"You are the light of the world. A city that is set on a hill cannot be hidden" (Matt. 5:14). In the kingdom of light where truth abides, the redeemed become spiritual cities that Christ will set upon hills so that the truth may be revealed so that other men may see... and come out of the darkness to be set free by the truth.

Lessons Learned

Jesus told us, "The kingdom of heaven is at hand." He was not only teaching us kingdom truth, He was also teaching us how to live and govern ourselves as His partnered representatives while we are engaged in this spiritual and heavenly operation to overcome the enemy and re-occupy territory stolen from God. It is impossible to put these truths into proper perspective unless we understand the big picture, and what it means "to have dominion." Verily, Jesus has given us a kingdom to rule and govern, as a kingdom in His kingdom... for His glory. It is not our planet to do with as we wish, even though we have done so; this earth is His possession and He sent us here as co-laborers with Christ, as His stewards and caretakers, to tend, take care of and manage the earth under His dominion as it orbits through the heavens.

> "So God looked upon the earth, and indeed it was corrupt; for all flesh had corrupted their way on the earth" (Gen. 6:12).

That generation in the day of Noah had become thoroughly corrupt and dominated by evil, having forgotten who they are and what they were supposed to be doing, whereby God caused a catastrophic flood upon the earth to wash away all remembrance of that generation of man.

When I first began to search for truth regarding the reason God sent mankind to earth, my limited understanding theorized we were sent here because of "something" we did – but now I know it was something the enemy did to us while we were in Heaven. We are spiritual beings and we came from God, to be certain, and I thought (erringly) that man needed to be "sanctified" because of something bad that he had done, but now I have a different perspective; we have always been the host of earth and our mission from the beginning has always been to reclaim, restore and re-occupy earth as a clean-up operation after the great rebellion in Heaven spilled over onto Earth. We did nothing wrong, per se; however, the enemy wronged us by sowing seeds of doubt in our mind to create fear, confusion and unbelief in the wake of his expulsion from Heaven. This "false perception" was the result of numerous "sinful nature" theologies that had been drilled into me my entire life. Just as inaccurate was this theology, so also were these inaccurate assessments of kingdom realities.

Therefore... the kingdom of heaven is like (or, in today's terms: here is the model, understand how it operates, now copy it... or... replicate the heavenly pattern you saw so that earth operates according to and becomes like the heavenly pattern you observed). Moses was told to copy the pattern he saw (Ex. 25:40; Acts 7:44; Heb. 8:5)... and since we know Christ, we are to live our life as His disciple, as imitators of Christ, to become sons of God, according to the pattern He demonstrated to us – as the Son of God.

> "Likewise, exhort the young men to be sober-minded, [7] in all things showing yourself to ***be a pattern of good works***; in doctrine showing integrity, reverence, incorruptibility, [8] sound speech that cannot be condemned, that one who is an opponent may be ashamed, having nothing evil to say of you" (Titus 2:6-8).

This world is corrupt because the spirit of this world has corrupted it – and mankind would do well to imitate Jesus and establish the heavenly pattern that He demonstrated for us to follow. This is our eternal purpose on earth... and yet another tribulation flood may become necessary.

Two Kingdoms In Conflict

> "For behold, the darkness shall cover the earth, and deep darkness the people; but the Lord will arise over you, and His glory will be seen upon you" (Isa. 60:2).

As mentioned earlier, it seems we have lost all understanding and comprehension regarding the kingdom of darkness upon the earth. Over the years, even some of my friends have regarded this word as merely a metaphor for sin and unbelief, which it is, and yet, darkness is also a veiled spiritual reality of evil that surrounds us – even now. The trick of the enemy is to deceive us and prevent us from perceiving the reality of evil and the existence of Satan wherein we remain unwitting slaves in bondage to sin and unbelief... thereby remaining unintelligent concerning spiritual matters and, thus, fail to establish the kingdom of heaven upon the earth.

The Apostle John knew Jesus more intimately that anyone on earth, and thus, he is able to communicate deep theological truth regarding Jesus Christ and the kingdom of God. John did not write his four gospels until about sixty years after Christ's resurrection, which allowed him much time for reflection and meditation regarding the "Word of Life" that he beheld... and the truth which Jesus taught.

When I read 1 John, it is crystal clear to me that he is presenting the truth of God within a compare-and-contrast framework to convey many principles:

- Jesus established the kingdom of heaven to expose and come against Satan's kingdom of darkness which Jesus referred to as "this world"
- The kingdom of heaven is based upon truth; darkness is based upon a lie

- Believers in Jesus will abide in Him and live according to the Spirit in truth and in love, but doubters will deny Jesus is Lord and be scoffers of the truth with unbelief in their heart
- Jesus is the Savior of the world; Satan is the destroyer and the accuser of the brethren
- The ruler of this world (Satan) is diametrically opposed to (anti) Christ
- Christ has His Spirit, and the Antichrist also has a spirit to deceive mankind

Spiritual Warfare

The kingdom of darkness that is upon the earth is opposed to Jesus Christ. It is antichrist! It seeks to compromise, undermine, and violently come against the church and God's truth every chance it gets. In order to comprehend the spiritual war that we are in, we must acknowledge the presence of evil and expose the lies of the enemy if we ever plan to succeed in piercing the darkness with the truth of Christ! John used the terms 'darkness' and 'world' more than any other gospel writer to convey this evil spiritual reality that surrounds us.

We are at war! To think otherwise means the Spirit of truth is not operational with you – yet. If the Spirit of God is in you, then the Spirit will bring fresh revelation to you every step along the path of discipleship to ensure "faith" is not compromised by the spirit of antichrist.

> "Every spirit that does not confess that Jesus Christ has come in the flesh is not of God. And this is ***the spirit of*** the Antichrist, which you have heard was coming, and is now already in the world" (1 John 4:3).

John uses a unique phraseology "τὸ τοῦ" that occurs only three other times in scripture:

- καὶ [and] πᾶν [every] πνεῦμα [spirit] ὃ [which] μὴ [not] ὁμολογεῖ [confesses] τὸν [-] Ἰησοῦν [Jesus] ἐκ [of] τοῦ [-] θεοῦ [god] οὐκ [not] ἔστιν· [in] καὶ [and] τοῦτό [this] ἐστιν [is] **τὸ τοῦ [the(spirit) - of the]** ἀντιχρίστου [antichrist], ὃ [which] ἀκηκόατε [ye have heard] ὅτι [that] ἔρχεται [it is coming], καὶ [and] νῦν [now] ἐν [in] τῷ [the] κόσμῳ [world] ἐστὶν [is] ἤδη [already]. (1 John 4:3)
- μηδεὶς [no one] τὸ [the thing] ἑαυτοῦ [of himself] ζητείτω [let him] ἀλλὰ [but] **τὸ τοῦ [the thing - of the]** ἑτέρου [other]. (1 Cor. 10:24)
- ἵνα [in order that] ὑμεῖς [ye] ὑψωθῆτε, [might be called] ὅτι [because] δωρεὰν [freely] **τὸ τοῦ [the - of]** θεοῦ [God] εὐαγγέλιον [gospel] εὐηγγελισάμην [I preached good tidings] ὑμῖν [to you] (2 Cor. 11:7)
- εἰ [if]ὀνειδίζεσθε [ye are reproached] ἐν [in] ὀνόματι [the name of] Χριστοῦ [Christ], μακάριοι, [blessed are ye] ὅτι [because] τὸ [the] τῆς [-] δόξης [of glory] καὶ [and] **τὸ τοῦ [the(?that) - of]** θεοῦ [God] πνεῦμα [spirit] ἐφ' [on] ὑμᾶς [you] ἀναπαύεται [rests]. (1 Pet. 4:14)

Consider how Satan set up a counterfeit kingdom as an alternate reality that seems deceptively good enough, but at its core is opposed to (anti) Christ. The counterfeit king is Satan, the counterfeit kingdom is "this world," he has a counterfeit christ [sic] and a counterfeit spirit. Much unnecessary attention has been given to the Antichrist (a word that appears only in 1 John (3x) and 2 John (1x); and conspicuously absent in Revelation) that many believe is a manifested being or person, as do I; however, I want to focus for a moment on the "spirit" of the antichrist.

Compare and contrast the attributes of these contradictory spirits:

- Spirit… of truth, of life, of wisdom, of justice, of faith, of gentleness, of holiness, of promise, of rejoicing, of strength with might, of freedom, of liberty, of unity, of wisdom and revelation, of prophecy, of grace, of supplication, of glory, of God, of Jesus Christ, of heaven and earth

- spirit... of evil, of error, of fear, of bondage, of harlotry, of infirmity, of divination, of deception, of stupor, of lying, of perversion, of chaos and confusion, of corruption, of demons, of darkness, of antichrist, of the world

Two spiritual forces are waging warfare in the heavenly realm – the Spirit of Christ and the spirit of antichrist[15] – and the mind of man is the only thing standing between (in the midst of) these two spiritual forces for dominion over the earth. The Spirit of the Lord will prevail upon the earth, but what spirit are you being influenced by? Is the Spirit of Christ conforming you into the image of Christ as His heavenly representative on earth – or are you being conformed to the pattern of "this world" to be an unholy tool and possession of Satan?

> "Now we have received, not ***the spirit of the world***, but the Spirit who is from God, that we might know the things that have been freely given to us by God" (1 Cor. 2:12).

Therefore, it is extremely important that we are able to discern and distinguish between these spiritual voices that speak into our mind, and thus, to know and thoroughly comprehend the Voice of Christ and His words of truth in order that we should live obediently to His commands. Once we know the sound of His voice, we must not obey the voice of strangers.

> "... and the sheep hear his voice; and he calls his own sheep by name and leads them out. [4] And when he brings out his own sheep, he goes before them; and the sheep follow him, for they know his voice. [5] Yet they will by no means follow a stranger, but

---

[15] The term "Christ" can be understood to mean: the manifested presence of God in or by a person. And likewise, the term antichrist can also be understood to mean the manifested presence of evil in or by a person; history has documented many such persons that fit this category... and they have always been among us... even today.

will flee from him, for they do not know the voice of strangers" (John 10:3-5).

Saints of God, we must understand who we are and what we are supposed to be doing because there is very much at stake. The term "*darkness*" occurs in the New Testament 42x – which John mentioned (6x) in the gospel John and (5x) in 1 John; similarly, the term "*world*" occurs in the New Testament 185x – which John mentioned (62x) in the gospel John and (17x) in 1 John in order to help us perceive the spiritual reality that we are in. But more importantly, John taught us that the way of escape from out of darkness is accomplished through faith in Christ Jesus – by building a permanent home within our heart for Jesus to abide within us… as we *abide* (27/32x) in Christ.

Consider, now, the message from Jesus to the Apostle Paul on the road to Damascus:

> "So I said, 'Who are You, Lord?' And He said, 'I am Jesus, whom you are persecuting. [16] But rise and stand on your feet; for I have appeared to you for this purpose, to make you a minister and a witness both of the things which you have seen and of the things which I will yet reveal to you. [17] I will deliver you from the Jewish people, as well as from the Gentiles, to whom I now send you, [18] **to open their eyes, in order to turn them from darkness to light, and from the power of Satan to God**, that they may receive forgiveness of sins and an inheritance among those who are sanctified by faith in Me' (Acts 26:15-18).

Understanding the darkness that surrounds us is essential to comprehending our mission on earth as we have dominion over the spiritual forces that are opposed to (anti) Christ. We all have a God-given purpose for being on earth and we need to seek the Lord Jesus to know what He wants us to do. His plan of redemption involves a predetermined purpose for you, and everyone as well, as sons of men having been predestined by God to live for Christ and establish His dominion on earth in newness, through truth, change and oneness. What you do (the will of God for your life) is determined by who you are (your identity) in Christ Jesus. If we do not know what the will of God is for our life… then it is because we have not taken time to inquire of the Lord and become His disciple. We are sojourners with a purpose according to His eternal plan of redemption for the earth – and mankind – which begins by hearing His voice!

The Lord has enabled us to operate with a renewed mind that is being transformed by the Spirit of God to be able to hear the plan of God on a continual basis, as in, all the time.

> "For God has not given us a spirit of fear, but of power and of love and of a sound mind" (2 Tim. 1:7).

> "For you did not receive the spirit of bondage again to fear, but you received the Spirit of adoption by whom we cry out, "Abba, Father" (Rom. 8:15).

When we declare Jesus our Lord, we are adopted into the Father's spiritual family; when we follow Jesus and become His disciple, we can adopt this next scripture… and own it:

> "The Spirit of the Lord shall rest upon Him, The Spirit of wisdom and understanding, The Spirit of counsel and might, The Spirit of knowledge and of the fear of the Lord" (Isa. 11:2).

What more could I possibly say beyond these scriptures to convince you so that you become thoroughly persuaded and convinced to live according to faith by the Spirit of God and live your life as a disciple of Jesus? In doing so, whatever things you forfeit "of this world" will be rewarded unto you as true riches in the new heaven to be revealed in the regeneration.

> "For whoever desires to save his life will lose it, but whoever loses his life for My sake will find it" (Matt. 16:25).

Are you willing to trade up? Listen to the Spirit... and be obedient to the Voice of Truth!

The kingdom of heaven is at hand!!!

Principalities and Powers

> "For by Him all things were created that are in heaven and that are on earth, visible and invisible, whether thrones or dominions or principalities or powers. All things were created through Him and for Him" (Col. 1:16); "to the intent that now the manifold wisdom of God might be made known by the church to the principalities and powers in the heavenly places" (Eph. 3:10)

Imagine the significance of this statement; Jesus created everything "through Him and for Him" including dominions, principalities and powers. And it was always the Lord's intent to reveal the manifold wisdom of God to all principalities, powers and dominions – through the church!

Jesus is – "far above all principality and power and might and dominion, and every name that is named, not only in this age but also in that which is to come" (Eph. 1:21).

> "Yet in all these things we are more than conquerors through Him who loved us. [38] For I am persuaded that neither death nor life, nor angels nor principalities nor powers, nor things present nor things to come, [39] nor height nor depth, nor any other created thing, shall be able to separate us from the love of God which is in Christ Jesus our Lord" (Rom. 8:36-38).

"For we do not wrestle against flesh and blood, but against principalities, against powers, against the rulers of the darkness of this age, against spiritual *hosts* of wickedness in the heavenly *places*..." (Eph. 6:12).

"... and you are complete in Him, who is the head of all principality and power" (Col. 2:10). "Having disarmed principalities and powers, He made a public spectacle of them, triumphing over them in it" (Col. 2:15).

Does this give you a larger perspective of what is happening on earth? Indeed, it should!

5. The Dominion

Dominion. What is it? Even though it is one of the most important words within Christian theology, I have never, according to my memory, ever heard a sermon about it, let alone heard the word used from the pulpit. Apart from the occasional use of this word repeated in doxologies and creeds, I wonder how many of us could define it. Certainly, I for one... could not. This chapter was written upon reflection, having already written the majority of text for this book, when I realized I have been writing about it – but I could not easily define it.

It would be the same if we tried to define the words... life, preeminence, or sustainable. These one words in singular take paragraphs to define, but we easily attribute this one word to the One who cannot be defined, even if a library of books were devoted entirely to Him: Jesus Christ.

Dominion, as best and as simply as it can be defined, is "the delegated right to act."

Included in this definition is "the right to exercise authority, and power, and judgment in all forms of governance, and we can see these three elements being used to form our three branches of government in America. All three can be independently acted upon, but all three operate in union as oneness in governance (or at least they should). So, let's take some time to understand this incredible principle.

Dominion, first and foremost, is a divine right. It is given by the Lord God to act, not with impunity, but to act on "His" behalf. This right comes with an authentication or "seal of approval" whereby someone can clearly demonstrate this right has been legally and officially given to them, or, they are operating in such a manner as to demonstrate they have been given this right. We can see an example of this when religious leaders asked Jesus:

> "Now when He came into the temple, the chief priests and the elders of the people confronted Him as He was teaching, and said, "By what authority are You doing these things? And who gave You this authority?" (Matt. 21:23).

These Jewish leaders had a right to ask Jesus this question because anyone who uses divine authority for their own motives to accomplish their agenda is swimming upstream against God's oncoming tsunami. They had a right to know, so it seems, but because they had already decided to reject His answer and remain in unbelief, Jesus answered their question with a question they could not answer without exposing their hypocrisy.

Dominion, secondly, is the authority to act upon this divine right and to enjoy all the privileges pertaining to this authority. Both the right and the authority to act can only be distributed by the One with the original right and the implicit authority to distribute – as they deem appropriate. If anyone operates in this capacity, it is because God alone has given them this authority, which is why we are told "to pray for those in authority over you" because, whether or not they recognize this position as a use of His authority, I can assure you that it most definitely is.

> "Therefore I exhort first of all that supplications, prayers, intercessions, and giving of thanks be made for all men, for kings and all who are in authority, that we may lead a quiet and peaceable life in all godliness and reverence. For this is good and acceptable in the sight of God our Savior" (1 Tim. 2:1-3).

As with all aspects of dominion, authority can be given – and taken away – and even returned. All authority was given to Jesus by the Father (John 17:2; Matt. 11:25-27).

Within the matrix of authority are various other manifestations whereby we come to know the term dominion best. They are:

- The Authority – is the means whereby a person has been granted permission to act
- The Power – is the use of delegated power and authority "exusia" to act "under, or out of" the authority of the original One who possesses all rights to this power and authority. The person or persons who operate according to this power must remain humble stewards of this operating as being from "out of *and* under" God's authority. People in leadership should not take this responsibility lightly, because if teachers of truth are held to a higher standard of accountability to God, then leaders are held to the strictest standard and, in this regard, should be done with as much humility as humanly possible.

None of these attributes reside within man as one of his personal gifts or talents. We are not born with them, per se; the Lord may have predestined some of us to live life with one or more of these attributes because He chose us or called us to operate in this manner from before the beginning of our way, but even in this regard, they are His attributes, not ours. We must always be mindful, "What God has given, God can take away" (Job 1:21) and we must "praise and extol and honor the King of heaven" who gives us these wonderful gifts (Dan. 4:36).

- We are alive because the life is in us, but the Life is not us.
- We have power and electricity flowing through us, but we are not the Power.
- We have glory hidden in these earthen vessels, but we are not the Glory.
- We have been crowned with glory and honor, but we are not the Honor and the Glory.
- We were made a little lower than angels, like elohims, but we are not Elohim.
- We are who we are, because of "I Am WHO I Am" abiding within us.

Our life is not our own. We were created in the womb and through the womb God gave us life, not just "a" life, but He gave us "the life" that belongs to Him as part of His dominion. The air and the water were created by Him and for Him, and in this regard, we cannot have a breath of life or red blood with the life in it – unless the Lord God had created both air and water for ruddy "adams" (men, mankind, humanity, or whatever you want to call us) to live upon the earth.

Even our intellect is not our own. We were blessed with intellect while we were being formed by the hand of God in the womb. We have the ability to cultivate this intellect – whether we choose to or not, but intellect is given to all men for the administration and operation of our physical bodies for the sake of His will and plan for your life. Our intellectual ability to reason and understand is a gift from God. King Nebuchadnezzar of Babylon had his intellectual reason (understanding) removed from the Lord God until he came to his senses and he did one thing: he lifted his eyes to heaven. He repented and did three things: He blessed and honored and revered the Lord, he acknowledges the Lord's sovereignty, and pledged his allegiance to Him as his sovereign Lord (Dan. 4:34-36).

"This is not the reasoning that initiates a debate that results in a compromise; on the contrary, it results in an agreement – with you completely agreeing with the sovereignty of God – on His terms – and with the Spirit helping you to understand what is happening. Nebuchadnezzar lost his reasoning, but it returned to Him when he lifted his eyes to heaven, he blessed the Most High and honored Him, and declared that God alone rules and reigns in the kingdom of men." [16]

This is dominion – and it begins by understanding with full reasoning of the intellect, that Jesus alone is sovereign. This is His kingdom and His dominion – and everything that happens, happens according to His perfect will and plan in order that He alone receives all the glory in it, whereby the Lord God is worthy to

---

[16] Excerpt from "Listen."

receive all honor and praise and exaltation and adoration in the glory of His holiness.

Dominion is not about what – but Who.

> "Then the kingdom and dominion,
> And the greatness of the kingdoms
> under the whole heaven,
> Shall be given to the people,
> the saints of the Most High.
> His kingdom *is* an everlasting kingdom,
> And all dominions shall serve and obey Him"
> (Dan. 7:27).

6. Dominion Defined

The terms dominion and kingdom have been explained and expounded upon by theologians, religious institutions, governments, five-fold ministers, clergy managers and pastors of local churches for thousands of years. They operated under various assumptions and it is through these lenses that they developed many doctrines and teachings.

There are primary and secondary lenses that we use to interpret scripture which are based upon the magnitude of truth we comprehend which influence our doctrines. The primary lenses are:

- Do you believe in a loving God who is in control of everything – or not
- Do you believe in God who is all good and without wrath – or not
- Do you believe that Jesus is the only begotten Son of God, Messiah and Savior – or not
- Do you believe Jesus is the only way of salvation – or not
- Do you believe there is a Holy Spirit – or not
- Do you believe spiritual gifts from the Holy Spirit can be manifested today – or not
- Do you believe that you can hear God's voice – or not
- Do you believe in the inerrancy of scripture in the original text – or not
- Do you believe that you are a human being in search of a spiritual experience – or you are a spiritual being that is having a human experience
- Do you believe you will spend eternal life either in heaven or hell – or not
- Do you believe eternal life will be spent upon the earth – or not

That last question represents a new "lens" that has not been asked for the past 2,000 years. If all doctrine and religious instruction have only presented the "non-earth eternal home" doctrine of heave versus the New Earth doctrine, then you can see how this alternative may significantly cloud our interpretation of scripture, as well as the perfect will of God.

What Is Dominion

- Dominion is the authority to act; it represents the legal right to exercise delegated authority, as a right granted (or given) by a sovereign to act as a representative of the sovereign, which can only be given or taken away by the sovereign

Of the 51 occurrences for "dominion" in the Bible, Jesus only used the term "dominion" once, and not in a good way; however, good examples of this principle were employed in many of His parables and teachings.

> "But Jesus called them to Himself and said, "You know that the rulers of the Gentiles *lord it over* [2634 *exercise dominion over* – KJV] them, and those who are great exercise authority over them" (Matt. 20:25).

The word "lord" is '*katakurieuo*' (2634)(4x) meaning, "to lord against, i.e. control, subjugate" from '*kata*' down and '*kurieuo*' (2961) to rule, have dominion (down), exercise lordship (over) [17]
- In Matt. 20:25, to exercise dominion over, as the "lordship" of Gentile rulers over their subjugates with absolute control
- In Mark 10:42, to exercise lordship over by exercising authority over, as a sovereign
- In Acts 19:16, as the ability of evil spirits (devils or demons) to exercise power over men (overcame - overpowered them and prevailed against them)
- In 1 Pet. 5:3, the evil of elders in "lording over" those who are under their spiritual care

---

[17] Strong's Concordance.

> "And He said to them, "The kings of the Gentiles exercise lordship (2961) over them, and those who exercise authority over them are called 'benefactors.' ²⁶ But not so *among* you; on the contrary, he who is greatest among you, let him be as the younger, and he who governs as he who serves. ²⁷ For who *is* greater, he who sits at the table, or he who serves? *Is* it not he who sits at the table? Yet I am among you as the One who serves" (Luke 22:25-27).

In these passages, we can clearly see that the 'nature' of having dominion as a worldly (and even demonic) concept as "a lording over others" is inconsistent with the spiritual paradigm of Christ's kingdom upon the earth. We have only one Sovereign, Jesus Christ, who is Lord over all, and we are His servants and ministers of the gospel of grace, never being called into a position of authority to exercise dominion "over" anyone, as in a hierarchical over-bearing worldly manner – but rather, we are to exercise authority in the paraclete model of coming alongside others as fellow ministers, servants, friends, partakers of grace, partners in the gospel, and joint heirs of eternal life according to the gospel of grace and faith in Christ Jesus.

The word "authority" (above) is '*katexousiazo*' (2715; Mark 10:42) and likewise, appears only one time and means "to have (wield) full privilege over; exercise authority upon."[18]

Thus, the worldly manner to lord "against and over" is inconsistent with the kingdom of heaven manner wherein we rule and reign "with" one another as we all serve and follow Jesus Christ our Sovereign Lord and King. We have another clear example of this heavenly dominion concept regarding our eternal home with God:

> "If anyone loves Me, he will keep My word; and My Father will love him, and We will come to him

---

[18] IBID.

and make Our *home* (*mone*) **with** him" (John 14:23).

Jesus said that He and the Father will make Their home "with" us, more specifically, not over us or under us but "in' us, that is made "with" us. This concept is transcendentally amazing!

The Lord and Supreme Commander over all creation, including heaven and earth, operates under a very different dominion model as our Sovereign who rules and reigns "with" us.

Is Jesus our Lord and Master? Yes! Are we to serve Him in a subservient manner? Absolutely! Must we obey His commandments? Without question! Does Christ partner with us as He co-exists in us and co-habits our earthen vessel? Well, you say, we may not have looked at it that way before. Jesus is a gentleman and He will never impose His authority over us, but rather, He chooses to rule and reign "with-in" us as we yield our sovereignty to His Sovereignty. He rules and reigns in your life depending upon how you yield your sovereignty to the sound of His voice that says: Come! Become My disciple.

If this model of jointly-partnered, sovereign-servant, co-authority dominion whereby both are engaged in exercising dominion through the delegated authority of Jesus as Lord is inconsistent with your perspective of how the universe is supposed to work, then how on earth can Jesus call you "friend"? How can Jesus refer to us as his brethren and beloved brethren? (See John 15:14; Rom. 1:7; Eph. 1:6; 1 Thess. 1:4; 1 Cor. 15:58). This, my friends, can only happen when we live as His disciple under His Lordship; no longer enemies of God, but friends "with" Christ.

What can I liken this type of dominion to? It would be like a potentate, ruler, magistrate or even the President of any great country coming into my house to ask me how "we" should shape the long-term sustainable growth of "our" community so that it remains vibrant and healthy, both socially and economically, for the next seven generations.

This is exactly how God wants to govern the universe with us, over us – and "with-in" us!

> "When the righteous are in authority, the people rejoice; but when a wicked man rules, the people groan" (Prov. 29:2).

The Apostle Paul had the "authority" and boldness to impose his opinion on Philemon regarding Onesimus, indicating that Philemon owed to Paul "his very life;" however, Paul did not command or impose that authority "over" Philemon in a worldly manner, but rather, he beseeched him on the basis of love – "yet for love's sake" – to do the right thing. This, my friends, is how the kingdom of God is supposed to operate now, and eternally, in the New Earth.

New Earth Dominion

Now, let us examine a new-earth model within the scriptures to glean truth upon truth:

> "Therefore I exhort first of all that supplications, prayers, intercessions, and giving of thanks be made for all men, ² for kings and all who are in *authority*[19], that we may lead a quiet and peaceable life in all godliness and reverence. ³ For this is good and acceptable in the sight of God our Savior" (1 Tim. 2:1-3).

We are to pray for all our leaders (spiritual and worldly) who are in authority, regardless if they are good or bad. How can I say this? It is because their position as an "authority" operates as one with

---

[19] *Huperoche* (2x, 5247) prominence, superiority (in rank or character); the position of magistrates (1 Tim. 2:2) and is also used for excellence of speech (1 Cor. 2:1); Strong's Concordance. They are not hierarchically "over" us, but are placed in a position alongside us to govern on God's behalf. This is not to be confused with '*exousia*' the only term Jesus used for lawful and legal authority to exercise the power that resides within His authority.

delegated authority with delegated power that employs the power and authority of the Almighty; regardless if they recognize it as such – or not – they are using God's power and authority in whom *is* all power and All might and All authority and All dominion.

We need to see dominion and delegated authority from "God's" perspective, not man's.

We are partners with Christ in the gospel of good news, and partakers of grace, having been commanded to have dominion, as stewards and caretakers of the earth, as partners and co-laborers with one another, to exercise His dominion that utilizes His sovereign authority within His kingdom. So now, let's look to the scriptures for good and godly, as well as worldly, examples of dominion.

Dominion (*kurieuo*-2961): to rule, have dominion over, exercise (***worldly***) lordship over:

- Rom. 6:9 – death no longer has dominion over Christ (or us – according to faith)
- Rom. 6:14 – sin shall not have dominion over believers (we are under grace)
- Rom. 7:1 – the (old) "Law" has dominion over a man while he is alive (unless we are rendered dead to the law, having been made alive again in the birthing anew by the Spirit according to the (new) "law according to the Spirit of life in Christ Jesus" (Rom. 8:2)
- Rom. 14:9 – "that Christ (*might be Lord*-2961) of both the living [ones] and the dead"
- And most importantly, the good example of dominion:

    "Not that we have dominion over your faith, but are fellow workers for your joy; for by faith you stand" (2 Cor. 1:24).

Dominion (*kuriotes*-2963): mastery, rulers: denotes (***godly***) lordship, authority, power, dominion, government:

- Eph. 1:21 – Christ is seated at God's right hand in the heavenly places above all principality and power and might and *dominion* (whether angelic or human)
- Jude 8 – debased men with sinful affections, despise *authority*, even man's governance
- Col. 1:16 – Jesus created all things, visible and invisible, even heaven, earth, thrones, *dominions*, principalities, and powers, all – having been created through Him and for Him
- 2 Pet. 2:10 – the unjust, reserved for judgment, walk after the flesh and despise *government*

Dominion (*kratos*-2904): great vigor – dominion, might, (**manifested**) power, strength:

- 1 Pet. 4:11; 5:11 – to Christ belongs the glory and the *manifested power* forever and ever
- Jude 25 – to the only God our Savior through Jesus Christ our Lord – be glory, greatness, *might* and (*exousia*) authority (literal Greek)
- Rev. 1:6 – to Jesus Christ belongs the glory and the *manifested power* forever and ever

The common theme coursing though all scripture is… Jesus has all dominion with (exousia) authority and (kratos) manifested power and greatness and glory forever and ever – and it is His plan to dispense delegated authority and power into the hands of men to govern this earth to have "dominion" over His enemies, those authorities and principalities in heavenly places – that are in opposition to Him and His dominion for the earth.

Anytime anyone operates outside of this paradigm, their actions are considered evil because it robs Jesus of the glory that is rightfully His. The dominion does not belong to us – it belongs to Jesus – and He has given it to us as His representatives to operate upon the earth to accomplish perfectly all that He planned. Not only are we to operate according to this manner now, but we will also operate in this manner in the New Earth when kingdoms are given to His obedient servants to rule and reign for all eternity. We are being tested and sanctified during this season of eternity on earth to determine whether we are trustworthy to receive kingdoms and dominion.

As is always my custom, I begin with the very words of Christ Himself… never beginning any teaching with Old Testament truth because we need the light of truth abiding within the New Covenant to illuminate *all* scripture. [20] So now, it is essential to understand the term "dominion" as a concept that is, foremost in principle, our first "commandment" given to us by God Himself.

> "Then God said, "Let Us make man in Our image, according to Our likeness; **let them have dominion** over the fish of the sea, over the birds of the air, and over the cattle, **over all the earth** and over every creeping thing that creeps on the earth" (Gen. 1:26).

Dominion, in this context, is '*radah*' (H7287) meaning: "to tread down, subjugate, subdue, crumble, and prevail"[21] with the idea of bringing into submission, to conquer. We are not supposed to exercise this type of dominion over people or the earth, which is the worldly manner of ruling and reigning, but rather… we are subjugate principalities and powers that have set up a counterfeit kingdom on earth that is opposed to (anti) Christ. We are to tread down, prevail against, reign, rule over, disregard and '*kibosh*' every principality, authority, power, demon, evil spirit, all strongholds and wickedness in high places, and every spirit that is antichrist including Satan Himself that is raised up against the knowledge of Christ… by operating under the delegated authority Jesus gave us, using His delegated power through the anointing of the Spirit to subjugate Christ's enemies to have dominion over this earth – in the name of Jesus.

---

[20] We must look at the Old in the light of the New Covenant, never the new in the light of the old.
[21] Strong's Concordance.

> "Then they were all amazed and spoke among themselves, saying, "What a word this is! For with authority and power He commands the unclean spirits, and they come out." (Luke 4:36).

> "And when He had called His twelve disciples to Him, He gave them power over unclean spirits, to cast them out, and to heal all kinds of sickness and all kinds of disease" (Matt. 10:1).

We were sent to have dominion, not over one another, but over God's enemies and the residual effect of their counterfeit kingdom upon men. The problem we face is complex: we are *not* to war against people who have been deceived to believe the lies of the enemy, as they are just like we once were without the truth of Christ abiding within us (here but by the grace of God go I), but we MUST come against these lies with truth – with authority and with power!

> "For we do not wrestle against flesh and blood, but against principalities, against powers, against the rulers of the darkness of this age, against spiritual hosts of wickedness in the heavenly places" (Eph. 6:12).

We are not to come against people with worldly weapons but with only the sword of truth. We are to speak the truth of God – in love – with power – under the anointing of the Spirit whereby our enemies are vanquished by the power of God – and other souls are saved alive.

> "And my speech and my preaching were not with persuasive words of human wisdom, but in demonstration of the Spirit and of power, [5] that your faith should not be in the wisdom of men but in the power of God" (1 Cor. 2:4, 5).

> "For the kingdom of God is not in word but in power" (1 Cor. 4:20).

Ok, then, since the Lord wants us to use His authority with power, when do we get this power?

> "But you shall receive power when the Holy Spirit has come upon you; and you shall be witnesses to Me in Jerusalem, and in all Judea and Samaria, and to the end of the earth" (Acts 1:8).

Therefore, this is the primary purpose of Christ's church upon the earth: to love one another…

> "… and to make all see what *is* the fellowship of the mystery, which from the beginning of the ages has been hidden in God who created all things through Jesus Christ; [10] to the intent that now the manifold wisdom of God might be made known by the church to the principalities and powers in the heavenly places, [11] according to the eternal purpose which He accomplished in Christ Jesus our Lord" (Eph. 3:9-11).

> "Now may the God of hope fill you with all joy and peace in believing, that you may abound in hope by the power of the Holy Spirit" (Rom. 13:15).

The enemies of Jesus will come against His beloved servants and disciples to hinder our dominion mandate and minimize our power over them, and they will stop at nothing to diminish our capacity to govern this earth in the authority of Christ. When I encounter the enemy, my approach is simple: disregard them. Hit 'em hard and keep moving forward… even taking the fight to them by binding them to prevent them from operating (Matt. 16:19; 18:18). Don't look back – keep your eyes upon Jesus – and advance against our enemy with the truth of God. They are a vanquished foe and already know that Christ is victorious over them, and they know that Christ has given us His authority… and His Spirit *with* power… to come against them! So, then, if you are under spiritual attack, then know this: if you are valuable, then you are vulnerable. Don't give up or give in! The enemy will discourage us with temptation and attempt to steal our integrity and our calling by causing us to fall into sin, but Christ is victorious even over sin and death! Ask God's forgiveness, get up and get back in the fight! The enemy wants you to stay down as a defeated foe, but don't succumb to their spirit of discouragement. Forgiveness restores us to God, and therefore… you are "the redeemed of the Lord." Shake it off and get back in the fight to have dominion over the enemy with renewed vigor! If you have fallen victim to sin in one area, then you are now an experienced warrior that understands the modus operandi of the enemy – and now you must teach others to avoid it – and come against the trick of the enemy by coming against that manner of warfare *by exposing it to the light*… in spirit and in truth.

Again, I say… we are at war! Love Jesus. Live the truth. Hate the lie. Have dominion!

Let's recap a few thoughts: Whose dominion is it? Who gave it to us? Why did Jesus give it to us? What comes with this dominion? And, how do we operate within this dominion? And here are the answers: the dominion belongs to Jesus (all things having been created through Him and for Him), He granted it to us for the purpose of governing the earth in His name, and we are operating under His delegated authority and power to do His will – not ours.

And why did He do this, you may ask? For what reason? Exactly… He did it for "the what" reason – i.e. He did it for His glory, "for Whom belongs the glory and the manifested power forever and ever. Amen."

Now, there may be some who protesteth that Jesus gets the glory and not the Father, but this line of reasoning is faulty on several levels:

- Jesus is God, through whom all things were created
- Jesus is Lord of heaven and earth, Lord God and Lord Almighty
- Jesus has always been the Father's manifest representative for earth, appearing upon the earth for Him and as Him as "the Living God"
- Jesus and the Father operate in Oneness of glory

When Jesus gets the glory, the Father is glorified.

It is all about Jesus – and God gets all the glory. And there is no contradiction in terms!

Now, let's backtrack for just a moment by reexamining Col. 1:16 (see above). Who does the scripture say "created all things?" Indeed, it says Jesus did. This is not a singular reference, so look up the many other references that confirms Jesus created all things, visible and invisible, material and immaterial: John 1:18; 17:5; Col. 1:15-17; 3:10; Eph. 3:9: Phil. 2:5-7; 2 Cor. 4:4; Heb. 1:2, 3; 2:10; Rev. 4:1; and Old Testament verses: Gen. 1:27 (His own image); Isa. 41:20; 43:7; including all other references to "Creator" as well.

All creation exists to create and sustain life… and Jesus told us that He is the life (John 14:6). Now, assemble these thoughts together in your mind… where does creation get its life from? Jesus. And why was man created and then given the breath of life? A: To give glory to God. And likewise, what does creation do? It manifest God's glory. All things were created with Life to give glory to God – and Jesus is God, who created all things, so then, creation itself is one expression of Life Himself. Creation is "one" expression of how Jesus chose to express Himself and manifest Himself – through His creation and within His creation, which includes you and me as His living tabernacles.

Why is this important? Jesus created all things, both visible and invisible, before anything was created, and Jesus is God, so now let's see what the scripture says following the "let them have dominion" verse in Gen. 1:26.

> "So God created man in ***His own image***; in the image of God He created him; male and female He created them" (Gen. 1:27).

Look closely at the subtle personal pronoun change in the Genesis creation account from "Our image" (v.26) to "His own image" (v.27).

Jesus is God. And "God created man in <u>*His own*</u> image." Once again, who is the creator? Jesus. Who created man? Jesus. Who formed man? Jesus. In Whose own image was man created in? Jesus. Who has all dominion? Jesus. Who gave man His own dominion? Jesus. Who gave man His Own glory? Jesus. If the epiphany has not happened yet, then consider this: who said that He is the light of the world? Jesus. And who told men that they are the light of the world? Jesus (Matt. 5:14). I could fill another fifteen pages of similar questions and answers to illuminate the same truth to you so that everyone can confidently proclaim: Jesus only![22]

Who you are (your identity) is because of Who Jesus is!

> "And the Lord God [Jesus] planted a garden eastward *in* Eden, and there He put the man whom He had formed" (Gen. 2:8).

Jesus planted a garden, also known as the Garden of Eden and the Paradise of God (Rev. 2:7), and in this garden He "placed" man – as a seed. It is way beyond this teaching to elaborate on man "as the seed"[23] of Christ, through whose direct lineage came Jesus, the

---

[22] To read these fifteen pages, read "Image" to discover who Jesus really is, as Lord God and Lord Almighty.
[23] Read "Understand" to see man as seeds of God's glory sown unto the earth.

Messiah, from Adam through Mary (and Joseph), but the spiritual implications are phenomenal, to be sure. Moving on...

We have been operating with theological terminology regarding "God" without any regard for who God really is. The all-inclusive, nebulous, ubiquitous "God" word that is casually used in all of our public prayers does not give the listener any indication if we are referring to the Father or Jesus or the Holy Spirit. Jesus created the earth, as well as you and me, and this earth is His dominion, which He has given to you and me; and He sent us to earth to be "the light" in a world swamped in darkness; and even though Jesus taught us to ask the Father for our daily bread (basic needs), Jesus "told" us to ask Him *for all things* (John 14:13, 14; 15:7; 16:24) not for our personal gain, but to assist us in our efforts to exercise His authority *to have dominion over His earth*. Now do you see prayer from a different perspective? It is not for our selfish gain or personal pleasure, but for His glory *and His dominion*! If you need a tree, then plant a mustard seed; and if there is a "mountain" obstruction that is blocking your way that prevents you from accomplishing the mission Jesus called you to perform, then speak to the mountain and cause it to be cast into the sea – in His name. Jesus gave us this authority, and if Jesus has called you to do something, then He will also give you the power, the authority and the provision necessary to accomplish His will (not yours) through you. May Jesus be glorified in us – and through us!

> "My Father is with Me" (John 8:16, 29).
>
> "I and My Father are one" (John 10:30).
>
> "He who has seen Me has seen the Father" (John 14:9).
>
> "You shall call Me, "My Father," and not turn away from Me" (Jer. 3:19).

Jesus is God! Jesus is our Creator, Sustainer, Deliverer, Redeemer, Savior, Sovereign Lord... and our God. Jesus operates in oneness *with* the Father. The word "God" has seemingly become a religious byword to placate our ignorance with pious-sounding terminology. So now, if you know who God is, then tell someone what He is like, but if you cannot, then tell them about Jesus who is "the image of God" (2 Cor. 4:4; Col. 1:15) and the "express image" of the Father (Heb. 1:3). He not only came to show us the Father… He lives in Oneness with the Father.[24]

Jesus has always been the Father's representative for earth – and also our Example for the host of earth, i.e. the sons of men (you and me). Jesus is the Savior of the world – and *also* the Savior of men.

> "And beginning at Moses and all the Prophets, He expounded to them in all the Scriptures the things concerning Himself" (Luke 24:27), "And He opened their understanding, that they might comprehend the Scriptures" (v.45) that all scripture points to the reality of Jesus as Lord and Creator of all (John 5:39).

Therefore, since we have a "New Earth Doctrine" with "Jesus only" whereby men have been "let" or "been granted dominion over the earth," having been "formed and put" on the earth by Jesus to operate under His authority, perhaps now we are able to decipher all the terms contained within the Old Testament and Old Covenant (which, by the way, was atoned for and rendered obsolete by Christ's sacrificial death upon Calvary's cross), as types and shadows preceding the revelation of this new and better Way – and to see "all things which are in Christ Jesus" – from His perspective.

The Domain

> "And the angels who did not keep their ***proper domain*** [first estate-KJV], but left their own ***abode*** [habitation-KJV], He has reserved in everlasting

---

[24] Read "Image" for a more comprehensive teaching on the identity of Jesus.

chains under darkness for the judgment of the great day" (Jude 1:6).

This scripture is far more important than theologians consider.

- Domain – (*arche*-746) a proper place, principal home, place of residency; "a beginning; first place; first estate."[25]
- Abode – (*oiketerion* – 3613; from *oiketer*, inhabitant, and *oikos*, a dwelling place); a habitation.

Most Greek words have very specific meanings, but some have cross-referenced interpretations wherein multiple meanings are derived from the same original word, like: house, abode, dwelling, home, habitation, room – as well as: house, estate, place, regions, dwelling places – as they relate to where we are now, as in physically, spiritually or geographically (in the body) or where we will be (in transition, and eternally – in glory).

Words without context often become words taken out of context. '*Arche*' for example is translated as: "beginning (40x), principality (8x), corner (2x), first (2x), misc. (6x)" to imply the commencement or first beginning of something from an origination point "in various applications of order, time, place or rank."[26] It can get confusing, at times… especially in regard to places within the kingdom of God that are allocated to specific persons *that change over time.*

Heavy and Wordy

This next section is very heavy and wordy, so keep this in mind and extend much grace to me, even as I extend even greater grace to the reader…[27]

---

[25] Strong's Concordance.
[26] Strong's Concordance.
[27] All terms and definitions in this section were taken from Strong's Concordance.

As best I can ascertain from a detailed review of specific Greek words: there are temporary and permanent places of residency for men (as well as for angels). Existing (first) habitation places were established for man, as well as for angels, and future permanent (eternal) habitation places have been promised to angels and men according to obedience... which can be forfeited on account of disobedience (to then reside in other places; see Places: Chapter 7).

- Home – applies to the place we can always return to, our permanent residence
- Abode – can be a temporary residence, as in the place occupied while on a long journey or sojourn in this reality, or as a permanent residence in the eternal dimension wherein residency is established based upon criteria (and in this regard... according to faith)
  - *Mone* – (3438), occurs only 2 times (John 14:2, 23) said by Jesus, and implies a residence, "the place of staying," and corresponds to the English "manse" as a dwelling place for a minister.[28] This is the place where one abides (*meno*, 3306, to stay in a given place) in, at or within the *mone* (abode) of the Father's *oikia* (house) within the *oikos* (estate)
  - *Oikia* – (3614) the actual dwelling place (or building) Matt. 5:15; 7:24-27; 2 Tim. 2:20; 2 John 10; it can also include inhabitants; of note, it is never used of the Tabernacle or Temple
  - *Oikos* – (3624) the whole estate to include the *oikia* dwelling (house) and *meno* (staying place), as in the place where family members or households dwell/inhabit (Matt. 9:6, 7; 11:8); it is also used of the Tabernacle as a House of God (Matt. 12:4) and the Temple (Matt. 21:13; Luke 11:51; John 2:16, 17); the house of believers where Christ is spoken of as "over God's house" (Heb. 10:21; 1 Pet. 2:5; 4:17); a household (Titus 1:11); a local church, (1 Tim. 3:15).

---

[28] IBID.

(Note: *oikia* includes the *inhabitants* of a house or household, Matt. 12:15, whereas *oikos* includes only *members* of a household or family, Luke 10:5; Acts 7:10).

❖ The main distinction being: the Father has abodes (*mone*) in His (*oikia*) house or estate, though many have assumed this location is always Heaven, as the "eternal dwelling place of believers" (to be certain [29]); however, the Lord Jesus makes a permanent abode (*mone*) "with-in" us as an out-of-country residence within sojourners wherein They (Father and Son) commune in Divine relationship and fellowship "with-in" us as living tabernacles (John 14:2, 24). In this context, men are "houses" and "tabernacles" to host the presence of God whereby men are the abodes (houses or rooms) within the Father's estate (read Acts 7:49).

- House – an *'oikia'* (3614) actual physical building, structure; or spiritual dwelling place that serves as a residence, where God has an *oikia* home with many abodes (*mone*, rooms, mansions), and so do we (when we make places in our heart where others may dwell)
- Place – the *'oikos'* entire estate that surrounds and includes the *'oikia'* home; it can also represent *'topos'* as in "the place" that Jesus goes to prepare for us (John 14:2)
- Dwell – *'oikeo'* (3611) to occupy, dwell, cohabit, inhabit an abode (house) as in our earthen tents/bodies; of God dwelling in light (1 Tim. 6:16); of sin dwelling in the flesh (Rom. 7:17, 20); of the Spirit dwelling in us (Rom. 8:9, 11); (Note: there are two references for dwell in Rom. 8:11 – the Spirit of Him (i.e. God) who raised Jesus from the dead dwells *'oikia'* **with** you – will also give life to these mortal bodies through His Spirit (i.e. of Christ) who dwells *'enoikio'* **in** you (1774)).
- Dwell – 'enoikeo' (1774) occurs only 6 times as it relates to the indwelling of: God in believers (2 Cor. 6:16); His

---

[29] Strong's Concordance, study on house (*oikia* - 3614, see #3) and Vine's Expository on heaven (*ouranos* -3772) "as the eternal dwelling place of saints in resurrection glory" in reference to 2 Cor. 5:1.

Spirit (Rom. 8:11) and the Holy Spirit in believers (2 Tim 1:14); the Word of Christ in believers (Col. 3:16); faith (2 Tim. 1:5); sin in the believer (Rom. 7:17). In this latter regard, sin cohabits us by indwelling a person (in the flesh, but never the inner man or soul); likewise, the Holy Spirit cohabits us by indwelling and partnering with our spirit (inner man), whereby the lukewarm person with a double indwelling (flesh and spirit) is rendered unstable because the spirit-man wrestles and contends with the flesh-man in double-minded doubt (James 1:8).

- Dwelling place – where your heart and mind wills to makes a permanent home that may or may not be secondary to the temporary residence
- Habitation – a dwelling place and established residence, the (*oiketerion*-3613) for angels which is heaven (Jude 6), our future habitation for the redeemed in the New Earth (2 Cor. 5:2) and tabernacles for the unredeemed (Luke 16:9); the church as the "permanent" dwelling place (*katoiketerion*-2732) of the Holy Spirit (Eph. 2:22); of localities Divinely appointed for the nations (Acts 17:26); as the Temple as God's dwelling (Acts 7:26); and as the place of demons (Rev. 18:2).[30]

Thus, there are two scriptures that are worthy of greater scrutiny. Either you can *invest* in an eternal inheritance and future residence that comes to you from *'ek'* (out of) heaven, or you can *divest* (forfeit) your inheritance to dwell in (be cast into) the "place of outer darkness" on account of unrighteous mammon and disobedience.

> "For in this we groan, earnestly desiring to be clothed with our *habitation* which is *from* [*ek-out of*] heaven" (2 Cor. 5:2; the word habitation (house-KJV) is 3613).

---

[30] All references from Strong's Concordance.

> "So the master commended the unjust steward because he had dealt shrewdly. For the sons of this world are more shrewd in their generation than the sons of light. ^{9} And I say to you, make friends for yourselves by unrighteous mammon, that when you fail, they may receive you into an everlasting home (tabernacle). ^{10} He who is faithful in what is least is faithful also in much; and he who is unjust in what is least is unjust also in much. ^{11} Therefore if you have not been faithful in the unrighteous mammon, who will commit to your trust the true riches? ^{12} And if you have not been faithful in what is another man's, who will give you what is your own? ^{13} "No servant can serve two masters; for either he will hate the one and love the other, or else he will be loyal to the one and despise the other. You cannot serve God and mammon" (Luke 16:1-13).

This story by Jesus is about an unjust steward and "a certain man" (which Jesus often referred to as Himself). In the middle of this teaching, He tells "sons of light" that they are not as shrewd as "sons of this world," never implying that sons of light are to become shrewd like sons of this world through unrighteous (evil) gain… but… they at least know how to plan ahead and prepare an eternal place that will take care of them, even if this place is "outer darkness."

The real message is: there are two eternal dwellings, one established by righteousness and the other by unright stewardship. Are you planning ahead by store-housing righteousness into your heavenly account or are you going to succumb to the earthly manner of seeking after worldly mammon and, thus, forfeit Paradise with true riches?

> "And the Lord said, "Who then is that faithful and wise steward, whom his master will make ruler over his household, to give them their portion of food in due season?" (Luke 12:42). "It is like a man going

to a far country, who left his *house* (*oikia*) and gave authority to his servants, and to each his work, and commanded the doorkeeper to watch" (Mark 13:34).

Jesus used compare-and-contrast terms to explain how the kingdom of God operates so that we may all understand and thoroughly comprehend what is at stake: receiving a permanent kingdom on earth with true riches. The earth abides forever, but everything of "this world" is temporary and will be shaken and tossed into the fire. In the resurrection, we will either receive an eternal inheritance for dominion on earth… or be sent into outer darkness to experience eternal torment on account of disobedience and unrightness.

> "For thus says the Lord of hosts, the God of Israel: "Houses and fields and vineyards shall be possessed again in this land." (Jer. 32:15)

We have a future and a hope that has been placed within these earthen vessels which will be redeemed later in the Paradise of God (read all of Jer. 32). Our obedience to have dominion in this life determines our inheritance in life eternal. Nothing in this world can compare to the exceeding greatness and glory that awaits us in the New Earth when we remain faithful to Jesus.

> "So ***I will restore to you*** the years that the swarming locust has eaten, the crawling locust, the consuming locust, and the chewing locust, My great army which I sent among you" (Joel 2:25).

And finally, consider the spiritual implication of your life now… and eternally:

> "If the righteous will be recompensed on the earth, how much more the ungodly and the sinner" (Prov. 11:31).

[page left blank]

7. Places in the Kingdom [31]

"I go to prepare a place for you" (John 14:2).

Much of our misunderstanding regarding where we go after our body dies is born out of a "heaven-only" doctrine as our eternal destination; however, there are two other places in God's kingdom that are mentioned within numerous scriptures that cast a different picture on where we might go and Who holds the keys of Hades *and* of Death:

> "I am He who lives, and was dead, and behold, I am alive forevermore. Amen. And I have the keys of Hades and of Death" (Rev. 1:18).

Jesus is speaking these words to the Apostle John as he is having a heavenly vision while upon the island of Patmos. This is the first of seven encounters John has with "One like the Son of Man," who clearly presents Himself in this moment as Jesus Christ: the Ancient of Days.

Most of us have been taught that Hell and Hades are the same place, but they are not. And most Bibles translate the word Hades (G86-*hades*) as Hell (G1067-*gehenna*), especially the KJV; however, Hades and Hell are very different places, and Hades and Death are separate places as well because they each have their own key(s).

So, let me ask you this: since Jesus talked about Hades as much as He talked about Hell, then why is nothing ever said from the pulpit regarding Hades? And if there are only two places where men go after they die (i.e. Heaven and Hell), as we have been taught by the church, then why are these two places (Hades and Death) mentioned by Jesus at all?

---

[31] This entire section was copied from Chapter 6: "Here: The Kingdom of Heaven is."

Hades (G86) occurs 11 times in the scriptures, and is a combination of two words: '*a*' (G1-not) and '*oida*' (G1492-seen) and is regarded as "the unseen abode of the dead; the place of departed souls; a temporary destination."[32] To say that I was unexpectedly surprised to learn '*oida*' (meaning: to see, perceive, understand, comprehend, know experientially) is the root word for Hades is an understatement if there ever was one. Hades is "the not seen place" or perhaps "the place of not understanding."

The Hebrew equivalent for Hades is *Sheol* (H7585), which has its' root from (H7592-*sha'el*) and means: "to inquire; to request, to demand." Sheol is regarded as: "the abode of the dead, the place of degradation; as far as the world is concerned, they have perished, yet they are still in a state of existence"[33] from God's perspective. Sheol, then, is "the ultimate resting place of all mankind"[34] (Gen. 37:35) for a season while we await the judgment according to our deeds.

Hell (G1067-*gehenna*) occurs 11 times, and is regarded as "the place (or state of) everlasting punishment."[35] It is interesting to note that all occurrences in the New Testament for Hell were uttered by Jesus – except one (James 3:6) – and one occurrence refers to "*tartaros*" (G5020).

Death is referred to as a place less frequently than these other places in God's kingdom, which is regarded as a destination for souls in rebellion and disobedience to Jesus the Lord and, therefore, are already spiritually "dead in death" – being eternally separated from God.

So then, when we die, our body leaves us (our soul) to disintegrate and return once again where it came from: the earth. At this point, our soul is either "in Christ" waiting in Hades/Sheol or it is dwelling in nakedness in Death. All souls will wait for the

---

[32] Strong's Concordance.
[33] IBID.
[34] IBID.
[35] IBID.

resurrection, the redemption, and the judgment; some will be resurrected into life eternal and others resurrected to condemnation in Hell. If you are "in Christ" and, having been clothed with Christ (Rom. 13:14; Gal. 3:27; Eph. 4:20-24; Isa. 61:10), you will receive a new resurrection body in the regeneration, which will be superimposed upon you as having come down "from out of heaven."

There are three other scriptures that will help us understand this concept of Hades in detail:

> "The sea gave up the dead who were in it, and Death and Hades delivered up the dead who were in them. And they were judged, each one according to his works" (Rev. 20:13).

> "For as the Father has life in Himself, so He has granted the Son to have life in Himself, *[27] and has given Him authority to execute judgment also, because He is the Son of Man. [28] Do not marvel at this; for the hour is coming in which all who are in the graves will hear His voice [29]* and come forth—those who have done good, to the resurrection of life, and those who have done evil, to the resurrection of condemnation" (John 5:26-29; see the footnote regarding "graves" [36]).

> "Then Death and Hades were cast into the lake of fire. This is the second death. [15] And anyone not found written in the Book of Life was cast into the lake of fire" (Rev. 20:14, 15).

---

[36] Grave (*mnemeion*-3419) means, "a remembrance" and primarily denotes "a memorial" as anything done (like a monument) "to preserve the memory of things or persons." Strong's Concordance. The remembrance of "who" we are and what we've done remains with us and will be remembered by God in the '*mnemeion.*'

Hades, then, is one of three *temporary* places that "holds the dead" until the judgment of Christ, yet Hell is a *permanent* place of eternal torment. On the Day of Christ, three places (Death, Hades, and the sea) will give up the dead for judgment; those who are "in Christ" will be raised in resurrection whereby a new body is superimposed upon them, but for those who are not saved "from out of" Death and Hades, they will remain in those places which are then cast into Hell where they experience not only the second death… but also eternal torment.

For many of us, our greatest fear and nightmare is being seen naked and ashamed, but today – our society flaunts it and unregenerate man's spirit is desensitized to it. Consider this point: three of man's greatest fears – falling, fire and nakedness – are related to eternal condemnation in Hell, and yet, eternal torment and torture as well is still not enough to change them.

Thus far, we have talked about Hades and Death, yet there are at least fourteen specific places within the kingdom of God that are mentioned in the scriptures, and Jesus alludes to many of them; so, why isn't the church teaching us the whole truth about the kingdom of God? Pardon my skepticism, but it is because, just like selling indulgences, you can still make money by selling heaven to people that refuse to listen to the voice of the Spirit.

Places With Purpose

As I was meditating upon these things, the Holy Spirit brought one word to me: "Places." It seems there are various places within the kingdom of God, and these places have specific purposes. There are three permanent realms in the kingdom (heaven, earth and hell) and within these realms are temporary places for various persons according to things done upon the earth.

Heaven: the presence of God:
- God's throne (Isa. 66:1)
- A place for worship before the throne with living creatures, elders, angels and others

- A temporary place under the altar for martyred saints (Rev. 6:9; 20:4)
- The New Jerusalem that comes down 'from out of' heaven in the regeneration (Heb. 11:16; Rev. 21)
- Jesus used the term "the kingdom of the heavens" (plural) and "heavens" twice (Matt. 24:29; Luke 12:33) to describe multiple aspects of and/or places in His kingdom
- Heavenly places, the interface between Heaven and Earth (Eph. 1:3; 2:6)

Earth: man's eternal residence:
- The visible realm; the physical reality of earth we can tangibly see and experience
- Hades: the unseen temporary realm of departed souls (Rev. 1:18; 20:13) that many believe is somewhere within "the heart of the earth" (Num. 16:32).[37] The Jewish term "Sheol" (Psa. 16:10) corresponds to Hades (Acts 2:27) within complementary texts, and possibly "Abraham's bosom" (Luke 16:22, 23)
- Death: another unseen temporary realm for unregenerate dead (Rev. 1:18; 20:13) as the resting place for those who have judged themselves unworthy of judgment by unbelief
- The sea: a physical reality in the visible realm that also temporarily holds the dead (which ceases to exist in the regeneration; Rev. 20:13; 21:1)
- Paradise, the Garden of God, Eden – that remains hidden behind the veil that will be restored in the regeneration at the culmination of all ages
- Heavenly places, the interface between Earth and Hell (the unseen realm of principalities, powers, demons, devils and evil spirits that wage war against mankind and the body of Christ – His church; Eph. 3:10; 6:12)

Hell: the absence of God (with many places reserved for judgment and eternal torment):

---

[37] Willmington's Guide to the Bible, p.683, section B.

- *Gehenna* (Hell) – the place for the second death after judgment (Rev. 2:11; 20:6, 15)
- The bottomless pit – a temporary place to hold "the dragon, that serpent of old, who is *the* Devil and Satan, and bound him for a thousand years" (Rev. 9:1; 20:1-3) that may also be "the abyss" to imprison demons awaiting judgment (Luke 8:31)
- The Pit – may be another reference for the abyss (Psa. 30:3; 49:9; 143:7)
- The Lake of Fire – a special place reserved for Satan (the devil), the beast and false prophet (Rev. 19:20; 20:10); in final judgment, Death and Hades are cast into this lake, as well as anyone not found written in the Book of Life (Rev. 20:14, 15)
- The Furnace of Fire – for those persons engaged in lawlessness as an offense to the kingdom of heaven (Matt. 13:41-42; 49-50) where there is wailing and gnashing of teeth
- *Tartaros* (5020- translated as Hell; 2 Pet. 2:4; Jude 6), "the deepest abyss of Hades," [38] a special place for fallen angels who left their proper domain, interfered with God's plan of creation and redemption for mankind (and the earth), and sinned against the daughters of men (Gen. 6:2)
- Outer Darkness – the place reserved for hypocrites, wicked, lazy, abominable and unprofitable servants, and unfaithful stewards where eternal torment following judgment occurs (Matt. 8:12; 22:13; 25:30; Jude 13; it is possible this place may be an element of earth, yet not as a place where joy or peace resides, which may explain why the wall around the Holy City is 240' tall)

There are specific places in the kingdom of God for specific persons according to deeds done upon earth; some according to faithful obedience – some according to disobedience and some according to unbelief. And there are specific places in Hell for specific persons as characterized by their crimes, as well as

---

[38] Strong's

varying degrees of torment, including "his own place" for Judas Iscariot who betrayed Jesus (Acts 1:25).

This next point is important – because we associate the statement by Jesus "I go to prepare a place for you" as being heaven only, and yet... Judas was also present when these words were spoken to the disciples, perhaps we should let Jesus decide which place you will be going to... not doctrines. Now then, within the context of these various places which have been identified in the scriptures, there are many places in the kingdom of God – each with a specific purpose for specific people according to their deeds done upon the earth.

These citations may also help us understand the kingdom of God as it relates to "in My Father's house (*oikia*) are many *rooms*" (*mone*-3488, meaning: a staying, residence, dwelling place; [39] John 14:2; 23)... or as I now perceive... "In My Father's estate are many dwelling places." This is why I refer to Earth as the sanctification room, Hades as the courtroom, Death as the rebellion room, and Heaven as God's throne room.[40]

Temporary Nations and Kingdoms

Heaven is the presence of God, Hell is the absence of God and Earth is the battlefield for conquest and dominion. When the Apostle Paul referred to the heavenly realm upon the earth, he was calling attention to the spiritual forces of hell (demons, evil spirits, principalities, powers and Satan) that are "of this world" that are waging war against the host of earth (mankind) upon the earth, and against the host of heaven (angels) as well. And this immense struggle for dominion on earth continues. Satan stole it from God and man was sent to earth as the clean-up crew... to deliver the dominion of earth back into the dominion of God's kingdom, but Satan tricked and deceived us into delivering our authority to him and, thus, the clean-up became a rescue and recovery mission for

---

[39] IBID.
[40] End of the excerpt copied from "Here: The Kingdom of Heaven Is."

mankind as well.

Earth, as we know it now, is in transition. Earth is the paradise of God which will one day be united in oneness with heaven in the restoration of the kingdom, but until that happens… there will be wars and rumors of wars, and calamities of every kind – in both the earth itself and in the families of man. In the meantime, the Lord continues to reveal Himself, as well as His purposes and plans, to those whose hearts are aligned with Him and have purposed within themselves to obediently do His will and live as His disciple.

This world, however, that is temporarily upon the earth, is under the dominion of Satan, the prince (or ruler) of this world (John 12:31; 14:30) and "prince of the power of the air" (Eph. 2:2). Man was sent to come against this ruler of rebellion, possess (take back, redeem) the land and occupy it until the Lord returns. We are more than over-comers… and we are more than conquerors... we are the redeemed of the Lord and we were sent by the Lord to redeem the earth!

> "How you are fallen from heaven, O Lucifer, son of the morning! How you are cut down to the ground, you who weakened the nations!" (Isa. 14:12).

The Lord, however, is a nation builder. We can see this by reading about the history of man upon the earth within the scriptures, as well as transcripts from secular historians. Nations arise and nations fall, yet the Lord Jesus is King over all the earth and His dominion rules over the nations… and His kingdom is an everlasting kingdom (Dan. 7:14).

> "Your kingdom is an everlasting kingdom, and
> Your dominion endures throughout all generations"
> (Psa. 145:13).

The kingdom of God (the <u>King</u>'s <u>Dom</u>ain) is the kingdom of Jesus Christ, and one day "every tongue should confess that Jesus Christ is Lord, to the glory of God the Father" (Phil. 2:11). Yet, in the meantime, the Lord will rise up nations and earthly kingdoms and leaders upon the earth according to His purpose, to have dominion, according to the sovereign will of God.

> "As for Me, behold, My covenant is with you, and you shall be a father of many nations" (Gen. 17:4).

The first time we see this Divine principle in action is the calling of Abram to live in faithfulness by the hearing of the Lord's voice. Abram had to be tested and perfected in faithful obedience before the Lord fulfilled His promise to him. Abram was considered a king already according to the territory (domain) of his father's family; however, the Lord called Abram to separate himself from his father's family and his father's land to go to the place the Lord would reveal to him. Abram took along his wife and servants, including his brother's son, Lot, comprising about 318 men (Gen. 14:14), not including herds and many possessions. Abram's estate was already large enough to be a city or a nation, but the Lord called Abram to become a special kind of nation… a nation that hosts God's Presence and Spirit as the focus of their life by the hearing of His voice.

> "So Abram departed as the Lord had spoken to him, and Lot went with him. And Abram was seventy-five years old when he departed from Haran" (Gen. 12:1-4).

It likely took Abram several years to make the estimated 680-700 mile journey from Haran to the place where the Lord appeared to Him (Gen. 12:7), and during this time, the Lord was teaching and instructing Abram how to walk in the way of the Lord. It is interesting to note, however, that the place where the Lord directed Abram to go was in a place experiencing a famine in the land. Once Abram got there, he had two choices at this point: either to stay in the land and consult (wait upon) the Lord regarding what they should do – or act independently of the Lord and take matters into his own hand.

> "Now there was a famine in the land, and Abram went down to Egypt to dwell there…" (Gen. 12:10).

Even though the Lord had provided for Abram along this multi-year journey (and this goes for all of us), there are times when the Lord will become silent to see what we will do with what we have learned along the way. This is Abram's first major test as the father of many nations, and he didn't pass; instead, he left the place where the Lord physically appeared to him (or let me say it this way – he left the Lord's manifest presence that was abiding in that place) and journeyed to a nearby nation: Egypt. Abram didn't stay there very long because he was caught deceiving Pharaoh of Egypt in an effort to protect his life.

Now, let me put this in context: when the Lord tells you what to do, He will guide you and instruct you along the way, and He will protect you and provide for your needs, and He will also give you the authority and power to perform the will of God so that you may faithfully do all that He commands; however… you will be tested along the way. If He calls you to do it, then He will carry you through it… and this, then, is a primary principle in the operating plan regarding man and how God's kingdom works on earth – *for all of us*, not just Abram! If He calls you to do it, His Presence and Spirit will carry you through it… with His authority and power made available to you to accomplish all that He has commanded you to do!

If you are able to hear God's voice and are obedient to do all that He commands, then the Lord will also build you up to become a mighty nation in the similitude of Abram.

Abram was learning the lessons of being obedient by the hearing of God's voice… and he was learning to trust the Lord regardless of the Lord's request. So, when the Lord told Abram to take his miraculously conceived and supernaturally born son Isaac up a mountain to sacrifice his only true begotten son, he may have had some initial doubts (like all of us)... but he trusted God.

Keep in mind, Abram is going through test after test after test, to learn lesson after lesson, to learn God's truth and gain understanding, and then the ultimate test from God comes to see if truth with understanding has taken root within him.

Abram passed the test! Hooray!

In this moment, a deep spiritual transaction happened in the heavens between God and Abram whereby the Lord (Jesus) enters into a covenant with Abram and changes his name to Abraham. The father of many nations now knows what he needs to know in order to pass along the keys of the kingdom to his son and all future generations through Isaac. Abraham hears, believes, obeys, understands and trusts.

When the Lord calls anyone to do anything, He will give them the authority, power and provision to do all that He commands… by the hearing of His voice (and not the voice of any other). This is how the kingdom of God upon the earth operates and we all need to learn this principle – and likewise, we will also be tested along the way to see if we will walk according to His truth only… and no other truth.

Back on point… the Lord is a nation builder. The Lord physically appeared to Abraham at least three times (Gen. 12:4; 17:1; 18:1), twice to Isaac (Gen. 26:2, 24; Ex. 6:3) and three times to Jacob (and, yes, I literally mean appeared physically; Gen. 28:13; 31:11, 13; 32:24-30). Jacob (renamed Israel by the Lord) begat ten sons… and then Joseph was born. Joseph was betrayed by his brothers and sold into slavery in Egypt, but…

The Lord (in Presence and Spirit) "was with Joseph." (Gen. 39.2, 21, 23)

Time and time again, Joseph was tested by others but he maintained his faith in God because "he trusted in the One" who gave him the spiritual gift to interpret dreams. When Joseph was able to correctly interpret Pharaoh's dream, he was elevated to second highest in command of a nation that was not his own to make preparations for an impending famine.

Joseph was made a slave of another nation for a God-given purpose. Through Joseph, one nation would be saved... and another nation, Israel, would be rescued as well. God's purposes under heaven are always prefect – even if we do not comprehend the reason why we struggle through many ordeals, trials and tribulations. Even though it seems our purpose and calling may have become sidetracked, the Lord will deliver us... and then He will deliver other peoples and even other nations as well, through us. So I encourage you... remain faithful... and steadfast... and trust in the Lord!

Fast forward nearly four hundred years and we find the nation Israel still dwelling within another nation. (Read that again and see if that makes sense to you). Then, from within that nation, God raised up Moses to deliver Israel out of bondage in Egypt. Consider, now, that Moses was born a slave within Egypt, sentenced to immediate death by order of Pharaoh that demanded all Israelite male babies be murdered when born, was "placed" along the Nile River where Pharaoh's daughter found him and raised him as a prince within the very nation that enslaved him. God allows things to occur that are far beyond our comprehension, which God always intends for our good... and yet (this next point is exceedingly important) sometimes bad things happen to us in "places" so that we may become the messenger of deliverance to lead others out of the very place that made us slaves.

As oftentimes happens, the Lord delivers us "from out of" bad situations, to go back under His authority and power to deliver others. It happened to Moses, and it may happen to you!

The nations within the Lord's kingdom are called by Him to follow in His ways, in order to host His Presence and Spirit, but we are never to be in bondage to any other nation because the Lord is a nation builder – and He is a deliverer of nations as well.

Fast forward again another 1,550 years and we find Israel in bondage once again, but this time under Roman occupation (as a nation within a nation). The problem with Israel, at this point in time, is that she has forgotten who the Lord is who calls them by name to do His will on earth. Israel had become very legalistic by observing statutes in obligatory obedience to a written code rather than hearing His voice and living out of (hosting) His Presence and Spirit – and being obedient to do all that He says.

Israel had become so deaf and blind along the way… that the Lord came back again to the nation He commissioned through Abraham, rescued through Joseph, and delivered through Moses in order to give them one more chance, as their Mesiah, to pass the test and, thus, save them. Jesus came to remind them and teach them the way and manner in which He originally intended them to live, but they not only rejected His message… they rejected the Messenger.

Jesus was born into a nation to lead His people out of bondage to sin into the Lord's salvation which only God Himself could orchestrate. If you can perceive God's recurring message of deliverance through Joseph, Moses and Jesus, then perhaps the Lord is also calling you in this hour to perceive your destiny and deliver others so they may enter into the Lord's salvation.

We have been commissioned by the Lord to be nation builders… and a deliverer of nations.

Israel, The Nation

There are some who, after having read many of my writings, may think that I am hostile or antagonistic to Judaism or the nation Israel. Nothing could be farther from the truth! It is my fervent hope that Israel may actually read and understand the truthful messages that I have received from the Lord and, thus, return to the One who came unto them as their Messiah, whom they rejected and brutally murdered in order to protect "their" religion and customs. Jesus physically appeared to their forefathers and spoke to them many, many times, but when Jesus appeared on the mountain in the presence of Moses and all Israel, they rejected the Lord's operational goal to hear and obey, so the Lord gave them over in disobedience to obey onerous written codes that no one could possibly become righteous by.

Hear His voice – or follow a bunch of onerous, arcane, obligatory rules and ordinances.

This seems like such a simple and easy choice to make; however, in order to hear God's voice, we must wait upon Him to hear Him speak, soften our hardened hearts, seek his face by turning (converting) the fullness of our affection and attention toward Him, seek His righteousness and live according to His truth in righteousness, diligently desire to host His Presence and Spirit – and (most importantly) be obedient to do all that He commands by the hearing of His voice.

Yup, sounds simple enough all right. And this is why the Lord tells us to press into Him in order to forsake the cares of this world that distract our attention, because being obedient requires patient endurance – which is impossible for the timid, cowardly or weak (doubtful in faith). The way of the Lord is righteous altogether, but it takes commitment and steadfastness to "continue" in life eternal versus living according to your own ways and customs in your self-directed kingdom. Following laws does not make anyone obedient or righteous – but – having a personal relationship with the Creator of the universe by hearing His voice and doing what He says – does! ***Hear***, trust and obey… for there's no other way (as the hymnal song sort-of goes).

Jesus came again – to reset the heavenly clock, to teach men how to walk in the way of God, and to fulfill the Old Covenant by appearing as Israel's Messiah; and His appearance served as either a witness for them – or as a judgment against if they reject Him.

> "Now as He drew near, He saw the city [Jerusalem] and wept over it, [42] saying, "If you had known, even you, especially in this your day, the things that make for your peace! But now they are hidden from your eyes. [43] For days will come upon you when your enemies will build an embankment around

you, surround you and close you in on every side, ⁴⁴ and level you, and your children within you, to the ground; and they will not leave in you one stone upon another, because you did not know the time of your visitation" (Luke 19:44).

Jesus created everyone with the ability to hear His voice whereby all manner of men must hear His voice, follow Him and obediently do all He commands. He never intended that any nation be governed by a worldly-minded, oppressive, godless sovereign because, when we attempt to live apart from His Sovereignty as King of kings and Lord of lords, we all become slaves in foreign lands.

He began by birthing a nation through Abraham; then, after many generations, the people demanded a king like all other nations. This was not what Jesus had in mind, so the Lord gave them Saul. Jesus is King over all creation, including heaven and earth, including every nation and dominion on earth, and the earth is within His domain "and His kingdom will have no end, and the government shall be upon His shoulders (Isa. 9:6). Therefore, any king, ruler, prince, monarch (or whatever the leader of a nation decides to be called) is merely an intermediary alongside us, but must never function as the mediator or intercessor between God and men.

> "For there is one God and one Mediator between God and men, the Man Christ Jesus" (1 Tim. 2:5).

Jesus promised He would come back… and when He did, He was brutally murdered and crucified upon a cross. When Pilate, the Roman governor, questioned Jesus and asked Him, "Are You the King of the Jews?" He answered and said to him, "*It is as* you say" (Luke 23:3); yet the Jewish leaders vehemently rejected Jesus and provoked the people demanding Jesus be crucified. "Now Pilate wrote a title and put it on the cross. And the writing was:

JESUS OF NAZARETH, THE KING OF THE JEWS" (John 19:19).

Jesus came unto His own (John 1:11) and the nation Israel rejected Him. Let me say this another way... Jesus is the King of Israel – they rejected their King – and then they murdered Him!

Jesus is King over every person and over every nation! Judaism, in this regard, is no different than any other worldly religion that has refused to declare Jesus Lord.

Now, then what are you going to do about this Man, Jesus? Everyone must come to a decision whereby their life is either governed by Jesus in every aspect, in spirit and in truth... or it is not. Are you willing to surrender everything – including your life – under His Sovereignty? Are you going to declare your complete allegiance and obedience to Him or are you going to continue standing in unbelief, rebellion and disobedience against His Lordship over your life?

JESUS is LORD

The dominion belongs to the Lord (Psa. 103:22), and yet Jesus created us and commanded us to have dominion over the earth (in His name), and then commissioned us to exercise His authority and power to have dominion over the earth, and He even gave us the keys of the kingdom... but He never intended us to be "kings or priests" over other peoples or nations "like the gentiles" but rather... to operate like Him as kings and priests alongside Him... submitted under His Lordship.

Does this mean that we are not supposed to have rulers and governors in authority over us? Absolutely, not! Earthly rulers are commissioned by the Lord (Rom. 13:1) and are merely exercising the Lord's power and authority that He granted to them to govern upright and rightly in rightness... and this is why we are told to pray for those in authority (Titus 3:1; 1 Pet. 2:17); however, we are not to have any king over us other than King Jesus, Who is Lord of heaven and earth. When earthly rulers become kings, there is a worldly (and demonic) tendency to become oppressive dictators that exercise domination rather than godly dominion. They are using His authority and His power, but they are using it in an ungodly negative manner to build their kingdom and, therefore, are not establishing the kingdom of God on the earth as God intended.

In the new earth, there will be one Lord, one King, and one dominion… and all will live as one to serve the Lord in the beauty of His majesty, united in oneness by the Spirit, for all eternity.

People have tried many times, unsuccessfully, to build a kingdom of their own, but no kingdom will last that refuses to operate according to God's operating system – i.e. according to the Spirit.

The Lord is a nation builder. Nations rise and nations fall; all the nations are as temporary places, but the Lord governs them all.

> "For the kingdom is the Lord's, and He rules over the nations (Psa. 22:28).
>
> "Oh, let the nations be glad and sing for joy! For You shall judge the people righteously, and govern the nations on earth. Selah" (Psa. 67:4).

Jesus taught us "You are the salt of the earth" (Matt. 5:13) and taught us parables that we are "good seed" (Matt. 13:38). We are good wheat seed sown upon the earth by the Lord, created upright to live according to uprightness, and God commanded all men to have dominion over the earth, and we were commissioned with a blessing to bear fruit and multiply upon the earth. Both wheat and the salt are synonymous for man's heavenly ordination to influence this world, have dominion over it, exercise (infuse) His authority and power in it, and multiply His glory within it. We are a royal priesthood by divine ordination to be as kings of nations by walking in obedience to the King of kings and the Chief Governor of all nations.

> "And every offering of your grain offering you shall season with salt; you shall not allow the salt of the covenant of your God to be lacking from your grain offering. With all your offerings you shall offer salt" (Lev. 2:13).

> "Should you not know that the Lord God of Israel gave **the dominion over Israel** to David forever, to him and his sons, by a covenant of salt?" (2 Chron. 13:5)

Are you now able to perceive the reason why Jesus referred to us "seed" and sent us to be "the salt of the earth"? We were sown onto the earth to influence this world as kingdom salt to effect a regime change by subjugating the enemies of God in "this world" and disperse darkness with "the light of truth." We were sent in as the clean-up crew, as conquerors – in the name of Jesus!

The Lord raises up nations – and then renders them low; the Lord raises up leaders – and then replaces them; the Lord raises up priests and prophets to live consecrated lives set apart wholly unto Him to guide both nations and leaders of nations… but woe to those priests who keep saints in bondage to rules, doctrines and ordinances by refusing to deliver the people with the Gospel of Truth. Woe… and again I say… woe unto them!!! We were sent here as deliverers and redeemers to liberate men from darkness to walk in the light… to become a nation of priests and prophets and kings in His dominion.

This dominion over Israel applied to David and his sons, and Jesus is not only a Son of David…

> "I am the Root and the Offspring of David, the Bright and Morning Star" (Rev. 22:6).

… Jesus is *also* the Root and the Source of David, as the One who was before him, as the Origin of all peoples and nations upon the earth, and as the Fulfillment of all Divine promises made to Abraham and Israel… and the Church, which includes you and me today. Jesus is not just a historical figure that came and left; Jesus continues to manifest Himself within us, by grace through faith, and manifests Himself through us by the empowering and outer working of the Spirit to accomplish the will of God and establish His kingdom and His dominion over all the earth. His kingdom will not fail… and the gates of Hades will not prevail against His church!

Our mission mandate to have dominion is never to be taken lightly; we will be held accountable for what we did and didn't do – in our life, in our family, in our profession and in our nation.

> "I will make you exceedingly fruitful; and I will make nations of you, and kings shall come from you" (Gen. 17:6).

Like Abraham, you are also a holy nation, a royal priesthood, the ecclesia called out from this world to be set apart as one person yet also as someone with a nation within you. Saints of God, it is time to start giving birth to the nation within you that the Lord preordained, predestined and predetermined within you "since before the foundation of the world." All of your ways have already been ordered and set before you, but you must surrender your will in order to walk according to this way – according to the way of Christ in you, by the empowering of the Holy Spirit, and give Jesus the glory in it and through it.

We are kings in the kingdom of our God and we are seeds that were sown to produce and bear much fruit and beget nations through faith in Jesus Christ. Jesus established Israel as an archetypal nation according to this pattern, through Abraham, but they forgot the lessons learned by Abraham, they refused to hear His voice, they walked in disobedience and then Israel rejected their Lord and King… whereby Jesus rendered that covenant obsolete.

> "For everyone will be seasoned with fire, and every sacrifice will be seasoned with salt" (Mark 9:49).

And yet, the church is not much different than that former way! The institutional church has imitated the pattern of Judaism and set people in hierarchical authority over us, telling us what to believe and how to live, being obedient to follow the doctrines and ordinances rather than hearing the Voice of Truth – whereby we might be set free from the doctrines of man to live according to the Spirit of Christ. And modern-day prophets within this hybrid lukewarm Judeo-Christian church system are imitating the prophetic customs of that worn out and obsolete way and, thus, pontificate incessantly about the Law of Moses and quote the promises within the Old Testament liberally, but rarely have I found a new covenant prophet that clings to the Good News of Jesus and speaks exclusively with new covenant truth, with Spirit-anointed authority and power, with Spirit-guided wisdom and understanding… and with new earth comprehension about the fulfillment of God's eternal plan for man upon the New Earth. We were sent to have dominion and establish nations, but instead… the church has built denominational kingdoms that are fearful of deacons and elders that were put in place to support the primary mission and ministry of pastors and priests – to make disciples for Jesus – not control pastors and priests.

> "Go therefore and make disciples of all the nations, baptizing them in the name of the Father and of the Son and of the Holy Spirit" (Matt. 28:19).

We need to get back to Faith 101, and back to the basics of faith, to understand who we are and the reason we exist on earth. We are here to accomplish the dominion mandate – in the name of Jesus – and under no other name or authority or denominational pretext. Jesus only!

Vatican, the Nation

It is one thing to bring a critical word to a minor world religion, but it is quite another matter to bring a critical word to a major world religion that comprises nearly one-sixth of the world's 6.2 billion people. As a former Catholic whose extended family is still deeply Catholic, I have never attacked, nor defended, their tradition to which I once belonged. I only speak the truth in love.

So, I ask just one question: how come only a few people are regarded as saints when we have all been called to live like saints to manifest all the wonderful promises made by Jesus to perform miraculous signs, wonders and greater works through us by the Holy Spirit according to faith?

How come? Because unless you teach the faithful the truth and to live whole-heartedly according to the Way of Christ, then people will continue to believe the less-than gospel version of Christianity, which by the way... is not a religion... it is based upon people having a personal relationship with Jesus, being firmly rooted and established in you in fullness of understanding, as your Lord and your God.

Does the church actively teach the faithful how to hear the voice of Jesus? Are sacrifices still being offered upon an altar according to an obsolete pattern when Christ Himself came as the Lamb of God, as the final heavenly sacrifice, to take away once and for all the sin of the world thus taking away any and all future need for any sacrifices – except one?

> "I beseech you therefore, brethren, by the mercies of God, ***that you present your bodies a living sacrifice***, holy, acceptable to God, which is your reasonable service. ^{2} And do not be conformed to this world, but be transformed by the renewing of your mind, that you may prove what is that good and acceptable and perfect will of God" (Romans 12:1, 2).

> "I have been crucified with Christ; it is no longer I who live, but Christ lives in me; and the life which I now live in the flesh I live by faith in the Son of God, who loved me and gave Himself for me" (Gal. 2:20).

Therefore, there is no longer any reason to adopt or continue to perform any of the religious practices in the Judaic model which served only as a type and shadow of the things to come.

> "Therefore purge out the old leaven, that you may be a new lump, since you truly are unleavened. For indeed Christ, our Passover, was sacrificed for us" (1 Cor. 5:7)
>
> "You also, as living stones, are being built up a spiritual house, a holy priesthood, to offer up spiritual sacrifices acceptable to God through Jesus Christ" (1 Peter 2:5). [9] "But you are a chosen generation, a royal priesthood, a holy nation, His own special people, that you may proclaim the praises of Him who called you out of darkness into His marvelous light; [10] who once were not a people but are now the people of God, who had not obtained mercy but now have obtained mercy" (v.9, 10).

Now therefore, the Church, in all variety of manifold expressions, including Catholicism, must become the New Wineskin (i.e. the unified body of Christ) that is filled to overflowing with the Holy Spirit, not as a meager taste, but "be filled with the Spirit" (Eph. 5:18) as the means whereby we manifest the goodness and greatness of Jesus our Lord as a demonstration of His greatness and His goodness abiding within the heavenly abode we established within our heart.

My continuous prayer for the Vatican, as one of four nations for which I have been praying and interceding for many years, is that one day She would awaken from her spiritual slumber to realize she is nothing apart from the Spirit of God, to focus her attention on Jesus only, to teach His truth and not her truth, to examine her doctrines to base all truth upon scripture and not man-centered opinions and traditions… in order to become the single greatest spiritual awakening within all of human history. The host of

Catholicism is about to enter into an incredible spiritual transition unlike anything anyone has ever seen before – to the glory of God in Christ Jesus!

Saints of God – it's time to arise!!!

8. Have Dominion

Our mission since the very beginning of time on earth is directly related to our creation as *adams*: human beings and ruddy sons of men – on earth. We were created by Jesus according to His likeness to be His image bearers, and then we were told, or more precisely – commanded – to have dominion. But what does this mean? And what does dominion look like? Before we discuss what it looks like, we need to understand this concept of dominion from God's perspective, and not as the world understands it. Consider these terms:

- King – a ruler in a position of authority in a place
- Domain – the principle place
- Kingdom – the king's domain
- Dominion – the authority to act given to a ruler

But… what does dominion look like?

Dominion is not authoritative control, per se; it is delegated authority with delegated power to operate according to one plan for one purpose: to establish God's sovereignty. Our God Reigns! Dominion is about giving God all the glory – all of it – in all things. God made creation, as well as the sons of men, and then He gave us dominion over His creation so that we do one thing: produce an increase to return in abundance with His glory attached to it. Any marvelous or incredibly awesome works that we return to Him without His glory attached to it is the lesson learned from Cain: God considered it unrightness (whereby his self-righteous vainglory works were considered evil).

We keep trying to save the world by changing people's opinions and ideologies, but what we really need most is: to be taught the truth. Jesus came as a teacher who was living out of an understanding that He received within a relational experience with His Father. Jesus was not an educator who taught one way but lived another; Jesus lived according to the way of truth – and He taught according to the way He lived as one unified expression. What people saw and heard – is exactly what they got – the truth of God manifested by a human being.

Step One

So, the first step in this process is to acknowledge that we are image bearers who were created according to our Creator, Jesus Christ, and to acknowledge Him in the fullness of His being. The time to quibble over which person in the Godhead made us or created us is abundantly clear in the scriptures and the Apostles Creed. God made us "in Our image" – and Jesus created us "in His own image," as two distinct authoritative actions: the authoritative act expressed (as thought conceived) and the authoritative act manifested (as spoken utterance), as the ratio and oratio of creation. And these are always followed by the authoritative act to perform it: creation became manifest (Gen, 1:26, 27; 2:7). And this leads us to our next step…

Step Two

Stay in oneness relationship with your Creator. Live in oneness with your Creator. Operate in oneness with your Creator. Be imitators of the Divine Nature – and live accordingly. Live like you mean it… with '*dianoia*' deep understanding – and give God the glory in it.

Step Three

Hear the Lord. Follow in the example of Jesus, who said what He heard His Father saying – and did what He saw His Father doing. Likewise, do what Jesus tells you, and say what He tells you to say. Jesus heard the thoughts of His Father – and then He did them according to how He was told... with '*oida*' understanding. It is for this reason that the first chapter of the Image Bearer series was written: to be able to hear the Voice of God. It is paramount in supreme importance to be able to hear His voice!

Jesus is in the Father, operating in oneness with the Father, as the only Begotten of the Father. Jesus heard the thoughts of the Father and then He implemented them as utterance words, which is precisely why Jesus is called the Living Word, Logos, as One in being (nature) with the Father, as Intelligence and Utterance, as "the Word of God."

We were created as spiritual beings with the spiritual ability to hear the voice of the Lord, which comes to us as a small still voice – as a spontaneous thought – as being distinctly and discernibly different than our own thoughts. This is how God speaks: as thoughts through the Spirit. And this is how Jesus speaks: with words through the Spirit. And this is how the Spirit operates: through love and power and a sound mind. The Father wants us to know His thoughts and Jesus wants us to know His ways, as the combined operation of a Triune God, in oneness of the Spirit.

> ***"My thoughts are higher than your thoughts and My ways are higher than your ways"***... is not a divine smack-down, but rather, the very key to knowing the will of God. When we know His thoughts, by hearing His spontaneous thoughts, then we have heard the actionable word and utterance of God, which should result in only one next step – to walk in obedience in the way of the Lord.

Step Four

Do it. Don't just think about doing it, or contemplate it, or say you are going to do it; let your yes be Yes and Amen! Anything less is from the evil one. When you hear the word of the Lord as His spontaneous thought, do it right there and then! Do not delay (unless the Holy Spirit puts a check in your spirit). If any part of this yes becomes conditional, as maybe, perhaps, possibly, conceivably, provisional, qualified, reserved, restrictive, uncertain, undecided, doubtful, speculative, hesitant, resistant, indecisive, tentative, faltering, timid, double-minded or anything that results in ambiguity, passivity, complacency or false contentment, then the word spoken to you has not been obeyed. We must be hearers that do.

Jesus heard the thoughts of His Father and He did what His Father said. Jesus demonstrated this Divine '*oida*' relationship with His Father over and over again (in everything He did) so that we may learn His pattern of living according to this way. Jesus came as the Archetype of a better way, and He showed us how to live… as the Way! He became the living Example whereby we can be imitators of Christ in obedient response to hearing the voice of Christ – and then doing it willingly – without conditions!

Step Five

Do it, but don't do it in your own power, or strength, or imagination, or authority, or talents, or reasoning, or ability. Jesus did not do what He did through human effort, nor did He operate out of His Divine position; He performed all His works and miracles as an ordinary man who yielded Himself completely and obediently, by relying entirely upon the Spirit of God to enable Him every step of the way. He did not do it in His own effort – He relied entirely upon the Spirit, and lived life according to the Spirit of life – one breath at a time.

Jesus showed us the way – as how to live according to the manner of *all* men, in a Spirit-filled and Spirit-directed manner, as spiritual beings having a human experience – in oneness with the Spirit. By doing all things according the Spirit, Jesus was able to glorify the Father in all His works, whereby all His works produced glory for the Father. Jesus never did anything according to the flesh or in the power of human effort; everything He did was done in the fullness of the Spirit so that God alone gets the glory.

> "Not by might nor by power, but by My Spirit,'
> says the Lord of hosts" (Zech. 4:6).

Jesus was around thirty years old when His public ministry began. Jesus knew all things and He knew who He was and He knew everything that was going to happen, but in everything He did, He did it from a position of yielded submission – as a servant. He did nothing on His own accord, but in all things, He did only what the Father told Him to do – and this was done in oneness with the Spirit. This is how Jesus lived – and this is how we are to live as well.

After Jesus was baptized by John in the Jordan River, the Spirit led Jesus into the wilderness to be tempted by the devil (Matt. 4:1). This creates a very interesting situation; Jesus told us the Father will not lead us into temptation (v.6:13), but such is not the case with the Holy Spirit. Jesus was tempted, just as in the manner that all men are also tempted, so that we may not lay a charge against Jesus using His Divinity to help Him through it, so that we may also be partakers of this way of entering into temptation, overcoming temptation and leaving the trial victorious – with angels attending and ministering afterward. The leading of the Spirit that is mentioned here, as well in Rom. 8:14 and Gal. 5:18, however, is not the Spirit who leads, but rather, the Spirit who guides, directs, drives, or figuratively, induces; the word is '*ago*' (71) and it means: to lead along, to bring, and connotes to bring (along).[41] And this is a good illustration of the Holy Spirit's role, as our Paraclete, Who comes alongside us and guides us in the way of Christ; never getting between us and Jesus, but always leading us in such a manner – so as to bring us along.[42]

> "For as many as are led by the Spirit of God, these are sons of God" (Rom. 8:14).

---

[41] Strong's Concordance; (along) added by author for illustrative purposes.
[42] Dynamic Fluidity is the influence of the Holy Spirit to guide us and direct us along the way of Christ. If we begin to turn to the left or to the right, the Holy Spirit will gently "push and pull" us so that we stay within the flow of the Spirit and the will of God. At times He may drive us, especially in regard to seeking Christ, but He will not control or manipulate us in any manner that compromises our free will to live according to righteousness – or unrightness.

"But if you are led by the Spirit, you are not under the law" (Gal. 5:18).

We are living within an open heaven, and we are able to hear God's voice, so the third element we can expect as spiritual beings that operate in yielded submission is this: angelic activity. And this is what Jacob experienced as well (Gen. 28:10-17): an open heaven, the Voice of God, and angelic activity. How much land did the Lord say belonged to Jacob? Was it land as far as the eye can see – or – was it the land that he laid upon (occupied)? When the Lord said, "spread abroad to the west and the east, to the north and the south" (v. 14), He was telling Jacob the land and territory he has been given was not restricted by borders or boundaries… it was a spiritual dominion. This is the true dominion of Jacob, not just a place as was given to Abraham, but an entire celestial planet under the command of the Lord our God, Jesus Christ. Every place he put his head was under Jacob's authority… and this was given to him on his way to Haran.

Consider, now, the ladder that was set upon earth which is the dominion mentality that followers of Jesus need to comprehend. The ladder, in this regard, represents the thoughts of our mind and intellect that are influenced by the Lord of Heaven who stands in authority above us (as above the earth)… with angels being sent to assist us in this dominion mandate. We need to perceive our dominion mandate from the perspective of the One who was speaking 'words' to Jacob and standing '*anothen*' (atop/above) a ladder that is set upon the earth … and not to perceive spiritual matters from the worldly perspective of things below.

> **"Set your mind on things above, not on things on the earth" (Col. 3:2).**

Our command to have dominion was never about one place or a region or a country or a nation; our inheritance is "the land we lay upon" – all of it – an entire Lion of Judah planet!

The Lord may give us kingdoms in regard to specific geographic locations on earth as He determines; however, we have all been called to have dominion over the things of this world *wherever* we are – in the name of Jesus. Wherever we go, the Lord will speak to us and tell us what He wants us to do. This is our dominion mandate... without borders or boundaries!

The biggest problem with man... is his small-minded thinking!

Step Six

After the temptation, Jesus returned to Galilee "in the power of the Spirit" (Luke 4:14). As spiritual beings, we are to walk according to the Spirit...in spirit and in truth, to worship the Lord and give Him glory in everything we do. If we cannot give Him the glory through it, then there is no glory in it! We are to live according to our inward being, according to our inner man, as a soul with spirit, with our spirit partnering with the Holy Spirit so that we may live according to the Spirit. There are no more laws or commandments other than those given us by Jesus, such that... we live by faith with a clean heart and a pure conscious toward God and man. There is only one law, one commandment... and one new Commandment:

> "For the law of the Spirit of life in Christ Jesus has made me free from the law of sin and death" (Rom. 8:2).

> "This is My commandment, that you love one another as I have loved you" (John 15:12).

> "A new commandment I give to you, that you love one another; as I have loved you, that you also love one another (John 13:34).

Step Seven

Continue to walk in obedience to the Lord by listening to the Voice of the Spirit, imitate Jesus, live according to the Spirit...and you will do greater works!

> "Most assuredly, I say to you, he who believes in Me, the works that I do he will do also; and greater works than these he will do, because I go to My Father" (John 14:12).

When the Lord commissioned the disciples to go out in pairs, He sent them out under His authority. They did not have the Holy Spirit at that time, and neither did they need it (John 7:39). They were operating "in" the authority of Jesus because they were abiding in His presence. "Behold, I give you authority to trample on serpents, and scorpions, and over all the power of the enemy, and nothing shall by any means hurt you" (Luke 10:19). Likewise, when we live out of Christ's presence that we host in us, we shall also do the same marvelous works the disciples did.

However, we do not have the tangible presence of Jesus within our midst, as the disciples had, which is why Jesus sent the Holy Spirit so that His presence may always remain with us.

> "… and lo, I am with you always, even to the end of the age." Amen" (Matt. 28:20).

The Holy Spirit is the Spirit of Christ (Rom. 8:9) and the Spirit of Christ (Phil. 1:19), who has all the similar attributes of Jesus Himself (Way, Truth and Life), who was sent by Jesus as our Paraclete, to come alongside us, to help us and comfort us (John 14:16), to guide and teach us, and bring to remembrance all things (v.26) whereby we maintain the divine relationship and remain in His presence, which leads us to…

Step Eight

Testify and bear witness – and thus, we begin the entire hearing process again and again by converting other souls to the way, truth and life.

The gospel is simple. The process is simple. Salvation is simple, so keep it simple. Hear and obey – there is no other way. Jesus only! Keep your eyes upon Jesus, and in all you do – give God the glory! I wish this truth did not have to come by way of a manual with written words, because the truth of the gospel is simply this: listen to hear the spontaneous thoughts of the Lord's voice in your mind – and obediently do it. Written words can be restrictive as well as prescriptive, but the utterance of the Lord is sharper than any two-edged sword.

> "The utterance of the Lord endureth forever" (1 Pet. 1:25; KJV).

9. Christianity Is Not A Religion

Christianity is not a religion based upon the teachings of Jesus, per se; Christianity is a relationship with Jesus that is firmly established in Him by living according to His truth.

Believers oftentimes claim to know Jesus as their personal Savior, but more often than not, they are unable to describe this relationship beyond that of the superficial religious perspective. Christians have come to believe they are members of a special institution that is superior to all other religions because they accepted Jesus and invited Him into their heart, yet this is a misnomer. God is everywhere and God is in everyone and Jesus is already dwelling in everyone regardless of where they are or what they believe; however, we must surrender the lordship of our life to Jesus and declare Jesus Lord upon the throne of our heart and enter into Him – the Door of salvation – Who waits patiently in our heart for us. We must declare Him Lord and exalt Him upon the throne of our heart… and become His disciple, being obedient to His truth.

Jesus wants us to enter into Him and have a personal relationship with Him and establish Him firmly upon the throne of our heart. Once this divine relationship has been established, a new "inner" man is created and then birthed as a new habitation by the Spirit whereby the temporary old man house is rendered obsolete. Formerly, we were a temporary dwelling place, as an earthen vessel, but now – we have become a permanent abode for the Lord to abide and, therefore, we have become a heavenly tabernacle for the Father and Son and Holy Spirit to rest – for the praise of His glory.

> "Heaven is My throne, And earth is My footstool.
> What house will you build for Me? says the Lord,
> Or what is the place of My rest?" (Acts 7:49).

Sadly, it seems the Christian religion has been building doctrine upon the wrong mountain of man-centric traditions. Believers are often regarded as members of a club that accepts them and transfers them between churches and parishes based upon the denominational doctrines they want to believe which tends to divide and segregate us rather than unify us in oneness. Jesus came to teach us the truth so that we live according to His truth; what *we want to believe* is inconsequential and immaterial to the discussion of faith unless it is firmly established and fully rooted upon His truth and only His truth.

In this regard, the church that Jesus commissioned has been only partially birthed by the Spirit of God. Much like the old man within us that needed to die in order for the new man to be birthed and revealed in us, the old manner of religious traditions that were carried forward into Christian theology from Judaism need to thoroughly be brought to the cross and crucified unto death in order for resurrection newness to begin again in the church according to the truth, as was experienced by the first century church. The current church model has embraced many of the teachings of Christ, but these truths were placed within old wineskins and now the new wine has become spoiled through and through. In fact, the gospel truth of Christ has become diluted, otherwise – it should have burst the old wineskin completely. The church, it seems, is merely a Messianic version of Judaism with contempt for the basic doctrine of freedom from the Law.

> "Then He spoke a parable to them: "No one puts a piece from a new garment on an old one; otherwise the new makes a tear, and also the piece that was *taken* out of the new does not match the old. [37] And no one puts new wine into old wineskins; or else the new wine will burst the wineskins and be spilled, and the wineskins will be ruined. [38] But new wine must be put into new wineskins, and both are preserved" (Luke 5:36-38).

We have preached many great sermons about new wine being the Holy Spirit that abides in new wineskins as it pertains to man's eternal salvation in Christ, but think about this for a moment: did new converts get new wineskins (bodies)? Absolutely not! Our inner man was made anew from above by the Holy Spirit who is dwelling in us whereby we were given a new heart and a new spirit – and the Holy Spirit was given to us in greater measure to completely fill this new inner man (Ezek. 36:26-28) and make us a holy habitation for the Lord. The new wine of the Holy Spirit was poured into the new "inner man" wineskin in our "new birth" conversion (John 3:3-8) in order to complete our primary mission upon the earth: have dominion. And once the Spirit was firmly established with the truth becoming firmly rooted within us, the third component of our soul (the mind) is being renewed by the Spirit to be conformed to the image of Christ so that we may fully, completely and thoroughly be transformed into the image of Christ as His representatives, as ambassadors of His dominion, and as gateways of love and grace to establish His dominion in the earth according to the truth – i.e. *His truth*.

This next point is revolutionary in application: the church is a wineskin – also. Humans are not given a new outward body or form in the new birth, so this message by Jesus is in regards to His church. Remember, now, Jesus instituted Judaism and made a covenant with Israel to be His chosen nation as a people set apart from the world to manifest the goodness, grace and glory of God, but… it got bogged down in institutional doctrines, laws, sacrifices and outward displays of performance. Holiness was perfected, but it wasn't personified. Judaism made a big show of having the knowledge of God and being His special nation, but they kept their distance from the Lord by refusing to hear His voice and enter into a personal relationship with Him.

When Jesus came, He fulfilled His covenant obligation to Judaism and then rendered that covenant obsolete! (Heb. 8:7-13) And while He was fulfilling this old covenant, He was also teaching us how to walk within "the way" of a new covenant in order to live in proper relationship with God, whereby Jesus instituted this New Covenant established by His shed blood – whereby He also created and established a "new wineskin" – the church. An old body of faith was rendered obsolete – and a new body of faith was established in truth.

When Jesus died, the Spirit of the Lord was poured into the Jewish Temple and the veil was torn in two from top to bottom, thus rupturing that old wineskin and rendering it thoroughly obsolete!

God was no longer obscured from view (being seen by only a few), nor was the divine relationship restricted to observance in buildings. There is now... no longer any need for types and shadows of that former way to teach us anything according to the new Way commissioned by Jesus, the Chief Cornerstone, Who established "His Truth" as the foundation of the church Whose first living stone placed in this foundation was Peter's testimony – and not Peter himself.

The church is the new wineskin that is able to handle the new wine of the Holy Spirit, but sadly, the church has compromised her true identity by trying to adopt former practices within Judaism.

There are several times when Jesus said: "must be" – one is in reference to man and one is in reference to the church that is destined to become "the bride of Christ."

> "Do not marvel that I said to you, 'You **must be** born again.'" (John 3:7)
>
> "And no one puts new wine into old wineskins; or else the new wine bursts the wineskins, the wine is spilled, and the wineskins are ruined. But new wine **must be** put into new wineskins" (Mark 2:22).

Is it becoming more clear now? We (you and me) must be born again (literally, born anew from above) by the Holy Spirit for this purpose: that we become new tabernacles and holy habitations for the Lord of glory to abide within us – as gateways of greater grace, greater works and greater glory flowing through us. Our outward bodies never changed (though some miraculous healings have occurred); the manifestation of this new birth is revealed through us as an outward expression of an inward reality that has been birthed in us by the Spirit of grace *Who* began converting us to become like Jesus. If anything burst in the new-birth process regarding man… it would have been our soul exploding with inexpressible joy.

The church is the new wineskin and the new wine is the Holy Spirit. Yes, the Spirit was dwelling in the Jewish Temple just as the Spirit is dwelling within everyone even now, but (this is revolutionary in thought) both the old man and the old covenant were merely shadows of an earlier operating system of the Spirit and a foretaste of things to come. When Jesus fulfilled the old covenant and the Law, the prophets and the Psalms, He rendered all of that obsolete in order to reveal to us, in revelation truth, how to become regenerate in newness by the Spirit in order to return to a previous time when God walked in the cool of the day with us – in Paradise. And yet, somehow, the church has returned to the former things and teaches the faithful to adopt those former practices rather than entering into her destiny according to the truth… as the bride of Christ.

How did this happen? Where did the church go wrong? Who is to blame?

We are all to blame because we all forgot who we are and Who created us on purpose, and we forgot our reason and specific purpose for being on earth in the first place: to have dominion.

> "Therefore, leaving the discussion of the elementary principles of Christ, let us go on to perfection, not laying again the foundation of repentance from dead works and of faith toward God, [2] of the doctrine of baptisms, of laying on of hands, of resurrection of the dead, and of eternal judgment. [3] And this we will do if God permits" (Heb. 6:1-3).

Laying aside all elementary principles of Christ, the church needs to advance on into maturity – and return to her first love – Jesus Christ. It is hard to replicate the supernatural events of the first-century church that relied upon the Spirit of Christ to guide them in all truth – when the current church model does not honor the Holy Spirit on Sunday nor teach basic principles about the Holy Spirit that are rooted in truth – who is the Spirit of truth!

Every Sunday, the church spends all her time listening to the voice of man and participating in the man show rather than listening to the Holy Spirit, who is the Voice of Christ, who was sent by Christ to teach us the truth and establish us in this new way that Christ taught to us. Every name for the Spirit that is mentioned in the scriptures is attributed of Christ Himself, and it is His Spirit that He sent to birth the church in us – and through us.

Jesus was conceived by the Spirit, empowered by the Spirit (as an example for us), endured all things (with the assistance of the Spirit) and was resurrected by the Spirit (as the initial Firstfruit for our future hope). After Jesus ascended into heaven, He sent the Holy Spirit to us in a "greater than" new wine capacity in order to continue His kingdom revolution upon the earth. The Spirit has always been hovering over the earth and has always been dwelling within men, but this fresh release of the Spirit nearly 2,000 years ago is the New Wine that Jesus taught us to expect. We are no longer entertaining the old wine of the Spirit as in former days; we are suppose to be transformed by the new wine of the Spirit abiding permanently within us as the latter day outpouring that the prophets prophesized about… when young men see visions and old men dream dreams (Joel 2:28). Sadly, we cannot manifest what has never happened to us.

This permanent habitation by the Spirit within us is our seal of salvation and His personal guarantee the root of Christ's truth has been established in us and we are maturing in Christ, with understanding, to produce the fruit of righteousness in the earth. And this new wine reality is authenticated by greater grace, greater glory and greater works being revealed to us and through us as the work of the Spirit within us. The Spirit is our Paraclete who was sent to come alongside us and to help guide us in all truth according to the way that Jesus taught and demonstrated for us. Therefore, let us advance on to maturity – to follow Jesus, to hear His voice, to obey His commands and to imitate His example.

The Holy Spirit is the new wine that Jesus promised, and this is the promise that was given to those of the old way... that we may all hope in a better hope.

> "And being assembled together with them, He commanded them not to depart from Jerusalem, but to wait for the Promise of the Father, "which," He said, "you have heard from Me" (Acts 1:4).

Again, I say, the Holy Spirit is the new wine, and we cannot do anything apart from the Holy Spirit. Try as we may, we are woefully unable to do and be all that Christ created us to do and be – apart from the Spirit. Formerly, we had the Spirit guiding us to the truth to convert us and transform us to become like Jesus, as His representatives on earth – but we must continue to press in and abide in all truth and "wait" until the baptism of the Spirit occurs within us whereby He empowers us to do what Christ commissioned us to do – with miraculous signs and wonders.

- The Spirit of Promise
- The Spirit of Hope
- The Spirit of Wisdom and Understanding
- The Spirit of Righteousness and Peace

The Spirit who dwells in us yearns jealously!!! (James 4:5) He dwells in us jealously until we surrender our will to Jesus and establish Jesus upon the throne of our heart whereby the Spirit transforms us into a permanent abode, no longer waiting jealously – but now waiting expectantly until Christ is fully formed in us to release manifestations of God's glory and power through us to continue Christ's regime change upon the earth – from darkness to light – by His truth.

The Spirit waits patiently for us. The Lord is manifesting Himself in us, but He will not express Himself through us until the New Wine in us is ready for public consumption. Sadly, many people have jumped ahead of the Spirit, myself included, and have thwarted the fermentation process of the Spirit to prepare us for greater grace, greater glory and greater works through the Spirit. Many of us have been given a foretaste of the Spirit's empowering and enabling to walk in a certain measure of the Spirit's glory with the initial deposit of a preliminary spiritual gift, such as tongues, but what would happen to us if we were totally surrendered and totally committed to being changed by the Spirit and transformed into the manifest expression that Jesus purposed and planned for us since before the foundation of the world? Wouldn't that be great! Wouldn't that be absolutely marvelous! Imagine an unhindered release of the Spirit through you that would cause people to be healed when only your shadow passed over them, or when your handkerchief touched them, or merely the sound of your voice sent shivers up spines and caused members to feel electric pulses through their body.

I don't want some of this to happen to me… I want the total package. Jesus Christ is all I want and the Spirit is all I need in order for the new-wine reality to be manifested in me and through me. I don't just want more *from* Jesus – I want it all! I want **more of who Jesus is** in order to become just like Jesus as His manifest representative on earth to do all the things that He did… according to His promise to those who faithfully and obediently follow His example – and give Him all the glory as a result.

The best I will ever be – is according to He who abides within me – in oneness with the Spirit.

Who I am is irrelevant. He who abides within me is all that ever matters.

> "When He had called the people to Himself, with His disciples also, He said to them, "Whoever desires to come after Me, let him deny himself, and take up his cross, and follow Me" (Mark 8:34).

Discipleship is not something to be taken lightly. A disciple must count the cost because the '*agonizomai*' striving that is needed to enter through the narrow gate comes at a significant cost to the old man as well as your new man; your former self must completely die according to self and reject the ways of darkness that has sought to conform you in sin to the pattern of this world. This is not who God created you to be, nor were you ever intended to live in this manner. You were created upright and very good to live according to righteousness by the indwelling Spirit, but now, through faith in Christ Jesus, the Spirit's supernatural power abiding within you, as a new creation in Christ, will be released through you in order to accomplish Christ's greater works through you. You are not an accident! He called you out of the world, in order to be consecrated and set apart for divine service, to be sanctified and rendered holy and acceptable by the Spirit, and commissioned you to live intentionally for one reason: to establish the kingdom of heaven upon the earth – through you – in the midst of His enemies. Your life is not your own, nor is your life about you; your life is about He who dwells within you to establish you and build you up in the most Holy faith in order to continue Christ's mission on the earth as His new-wine tabernacle, and therefore… to have dominion and usher in a regime change! According to the Spirit… and by the Spirit's enabling…

> "I can do all things through Christ who strengthens me" (Phil. 4:13).

This is the work of the Spirit in you! You are not doing it, as many of us have been taught. Christ in you is doing it! You are merely the earthen vessel that your soul has yielded to perform the will of God in you, with you, and through you – to the praise of His glory. It is not about you manifesting your glory, which you truly have… it is about you manifesting the Lord's glory through you so as to be a faithful steward during this phase of eternity on earth as a consecrated instrument of His glory to produce more glory in the earth whereby we will, after this earthen vessel has released its hold on life, we shall enter into the Lord's glory… and into life eternal… with greater glory!

> "Most assuredly, I say to you, unless a grain of wheat falls into the ground and dies, it remains alone; but if it dies, it produces much grain" (John 12:24).

God created us as "His seed" with many grace attributes, as well as His glory placed within us to produce more glory. If we die with nothing more than this glory, without having created any more glory for the Lord, then this good seed placed within us (which is within all mankind; Matt. 13) enters into the ground and remains alone (without any glory; like the denarius). However… when we yield our life as obedient servants to the Lord of glory, then our grain of wheat will produce even greater glory as faithful stewards of His glory within us; and once we have completed our intended purpose on the earth, this seed will fall into the ground along with the mature fruit that was sown in righteousness whereby – much grain is produced! The glory placed within us is multiplied!

> "But others fell on good ground, sprang up, and yielded a crop a hundredfold. When He [Jesus] had said these things **He cried**, "He who has ears to hear, let him hear!" (Luke 8:8).

When your earthen vessel (literally, a seed) has devoted its life to producing more godly glory for the Lord, then… can you imagine what your glory will look like in the resurrection with all this righteousness credited into your account (Phil. 4:17).

> "But the ones that fell on the good ground are those who, having heard the word *with a noble and good heart*, keep it and bear fruit with patience" (Luke 8:15).

Bearing the fruit of righteousness does not happen immediately, especially when it takes the Holy Spirit ten, twenty, even thirty years (like it took me) to convert us and conform us into the image of Christ before we begin bearing fruit in righteousness. Through patient endurance and longsuffering, by struggling through faith and fighting the good fight of faith, to remain faithful and obedient to the very end... is a narrow gate that few enter in.

> "Eye has not seen, nor ear heard, nor have entered into the heart of man the things which God has prepared for those who love Him" (1 Cor. 2:9)... "Who acts for the one who waits for Him" (Isa. 64:4).

Are you using God's glory to build your kingdom? Does 'your' life glorify God? We get out of this temporary life what we cultivate – and the fruit of righteousness produced by our soul in obedience to Christ goes into our account.

> "And when the Chief Shepherd appears, you will receive the crown of glory that does not fade away" (1 Pet. 5:4).

"A man reaps what he sows in this life – and into the next. What is your focus for living on earth that will survive the test of eternity? What will your inheritance look like? Will it be that of a pauper, or as someone barely escaping the flames, or will it be that of a priest or a king with a kingdom, or sadly... none of the above?"[43]

Regrettably, what we have been taught in Sunday school and from the pulpit of man is an immediate gratification watered-down version of the hope we have in Christ. And this is my biggest complaint within the institutional church because we are actually teaching the faithful to be less-than followers of Christ by marketing the seemingly good but less-than gospels of Judaism and "this world" to keep us in bondage to the Law that we were delivered from – and this by sin merchants and sheep merchants selling emotional appeals that are building personal kingdoms for themselves rather than the kingdom of God upon the earth. Anathema. We are here for His good pleasure, not ours, and we are His sheep in His pasture to do His will – not goats living in pastoral pastures in doctrinal obedience to men, or denominational

---

[43] Excerpt from "Understand."

church factions, or the former pattern of Judaism, or even the former ways of the world in which we once lived.

> "Or do you not know that your body is the temple of the Holy Spirit who is in you, whom you have from God, and you are not your own? [20] For you were bought at a price; therefore glorify God in your body and in your spirit, which are God's" (1 Cor. 6:19, 20).

We are tabernacles for the New Wine that has been poured into us in order to release through us a greater outpouring of the Spirit in these last days. The fields are white with harvest, but workers are few who have been sealed and qualified by the Spirit, having been sanctified and purified by the Spirit of holiness, to release this greater glory. You are reading this because the Lord has activated you for duty in service to God Almighty who has called you according to a His great commission in these last days to put aside the failed works of the institutional church and enter into the promise in which we have placed our hope: the kingdom age tsunami of the Holy Spirit.

We have been called by the Lord to be more than conquerors through Christ… we have been called to become manifest expressions of Christ Himself *and His glory* upon the earth.

> "Now the Lord is the Spirit; and where the Spirit of the Lord is, there is liberty. [18] But we all, with unveiled face, beholding as in a mirror the glory of the Lord, are being transformed into the same image from glory to glory, just as by the Spirit of the Lord" (2 Cor. 3:17, 18).

> "***And the glory which You gave Me I have given them***, that they may be one just as We are one: [23] I in them, and You in Me; that they may be made perfect in one, and that the world may know that You have sent Me, and have loved them as You have loved Me" (John 17:22, 23).

We are the Body of Christ that willingly desires to do His will – as His hands and feet – as His new earth ambassadors dwelling in new wineskin embassies to be a fresh release of glory and grace in these last days.

Nothing will ever separate us from the love we have which is in Christ… yet we must be obedient to do all that He has imagined for us and purposed for us, even in death. Yet Death is merely a temporary place that holds those who wait without hope, and Hades is the temporary place that holds those who wait with hope, but there is a better place that is beneath the altar in heaven where the saints of God who were martyred for faithful obedience to Jesus are waiting as the first resurrection of the faithful (which is a better resurrection than the latter one from Hades; Heb.11:35) to rule and reign with Christ upon the earth for a thousand years before the final culmination of all ages takes place. And they will never see death! And then Satan will be released for a period of time and then the day of judgment when everyone will be resurrected, some to go into life eternal and others to go into outer darkness where there will be weeping and gnashing of teeth. It is important to understand this next point: make-believers (goats) and hypocrites will be cast into outer darkness.

It is not enough to know about Jesus and profess to have a personal relationship with Him. Either you know Jesus and understand the truth and are obedient by the hearing of His voice to do all that He commands… or else you are just a goat pretending to be one of His sheep

> *"My sheep hear My voice, and I know them, and they follow Me" (John 10:27).*

Do you have a personal relationship with Jesus – or do you believe in a theology that says you have a personal relationship with Jesus?

Jesus is not interested in passive believers, make-believers or religious spectators! Jesus came to call disciples into divine service who will enter into His reward in the regeneration. If God can raise sons of Abraham up out of rocks, then there is no shortage in His ability to accomplish His agenda to fill the earth with His glory; however, this may not include you. Search your heart and allow the Spirit to convict you if you are not standing in the way of Christ Jesus. It is better that we judge ourselves and convert… lest we come under judgment and thus forfeit our soul to the flames of hell.

> "For what profit is it to a man if he gains the whole world, and loses his own soul? Or what will a man give in exchange for his soul?" (Matt. 16:26)

Believing in Jesus is not enough to save you – "for even demons believe and tremble" (James 2:19). Jesus is not interested in saving self-righteous goats; He is calling believers into the way of truth to become His disciples as faithful sheep in "His" pasture.

You were not called to continue in the wayside pattern of this world; you were called to be converted and thus… transformed by the renewing of your mind so as to be commissioned unto divine service in the name of Jesus – for His sake. Salvation is not the goal for man on earth! Conversion is!!! Sanctification is!!! Transformation is!!! Dominion is!!!

Man's goal in life is not to get into heaven… but to get heaven into us!!!

Salvation into life eternal in Paradise *is our great reward* for those who live life as faithful servant/stewards that obediently do all He commands by the hearing of His Voice. Live according to the Spirit and deny the gravitational pull of the flesh to live according to sin. You were created upright to live according to righteousness so as to enter His Righteousness, i.e. Jesus Christ… and Jesus is the Resurrection and the Life!

> "But seek first the kingdom of God and His righteousness, and all these things shall be added to you" (Matt. 6:33).

Jesus is Jehovah Tsidkenu – the Lord our Righteousness, and we need to enter into His righteousness if we ever hope to get out of the dragnet of lawlessness and unrighteousness in disobedience through unbelief that is upon the earth.

If we have not entered into Jesus and we are not "in Christ" – then we have not entered into His salvation.

Brethren and saints of God… be encouraged… you are not alone. When we are in Christ, then we are already sons of God with resurrection in us! God has never forsaken us or abandoned anyone thus far. He gave us His Spirit to partner with our spirit to help us escape the dragnet of unbelief, Who waits patiently and jealously for us to yield the kingdom of our life into the Lordship and dominion of Jesus Christ whereby the Spirit guides us in all truth to become disciples of Jesus. We have all been predestined by God to live according to this plan, but whether we choose to enter into the Lord's righteousness – or not – is our choice. God will never forsake us, unless we have forsaken Him, and then he will forsake us in judgment into the eternal place we have chosen for ourselves. God does not send us to hell… it is we who judge ourselves unworthy of Him and His salvation, whereby those apart from faith are already living in Death, having chosen to remain separated from Him, and will forfeit their soul in defiance to Him in hell. The church has done an excellent job of making believers by promising them eternity in heaven, but Jesus never promised believers eternity in heaven.[44] Heaven does have a temporary place under the altar for those disciples who have been martyred for their faith.

Keep your eyes upon Jesus and seek Him only. Let His Righteousness dwell in you richly!

Seeking anything else by keeping your attention on anything else is part of the grand illusion of this world upon the earth – to tempt

---

[44] Read "Here: The Kingdom of Heaven Is" especially chapter six regarding the place(s) that Jesus has prepared.

you into sin, to make you a slave of sin and to keep you in bondage to sin so that you remain … in this world. Sin is anything that keeps us separated from God – according to what we do – and do not.

What more could I possibly say to help you understand and thoroughly comprehend what is at stake here?

We were created by Jesus, the Lord of hosts – to host God's Presence and Spirit within these earthen vessels. We are the host of earth – and earth is our proper domain and habitation, but this current generation upon the earth is temporary, as are these earthen vessels; the host of earth will be raised in resurrection to live again on the new earth in the regeneration when God makes all things new (again)… and the Lord will reward everyone according to their faithfulness (or lack thereof). What inheritance are you expecting in the resurrection to remain with you for all eternity upon the new earth? Will you be as one "barely passing through the flames" without even any garments credited into your account… or will you be one who surrendered all to become a disciple of Jesus whose works of righteousness credited into your account will be available for your use to purchase white linen and gold as part of your heavenly inheritance when you get to the other side, which you will enjoy as you walk in the cool of the day – every day (since there is no night) – with Jesus for all eternity. Will you be naked and ashamed – or will you be clothed in glory?

The church age is over and the kingdom age has begun. Believers can no longer remain standing in two ways regarding faith in Christ: either He is your Lord and your God… or He isn't. If Jesus is your Lord, then become His disciple and do what He commands. Be all in – or all out! Lukewarm faith is yet another illusion, as is mediocrity. Be hot or be cold. The kingdom of God is Yes and Amen!

This is the gospel of salvation that has been made known to me by the Holy Spirit. This letter was written under His inspiration and anointing within a couple hours (10/4/16) and I give Jesus all the glory for this truth, which is His truth manifested on paper through me for your benefit.

It's all about Jesus – and God gets the glory! Amen!

Jesus seeded His glory into us to produce more glory, and we were sent to earth with His authority and power to operate under His authority and power to have dominion over the earth. Man has been given this ability, via free will, to produce kingdoms and nations with His glory, power and authority resident within us – and this man has done – yet mainly for evil. But now the time of understanding is coming, with refreshing by the Spirit, to return to the truth and live obediently to the truth to fulfill our manifest destiny upon the earth as "Christ in us" with heavenly power and authority abiding in us and supernatural signs and wonders flowing through us. We are here to shift the atmosphere of this planet from darkness to light – with the truth – and to change this world from bondage to sin within the alternate reality of Satan's dominion – to liberty and freedom in Christ in His kingdom through the indwelling Holy Spirit.

Jesus sent the Holy Spirit to guide us in all truth, to empower us to live according to His way, to build us up in faith, to establish His church, to be the Administrator of His church......

Somehow, somewhere along the way, we forgot who we are, who Jesus is and what we are supposed to be doing. The New Earth Doctrine is to help reorient the applecart of faith and get it pointing in the right direction… toward Jesus only!

The church age is over… the kingdom age has already begun!

10. The Kingdom of God

Jesus came to teach us about the kingdom of God and to understand how the kingdom of God operates. Man had been behind enemy lines for so long and adopted many cares of this world, including the practices of wayward nations, that the times had been fulfilled and Jesus needed to reset the spiritual clock regarding man – so He came to teach us about the way, and what better way than to be a perfect manifest demonstration of how we were created and intended to live on this earth.

> "For the kingdom of God is not eating and drinking, but righteousness and peace and joy in the Holy Spirit" (Rom. 14:17).

To put everything into context thus far ... Jesus is the King of Heaven and Earth, He created man to occupy the earth, but man lost all remembrance of why he was sent here, so God Himself came to earth to show us the way, and in doing so... He established a forward operating position on earth called "the kingdom of heaven" within enemy territory (aka the kingdom of darkness). As the King of Heaven, Jesus was able to initiate this radical regime change by establishing a forward operating base deep within enemy territory by training twelve ordinary men as an insurgency to listen, obey, live according to the Spirit... and train others to become disciples.

Man was created to occupy earth so as to overcome this world with the atmosphere of heaven.

This is man's eternal purpose under heaven within the Kingdom of God: take back, redeem and occupy the earth in the name of Jesus... and give God all the glory in it. By faithfulness, in righteousness, by grace, through obedience, for His glory, we will receive an inheritance upon the New Earth in recompense for our sacrificial lives offered in service to Jesus.

Mone and Meno

There is an interesting correlation between two terms that Jesus used in John 14 to teach truth with understanding regarding the kingdom of God: '*mone*' (3438) and '*meno*' (3306). '*Mone*' is a permanent abode and '*meno*' is a dwelling place to abide temporarily, which is similar in meaning to '*katoikio*' (2730) as a quasi-permanent place to dwell while temporarily living '*kata*' (2596-down) on earth (Eph. 3:17) i.e. dwelling under '*oikia*' the Father's house.

The translation and meaning of these words can oftentimes be confused. Many things which are considered permanent dwelling places upon the earth, such houses and buildings, are actually temporary structures upon the earth at this present time. Much of what we consider permanent is actually only a type and shadow of the true spiritual reality that surrounds us (Col. 2:16-18).

Jesus came to teach us about the kingdom of God and oftentimes He contrasted it between things temporary and things permanent (as well as things old and new things; Matt. 13:52). Jesus taught numerous parables about the temporary nature of this world, as well as the operating system of this world that has ensnared all of us in sin by many temporal values and the care of worldly things. When these things, or anything (mammon), has become our focus and purpose in life, these temporary things will cause separation between us and the Lord… and for this reason Jesus also came:

> "Behold! The Lamb of God who takes away the sin of the world!" (John 1:29).

Sin, in this regard is "anything" that causes separation between us and the Lord; Jesus came and took away the sin of the world, which He accomplished on the cross. Jesus came to bear witness to the truth (John 18:37), as the manifest expression of God's word (John 1:14) by becoming the manifest expression of God's truth in Christ Jesus (John 14:6), in order to teach us about the truth… so that we may reject the deceitfulness of many lies that so easily ensnares us in sin which separates us from God and the promise of life eternal with Him. Jesus showed us the way of escape to get free from the dragnet that is over this world… and it is through faith in Him, by believing in His truth, by obeying His words of truth and abiding in His word that we are saved.

Jesus came unto us as "Immanuel: God with us," whereby His *parousia* permanently took away this sin by His ever-present nearness and presence abiding in us. He not only took away the veil of temporary separation that had been placed between God and man, but He also presented man with a permanent solution to the sin paradigm: grace through faith. Faith, in this regard, is not what we believe, but rather… the manner in which we live life according to what we believe. If we, through faith, continue to believe the lies of the enemy and continue to walk in doubt and unbelief, can this then be considered saving faith if we continue to live in a worldly manner according to sin? This question requires much personal and moral reflection.

Jesus presented everyone with a way of escape, but few enter into this way. The problem is, the majority of us do not even know that we are walking along the wayside path in sin that leads to destruction because we are simply doing what everyone else is doing, including some religious leaders. There seems to be no distinction in this world between those supposedly being faithful in righteousness and those believing faithful doctrines while operating in unrightness… because the absolutes in terminology have been redefined to accommodate a watered-down gospel.

The big picture regarding man living in "this world" is based upon a false operating system rooted in a lie by the enemy (Satan) that continues to deceive us and cause doubts to arise within our hearts, but (here is the good news) everything in this world is temporary… and I mean everything, that is, that does not give glory to God. This is merely an alternate reality that we have been deceived to embrace and live according to; it is temporary – and it is fading away.

The mystery of man upon the earth is sanctification whereby he is being changed, renewed and transformed by the Spirit of God to adopt the operating system of God's kingdom so as to live according to the Spirit (rather than sin) on earth as it is in heaven – and live like Jesus as His likeness. We are being transformed so as to live according to the kingdom *here and now*… as a foretaste of the true reality to come, and our faithfulness to God within this temporary season upon the earth will be rewarded with permanent "true riches" in our eternal residence.

The mystery of man is also transition – from that which is temporary to that which is permanent (or eternal). We are only in these temporary earthen vessels upon this temporary world and living a temporary life in temporary residences with temporary things (that we think belong to us) until we come to the full knowledge of the Lord's truth and we embrace this truth within a discipleship manner that produces a divine, personal and *permanent* relationship with the Lord Jesus… wherein our temporary earthly dwelling (*meno*) is being converted into a permanent abode (*mone*) within our heart and soul right now!

If Christ abides in you on account of faith, then you are living in eternity right now!

Our body is temporary, but our soul is permanent. You do not have a soul, per se; you are a soul – and your soul is eternal…

> "That he should *continue* to live eternally" (Psa. 49:9).

The operative word is "continue." Selah. We were sown by the Lord as "seed" of truth upon the earth to produce an abundant harvest of goodness in us and through us, and this is our God-given task and responsibility (Eccl. 3:10), but Satan has also cast his seed of doubt to perform deeds of unrighteousness in us and through us (Matt. 13:39). For this reason we must "continue" in the truth and live according to the manner in which we were created: as upright (in rightness) and very good… as sons of righteousness with the light of truth abiding in us.

There has also been some confusion in terminology between eternal and immortal; eternal has to do with spiritual things, like the soul; immortal has to do with physical things, like man's body. The body that we are given is mortal (never immortal), temporal and will die, "For it is appointed once that every man die" (Heb. 9:27), and after that... the judgment; however, there is a small group of people that will be in the kingdom in a future age that are eternal and immortal because they have already physically died once before (martyred) and will be raised in resurrection into new bodies before the regeneration (Rev. 20:4-6). And this, then, becomes an example of our eternal hope for everyone that lives according to the Spirit as a citizen of heaven (by God's adoption as children through faith in Jesus) in the kingdom of God... so that we who "continue" in faith will be raised in resurrection and given a new glorified body to serve the Lord eternally upon the new earth in the regeneration... when God makes all things new (again).

Our souls are eternal – and God has placed eternity in our hearts (Eccl. 3:11). God has also placed a seed of His glory in us, as well as His Spirit and His life, to help us "continue" through faith during this temporary transition period on earth. Jesus created us to be His likeness in every regard, including having a divine nature, so that we may operate our affairs upon the earth in the same manner that He would... in this life and the life hereafter. Everything concerning man upon the earth in this life is temporary... except one thing:

> "One generation passes away, and another
> generation comes; but the earth abides forever"
> (Eccl. 1:4).

The earth is also in transition, but unlike man, the earth abides permanently as one place within the kingdom of God... yet *it will not* be utterly destroyed as some falsely teach. The "things of this world" are temporary, fleeting and will fade away, and those things that do not give glory to God will be burned away in the judgment fire, but "the earth" abides forever because earth is our permanent place, our proper domain (dominion) and eternal "habitation" in the regeneration for the "host of earth" (aka sons of men).

> "And one cried to another and said: "Holy, holy, holy is the Lord of hosts; the whole earth is full of His glory!" (Isa. 6:3).

"The word "*habitation*" (in 2 Cor. 5:2) is '*oiketerion*' (G3613 – *residence*) a word that occurs only twice in the scriptures, which refers to: A) the former home of angels that did not keep their "first estate, proper domain" residence which was in heaven, but had to leave their abode/*habitation* on account of unlawful deeds (Jude 6), and B) as it refers to our new "habitation" residence ('*ex*' as coming "from out of" heaven) which we will inherit in the resurrection as we abide upon our "first estate and proper domain" – earth. Much like fallen angels whose proper domain was in heaven, who have been condemned by God in everlasting chains and darkness to await judgment, likewise mankind can also fall from his proper domain and first estate (earth) on account of sin and disobedience."[45] Do you now see the spiritual parallel between heaven and earth and what has been happening in the kingdom of God?"

Everything in heaven and on earth has gone through or is going through a transitional period whereby everything temporary that has been compromised by Satan's seed of doubt is being changed, renewed and transformed to be conformed to the image of Christ and the heavenly pattern where Jesus is Lord... forever and ever, Amen! If anyone refuses to "continue in righteousness" through faith and, thus, rebels against Jesus to continue in lawlessness and sin, and refuses to give God glory, then they will be burned in the fire.

> "Whoever commits sin also commits lawlessness, and sin is lawlessness" (1 John 3:4).

---

[45] Excerpt from "Here: The Kingdom of Heaven Is"; Chapter 3: "Do Men Go To Heaven?"

> "The Son of Man will send out His angels, and they will gather out of His kingdom all things that offend, and those who practice lawlessness, [42] and will cast them into the furnace of fire. There will be wailing and gnashing of teeth. [43] Then the righteous will shine forth as the sun in the kingdom of their Father. He who has ears to hear, let him hear!" (Matt. 13:41-43).

> "But there shall by no means enter it anything that defiles, or causes an abomination or a lie, but only those who are written in the Lamb's Book of Life" (Rev. 21:27).

Once the permanent and eternal relationship with Jesus has taken root within our mind and the truth continues to grow within our heart, we *shall* continuously desire to be converted by the truth to no longer be conformed to the pattern of this world but to have Christ "abide" in us and become fully formed in us by being conformed to His truth. This is the work of the Holy Spirit in us, who is the Spirit of truth, who brings understanding into our mind and is working to set us free from sin and the bondage of sin by empowering us to avoid (and reject) the temptation of sin. We are being liberated from bondage to lawlessness – to live according to righteousness!

Saints of God, we are truly and eternally children of God when we live according to this truth!

Yet… we have been slaves to sin behind enemy lines for so long that we do not even know who we are anymore. Jesus is the Word of God (John 1:1-5) and He manifested the word of God for us so that we may believe His word, follow His example and convert: return to the truth!

> "And the Word became flesh and dwelt among us, and we beheld His glory, the glory as of the only begotten of the Father, full of grace and truth" (John

1:14).

> "Then Jesus said to those Jews who believed Him, "If you abide in My word, you are My disciples indeed. ³² ***And you shall know the truth, and the truth shall make you free***." ³³ They answered Him, "We are Abraham's descendants, and have never been in bondage to anyone. How can You say, 'You will be made free'?" ³⁴ Jesus answered them, "Most assuredly, I say to you, whoever commits sin is a slave of sin. ³⁵ And a slave does not abide [*meno*] in the house forever, but a son abides [*meno*] forever. ³⁶ ***Therefore if the Son makes you free, you shall be free indeed***" (John 8:31-36).

The Jews had been behind enemy lines so long that they deceived themselves within their own denial. They said, "We have never been in bondage to anyone" and yet, somehow, they so easily forget their bondage in Egypt, as well as Assyria, Babylon, Persia and now, even, under Roman occupation. These Jews believed Jesus, as do a multitude of people today, but they did not understand their bondage dilemma because this is what "the sin of the world" does… it blinds us from seeing and understanding the truth that keeps us in bondage to lies, deception and most of all – doubt – to keep us from the truth.

When we forget who we are and why we are here and who God is and why we were created by God to be on earth in the first place, then this, my friends… it the work of the enemy in our heart who will contradict the truth of God to cause you to doubt God and believe a multitude of lies in order to rob you of any and all spiritual understanding. In this regard, if a person continues to live like this, as a slave to sin, then their temporary dwelling place, which has already been rendered obsolete on account of disobedience and rebellion, will be judged as insipidly worthless salt and tossed into the fire.

God is under no obligation to save us; "work out your own salvation with fear and trembling" (Phil. 2:12). Jesus gave us a way of escape, but we must enter into it and live according to it. Jesus has given us the truth and now *we* are obligated, through faith, to believe the truth and live according to the truth or else we will judge ourselves unworthy of the kingdom. God's mercy applies to covenant keepers, not covenant make-believers. Jesus is our Savior… and when we enter into His way, His truth, His righteousness, abide in His word, by being obedient to His truth as His disciples, then we have entered into His salvation – and we will never taste Death! Saints that live according to the Spirit of truth are no longer living within the temporary realm of this world, nor are they in bondage to sin… they are living as permanent residents of God's kingdom, and the death of these earthly bodies is merely a transitional change "out of" temporary clothing to enter into transformational eternal glory clothing. We will be changed from glory to glory, and transfigured to become just like Jesus – in glory!

Sounds too unbelievably true to be true? If you do not understand the concept of being changed from glory to glory, then read "Understand" to see how Jesus created you – and why! The term transfigured (*metamorphoo*-3339), as it pertains to the transfiguration of Jesus, is the exact same word that Apostle Paul used as being "*transformed*" into the image of Christ (2 Cor. 3:18) and, thus, we are being conformed to His image:

> "And do not be conformed to this world, but be ***transformed*** by the renewing of your mind, that you may prove what *is* that good and acceptable and perfect will of God" (Rom. 12:2).

We are being changed "back into" who we were to begin with – in preparation for the regeneration (*palingenesia* – literally: genesis again)! And we will return, to forever be with the Lord once again, to be "who" we were created to be – as sons of God abiding in Paradise, the Garden of Eden! When Jesus comes again – apart from sin – "we shall see Him as He is" in glory, and we shall be seen as we truly are "like Him" (1 John 3:12)… yet without these earthly garments (Heb. 9:28).

> "Beloved, now we are children of God; and it has not yet been revealed what we shall be, but we know that when He is revealed, we shall be *like* Him, for we shall see Him as He is" (1 John 3:2).

Jesus said we will become "like angels" in heaven (Mark 12:25)… but not as angels "in heaven." We shall become like Jesus as He is "in glory" … as heavenly citizens upon the new earth.

Everything that we are doing on earth right now is in preparation for the regeneration when the Lord makes a new earth for us to rule and reign with Him on this earth for all eternity – apart from sin – and yet somehow we have forgotten who we are and somehow think we will play harps on clouds. Argh!!!

Transition Through Temporary

Everything is in transition right now and everything will be changed and transformed; and man needs to understand the temporary nature of all things that are upon the earth, including himself. Our life is but a vapor, a brief breath… and then we pass away; yet where we came from is still somewhat of a mystery, but were we go after our bodies cease to be alive… is to yet another temporary place for an undetermined time. There are as many as fourteen places in the kingdom of God and the temporary place you go is based upon the things you did while on the earth.

- Death – the temporary holding place for those who reject God and have judged themselves as spiritually dead and unworthy of salvation
- Hades – the temporary holding place for those who profess faith in Jesus and are worthy of judgment by Jesus: some into His salvation in Paradise yet others into outer darkness
- Under the altar – the temporary holding place in heaven for martyrs who wait for the first resurrection and the millennial reign of Christ

And yet, we have been taught that everyone goes to heaven regardless of their crimes done on earth. Jesus never promised us heaven, the Apostles never preached it and our Creeds don't teach it![46] In the regeneration of all things, the temporary will be replaced by the permanent, and man's dominion (the earth) will be restored in oneness with heaven in the kingdom of God. The "restoration of the kingdom" is what the regeneration is all about, in newness, through truth and change becoming oneness again – under the Lordship of our King, Jesus Christ.

The earth is man's domain and this dominion was given to us by God (Gen. 1:26-28). Earth is our proper domain and eternal habitation – in this temporal life as well as life eternal.

The kingdom of heaven has come near; the kingdom of God is within you; the keys of the kingdom have been given to you (Luke 10:9-11; 17:21; Matt. 16:19). And Jesus says to us…

> "Repent, for the kingdom of heaven is at hand!" (Matt. 3:2)

The kingdom of heaven is neither up nor down… the kingdom of God is in! What you choose to do with the knowledge of this truth depends upon you working out your salvation with fear and trembling as you walk in the truth and abide in Christ. Either be converted by the truth to abandon the lies along the temporary wayside that leads to destruction or walk as a disciple of Jesus to live according to His way and His truth.

John 14

"Let not your heart be troubled; you believe in God, believe also in Me. [2] In My Father's house are many mansions [***mone***]; if it were not so, I would have told you. I go to prepare a place for you. [3] And if I go and prepare a place for you, I will come again and receive

---

[46] Read "Here: The Kingdom of Heaven Is"- Chapter 3 "Do Men Go To Heaven" by the author.

you to Myself; that where I am, there you may be also. [4] And where I go you know, and the way you know." [5] Thomas said to Him, "Lord, we do not know where You are going, and how can we know the way?" [6] Jesus said to him, "I am the way, the truth, and the life. No one comes to the Father except through Me. [7] "If you had known Me, you would have known My Father also; and from now on you know Him and have seen Him." [8] Philip said to Him, "Lord, show us the Father, and it is sufficient for us." [9] Jesus said to him, "Have I been with you so long, and yet you have not known Me, Philip? He who has seen Me has seen the Father; so how can you say, 'Show us the Father'? [10] Do you not believe that I am in the Father, and the Father in Me? The words that I speak to you I do not speak on My own authority; but the Father who ~~dwells~~ abides [*meno*] in Me does the works. [11] Believe Me that I am in the Father and the Father in Me, or else believe Me for the sake of the works themselves. [12] "Most assuredly, I say to you, he who believes in Me, the works that I do he will do also; and greater works than these he will do, because I go to My Father. [13] And whatever you ask in My name, that I will do, that the Father may be glorified in the Son. [14] If you ask anything in My name, I will do it. [15] "If you love Me, keep My commandments. [16] And I will pray the Father, and He will give you another Helper, that He may abide with you forever— [17] the Spirit of truth, whom the world cannot receive, because it neither sees Him nor knows Him; but you know Him, for He ~~dwells~~ abides [*meno*] with you and will be in you. [18] I will not leave you orphans; I will come to you. [19] "A little while longer and the world will see Me no more, but you will see Me. Because I live, you will live also. [20] At that day you will know that I am in My Father, and you in Me, and I in you. [21] He who has My commandments and keeps them, it is he who loves Me. And he who loves Me will be loved by My Father, and I will love him and manifest Myself to him." [22] Judas (not Iscariot) said to Him, "Lord, how is it that You will manifest Yourself to us, and not to the world?" [23] Jesus answered and said to him, "If anyone loves Me, he will keep My word; and My Father will love him, and We will come to him and make Our *home* [*mone*] with him. [24] He who does not love Me does not keep My words; and the word which you hear is not Mine but the Father's who sent Me" (John 14:1-24).

END

Jesus has invited us to partner with Him and to be partakers of the divine nature to accomplish all that He has *prepared beforehand* for us to walk in (2 Pet. 1:4).

> "For we are His workmanship, created in Christ Jesus for good works, which God prepared beforehand that we should walk in them" (Eph. 2:10).

When we have made a permanent habitation (*mone*) for the Lord to abide within us, then we are already citizens of heaven living in eternity right now… it just hasn't happened yet while we still struggle (*agonizomai*) in the flesh (in these '*meno*' temporary earthen vessels).

The goal of man is <u>not</u> to get into heaven… but for heaven to get into man!

Jesus came to re-start the spiritual revolution on earth and initiate a regime change, and this is why Jesus created us in His image according to His likeness, to become like Him, because we were commanded to have dominion and be regime changers that He created us to be – and become – as His representatives, in His name.

Jesus is our Divine example and He showed us how to do it. If Jesus did it – then so can we! Jesus is "with us always, even to the end of the age" (Matt. 28:20) and He sent the Holy Spirit to assist our inner man's efforts to effect this regime change!

> "As He is – so are we in the world" (1 John 4:17).

We are here according to His eternal purposes and we need to get back to the business of our Father's will and focus, once again, on being the light of the world to disperse the darkness with the light of truth by keeping our eyes upon Jesus! Live according to the

Spirit!

> "For those who live according to the flesh set their minds on the things of the flesh, but those who live according to the Spirit, the things of the Spirit" (Rom. 8:5).

Have dominion. Earth is our permanent habitation… and this is why sons of men were created and sent as "the host of earth." We were sent to effect a regime change by releasing the atmosphere of heaven abiding in us, and the church needs to align itself with this truth.

> "Go therefore and make disciples of all the nations, baptizing them in the name of the Father and of the Son and of the Holy Spirit" (Matt. 28:19).

11. It Don't Come Easy

One morning, this once-popular song popped into my early morning meditation.[47] The lyrics and the singer are irrelevant to me, but the message is very relevant to everyone living on earth.

Over the years, I have read many messages about living faithfully for Christ as something that is as easy as twelve easy steps, and this, then, was followed by similar sales pitches to the faithful with fewer and even easier steps to attain all the promises we have in Christ... "within this new book" or "CD offer" as if we can easily import the truth of God as patches on our old wineskin without even sensing the need for spiritual newness in new wineskins. Most of these patches are relatively easy to implement without much sacrifice to the old man, but when these patches fail – which is to be expected since these are temporary patches on the temporary man – then another seemingly "inspired" book will surface with more seemingly great patches... and the old man hobbles along in blissless ignorance without power apart from the truth.

There are no shortcuts when it comes to living according to the truth in righteousness. If someone tells you it's not that hard, then they have not been walking along the path of discipleship under the tutoring of the Holy Spirit. When Jesus said, "Many are called but few are chosen" (Matt. 22:14), it was in context to entering into life eternal resulting from a life of righteousness by struggling to live according to the truth of God abiding within you.

> "Then one said to Him, "Lord, are there few who are saved?" And He said to them, [24] "Strive to enter through the narrow gate, for many, I say to you, will seek to enter and will not be able" (Luke 13:23, 24).

The word "strive" (also translated "struggle") is '*agonizomai*' and

---

[47] This is the work of the Holy Spirit to bring truth to us... even truth within secular society, "All We Need Is Love."

the English equivalent is "agonize." If someone tells you the way of Christ is easy and faith is not that hard to attain, then I can confidently say… they are standing on the wayside (along but not on) the true path that leads to salvation and life eternal because an easy message contradicts the message of Jesus. Faithfulness in this world is a daily struggle when you live according to the truth of Christ.

"This word summarizes our struggle on this earth as we have dominion in His name while our adversary seeks to destroy the message of grace and truth that is being manifested in us and through us. This struggle is not easily won by simply flicking a wrist, or making a verbal profession, or signing a membership roster, or attending the Sunday morning fraternal order of any denomination. Folks, we are in a spiritual battle on this earth and our adversary has been deceiving us with many lies and eating the church's lunch to keep us captive to sin and controlled by sin for one purpose: to deceive us, obliterate us – and maintain possession of "this world." We must overcome the lies of the enemy and strive to enter through the straight and narrow gate, but in order to do this… we must know the truth and be obedient to the truth."[48]

Life eternal is not something that is easily attained with a verbal profession… it requires steadfast persistence, determination and patience to live according to the truth, and despite all manner of trial and tribulations that will come against you, and all manner of temptations to deceive you by the enemy to keep you in bondage to the many cares of this sinful world (the counterfeit reality), a disciple must agonize through these struggles so as to "continue" in faith to attain life eternal.

> "For the redemption of their souls is costly, and it shall cease forever— [9] that he should ***continue*** to live eternally, and not see the Pit" (Psa. 49:8, 9).

To continue in life eternal seems very contradictory to the messages we hear in the church, which teaches us we attain eternal

---

[48] Excerpt from "Understand" section titled, "Why Do You Strive?"

life as our great reward according to faith, but this is a misnomer. We are spiritual beings that are having an earthly experience. Our souls are eternal. Our soul is already living eternally; however, we need to live according to faith in righteousness if we are going to "*continue*" to live eternally. Our names have already been written in the Book of Life if we *continue*, by grace, in faithful obedience to Christ, but we can erase (blot out) our names on account of disobedience and unrightness living (Rev. 3:5). We were sent to earth to have dominion over our adversary who wages war against the kingdom of God, and we resided in Christ "just as He chose us in Him before the foundation of the world, that we should be holy and without blame before Him in love" (Eph. 1:4).

We are spiritual beings that have always been in existence in regard to God's creation; who we were and what we will become seems trivial and immaterial to the daily struggle we are experiencing during this season of eternity upon the earth. We are sojourners sent by the Lord to perform very difficult and dangerous godly service: to redeem the earth from the dominion of Satan. Who you are is really inconsequential to the matter at hand; you were sent to earth as a servant of God Most High as one soldier in the host (army) of earth (mankind) to come against worldly darkness with the light of truth. To assist us in this effort, the Lord entrusted us with His things, as stewards and caretakers, to establish the kingdom of heaven upon the earth.

So, if you think coming against Satan and his entire demonic army of principalities, powers, demons and evil spirits is an easy matter, and all you have to do is have faith and believe in Jesus whereby you will be saved, then consider this:

> "Even the demons believe—and tremble!" (James 2:19).

Saints of God, we have been deceived with many lies to believe many manmade doctrines that are inconsistent with the truth of Christ's message. We are servant warriors and we were sent to bring the fight to Satan and his army of rebellious angels and their onslaught of wickedness.

We have been taught "do our best and Jesus takes care of the rest," but we haven't even been taught about our true and rightful mission for the earth, so how can we even consider we are doing our best if we don't even know what we are supposed to be doing anyway? Let me say this another way…

How can we be faithful if we don't know what we are supposed to be doing?

If we don't know what we are supposed to be doing on earth, then how can anyone tell us how to be faithful – or even – if we are being faithful? Faithful in what? Faithful to whom? Faithful by following the denominational doctrines of our local church and the opinions of a preacher? Having been behind enemy lines for so long, we forgot who we are and what we should be doing, and it seems we have been faithful in building the wrong city upon the wrong mountain for 2,000 years.

We were sent as conquerors and redeemers seeking conquest, as servant soldiers being sent to overcome the enemy with three things: the truth of God, the word of our testimony and the power of the Spirit dwelling within us. That is all any earthen vessel has in their arsenal against demonic forces that seeks to kill and annihilate you… and out greatest weapon is truth. The Apostle Paul called it the sword of truth (or the sword of the Spirit) and the Holy Spirit is the Spirit of truth. Truth is our primary weapon and Jesus came as the Truth to testify to the truth in order to liberate us from our self-imposed bondage to sin and the alternate reality of Satan's dominion upon the earth.

If we don't know the truth, then how can the truth set us free?

> "And you ***shall*** know the truth, and the truth shall make you free" (John 8:32).

This message, and our worldly struggle, is not about man; the battle is between God and Satan! The host of earth (men of goodwill) were sent by God into the midst of a cosmic battle against the forces of evil, being clothed in human weakness, to war on His behalf. This battle is not about us! We are the weaker things of God, in the similitude of Job, that are being tested to prevail on God's account – with the knowledge of the truth – as manifest demonstrations of the truth – against all the weapons of the enemy – to give God all the glory. This battle involves us because we were sent as servant soldiers to come against the enemies of God who refused allegiance to Jesus Christ; however... the battle is the Lord's!!! And within this battle, we will encounter many brethren like us that have been deceived to live according to the lie of the enemy... but they are not our enemy!!! They have been deceived and have been taken captive to become a slave to sin, which is the operating system of "this world" because the truth is not in them... at least not yet. As servant soldiers of the Lord Jesus, who is "Commander of the Lord's Army" (Joshua 5:13-15), He has commissioned us and enabled us to live according to the truth through the operating system of the kingdom of God, which is: by the Spirit of God.

Many years ago, the Lord spoke two words to me back to back which I now comprehend:

> "I am plowing furrows in your mind."
> "I am training your mind for war."

The Lord has been plowing truth upon truth in my mind to live according to the truth and to trust Him, implicitly and unreservedly, in everything; and the Lord has been training my mind with the sword of truth so that it becomes my primary weapon against the enemy!

When this battle is over, we will turn our swords into plowshares and resume tending the garden as in the beginning – in Eden (Isa.2:4; Micah 4:3); but until that day happens, we must "continue" to "fight the good fight of faith" and give God all the glory, through Christ Jesus.

Jesus Our Conquering Redeemer

Jesus exemplified the servant soldier archetype in everything He did, being armed with the truth of God and the indwelling Spirit.

> "Or what king, going to make war against another king, does not sit down first and consider whether he is able with ten thousand to meet him who comes against him with twenty thousand?" (Luke 14:31).

Everyone serving in the military understands military culture and what it means to be under authority; there is someone over you that is taking responsibility for your life and you have entrusted your life into their authority. This type of trust does not come naturally because the operating system of this world is based on false disambiguation of truth, distrust, fear and self-interest. Trust must be embodied and demonstrated before it can be earned.

When Jesus was preaching the message of the kingdom and teaching us to trust God and return to God, He demonstrated the heavenly operating system and culture of the kingdom with many miraculous signs, wonders and healings. On one occasion, a Roman soldier came up to Him and asked Him to heal his servant who was ill, and Jesus marveled at the faith of this gentile servant soldier because be understood the heavenly operating system of being under authority.

> "The centurion answered and said, "Lord, I am not worthy that You should come under my roof. But only speak a word, and my servant will be healed. [9] For I also am a man under authority, having soldiers under me. And I say to this one, 'Go,' and he goes; and to another, 'Come,' and he comes; and to my servant, 'Do this,' and he does it." [10] *When Jesus heard it, He marveled, and said to those who followed, "Assuredly, I say to you, I have not found such great faith, not even in Israel*!" (Matt. 8:8-10).

This, my friends, is the operating system of the kingdom: we will do what we are told by hearing the Lord's voice (and not the voice of others). When Jesus sent the disciples out under His authority to heal the sick and cast out demons, He gave them this command: enter places that are worthy and do not take extra articles of clothing. They went out only armed with truth, being clothed with understanding, to operate under the authority and power of Jesus to come against demonic manifestations of darkness on people. Likewise, when we go out to do the will of the Lord, we are oftentimes like sheep lead to slaughter, but we shall return, just like the disciples did… rejoicing and marveling. They shared after-action stories of various experiences, and then Jesus said something somewhat unexpected:

> "Then the seventy returned with joy, saying, "Lord, even the demons are subject to us in Your name." [18] And He said to them, "***I saw Satan fall like lightning from heaven***. [19] **<u>Behold, I give you the authority</u>** to trample on serpents and scorpions, and over all the power of the enemy, and nothing shall by any means hurt you" (Luke 10:17-19).

Jesus gave us the authority!!! When we operate under the authority of Jesus, under His power, peace, protection, and provision, His Presence will go with us to do all that He purposed for us to accomplish. When we operate under His authority, we are able to do the exact same thing these disciples did (which was even before Jesus sent the Holy Spirit; John 7:39). When we do what Jesus commands, as being under His authority… Satan's dominion on earth will fail!!! This is the plan of God and the will of God for us through Christ Jesus! It is, literally, Jesus going out to make war against the enemy abiding within your earthen vessel, as one member in the body of Christ, to continue the fight against Satan. This is most important: it is not you taking the initiative to do it. We are to operate under His authority as servant soldiers to do all that He commands… and not operate according to what we think or feel He wants us to do. Know it, understand it, then do it. Jesus is working His power through us, by the Spirit, to do what we were created to do: host His Presence and Spirit… and usher in a regime change on earth.

While in training, don't be impulsive; wait for it! Wait for the empowerment of the Spirit!

The power, the authority and the truth with understanding are not in us – nor are they ours. We are merely earthen vessels "hosting" the fullness of the Godhead bodily within us to accomplish the will of God through us – with the tools God has given us… and continues to reveal in us. These are His tools and resources being made available to us as disciples and servant soldiers. God is doing it in us, to us, with us and through us – to the praise of His glory.

We are atmosphere changers sent to change the atmosphere of this rebellious world with the heavenly atmosphere of grace and truth, with His authority and power given to us, to overthrow the kingdom of darkness and set captives free. This is your primary mission – and mine as well. ***When we comprehend why we were created, then we will understand our identity comes from who we are – according to He who created us for a purpose***. The worldly system has perverted this heavenly principle by telling us…"who" you are is based upon "what" you do; however, the true heavenly principle is this: "what" you do is based upon "who" you are!

Ask Jesus to reveal your true identity to you – and let's get this dominion mandate started!

- You worship the Lord in spirit and in truth because you are a worshipper
- You pray and intercede because the Lord created you as a watchman and prayer warrior
- You preach because the Lord anointed you to proclaim the truth and God's deliverance
- You prophesy because Jesus has anointed you to make His thoughts and ways known
- You teach because you are His teacher to disciple the nations in the way of righteousness

- You heal because the Lord commissioned you to be a doctor and tend His flock
- You have a business mindset and the Lord enabled you to produce great wealth in business to support the work of His ministers that builds His church
- You are a lawyer, nurse, judge, politician, astronaut, carpenter, plumber, police officer, accountant, vet, horticulturalist, architect, soldier or whatever because the Lord has given you a task to perform and your identity is found in doing what Jesus created you to accomplish as you host His Presence and Spirit within your earthen vessel

We do not get our identity from "what" we do. We get our identity from Jesus, by being in a life-giving relationship with Him… whereby He tells us our unique task upon the earth. We most likely will be doing the same task after our conversion as before, but now we are doing it, not because this is what we do, but now… because this is who we are in regards to Christ; and we use these gifts and talents to establish the kingdom of God in accordance with His will for us.

Not long ago, my daughter began talking to me about the will of God for her life. As we chatted, she said she had many personal interests (desires) and talents that she wanted to use for kingdom purposes, but she felt this was self-serving, to which I said, "Who do you think gave you those gifts, talents and desires?" Her mind became at ease knowing the Lord created her with desires in her heart – and that she could operate out of those desires.

> "May He grant you *according to your heart's desire,* and fulfill all your purpose" (Psa. 20:4).

The goal is to see us doing everything on behalf of Christ in us rather than us doing anything on behalf of us. And again, I go back to build upon an earlier point:

1. You "do" and become according to "who" Jesus created you to be…
2. If you do not know who you are (your identity in Christ), then how do you know what you are supposed to be doing
3. If you do not know the truth, then how is it possible to say you are living faithfully

The Image Bearer series is built upon the knowledge and truth that mankind was created "in His image according to His likeness" so as to become exactly what we were created for: to bear His image and become exactly like Jesus in every respect according to His earthly example. We get our identity from "Who" we are in relationship with (Jesus) – and not from "what" we do – because you were intended to become and be another unique manifest expression and representation of Jesus upon the earth… and there will never be anyone one else like you! You were born for a purpose according to His plan of creation, redemption and regeneration. Walk according to the destiny Jesus established (and preordained) for you!

Saints, we need to know who we really are. My first book, "Regenesis: A Sojourn To Remember Who We Are" is based upon my exhaustive search within the scriptures to understand who we are according to He who created us, i.e. Jesus Christ. A pattern of His way was encoded within the spiritual DNA of our soul, and He planted a seed of His glory in us, and He created us with the spiritual ability to hear His voice so that we may "become and be" according to all that He created us to be, become and do… as servant soldiers, as servant stewards and as disciples of Jesus our Lord and King to do all that He commands.

The entire universe is under His authority and under His command… are you?

Before Jesus was arrested, falsely accused, illegally sentenced and brutally murdered, He told His disciples to take a sword with them. One of the disciples immediately produced two swords (a long knife) and showed it to Jesus…

> "And He said to them, "When I sent you without money bag, knapsack, and sandals, did you lack anything?" So they said, "Nothing." [36] Then He said to them, "***But now***, he who has a money bag, let him take it, and likewise a knapsack; and he who has no sword, let him sell his garment and buy one. [37] For I say to you that this which is written must still be accomplished in Me: 'And He was numbered with the transgressors.' For the things concerning Me have an end." [38] So they said, "Lord, look, here are two swords." ***And He said to them, "It is enough***." (Luke 22:35-38).

Jesus told them no weapon formed against them would prevail against them, but here we see at least one disciple carrying weapons. Was Jesus, at this moment, teaching His disciples to do something contrary to an earlier command of operating under His authority and power without weapons... or was Jesus referring to something entirely different, as He customarily did, from a heavenly perspective? In this moment, the sword carried by Peter produced yet another teaching opportunity by Jesus when Peter acts impulsively, as he customarily did, when he used the sword in an offensive rather than defensive manner.

The word "sword" is an instrument used for violence. Jesus has been teaching the disciples to be vigilant, because violence only begets violence.

The term "it is *enough*" employs the word '*hikanos*' (G2425) with a variety of meanings, including: "sufficient, competent (in terms of persons), enough (in terms of things), ample (in amount), fit (in character)."[49] We do not know whether Jesus was referring to persons or things; however, we do know there was a diversity of opinions by the disciples at this time, including some who betrayed Him and others who continued to doubt. Nonetheless, Jesus said it, but what did He mean by it?

---

[49] Strong's Concordance.

The Lord knows we have need of material items, like food and clothing, as well as knapsacks to carry these items, and moneybags to purchase supplies for the journey… because we are sojourners that have been sent to earth to say and do what He tells us, and to go wherever the Lord tells us to go. When we live according to this minimalist mindset, to take only those things necessary to do the will of God, we do so trusting our care into His protective hands.

Why, then, do any disciples of Jesus need swords? An earlier lesson may shed light on this – as well as a future lesson to follow in Gethsemane. When the Lord's disciples (James and John) saw the rejection of Jesus by a Samaritan village, they asked Him, "Lord, do You want us to command fire to come down from heaven and consume them, just as Elijah did?"

> "But He turned and rebuked them, and said, "You do not know what manner of spirit you are of. [56] For the Son of Man did not come to destroy men's lives but to save them." And they went to another village" (Luke 9:54-56).

Jesus came to save the lost – and gather us – not scatter abroad. Jesus came to heal the sick, not kill and destroy, like Satan. We are the host of earth and "the manner of spirit that we are of" is to operate in the likeness of Jesus – to save many souls alive! It is interesting to note that "the manner of spirit" that do command fire to come down from heaven are heavenly angels that have been commanded by the Lord of Hosts (Jesus) to do so (Gen. 19:13, 24). Therefore, Jesus "rebuked them" for having an agenda that was opposed to His plan of salvation by the "host of men" for "all" mankind. If we think, somehow, that we have been called to take up arms or perhaps even lead an armed rebellion, then we do not comprehend who we are – or our purpose under heaven.

In the Garden of Gethsemane, Jesus was being arrested by a mob being led by Judas Iscariot when one of the previously mentioned disciples decided to take matters into his own hands…

> "Then Simon Peter, having a sword, drew it and struck the high priest's servant, and cut off his right ear" (John 18:10).

Peter had the sword... because he didn't understand the word of the Lord. Peter acted impulsively and independently of Jesus, and yet Jesus knew this would happen, and this is why He said "Enough it is" when two swords were shown to Jesus earlier because He was going to demonstratively teach four things:

1. When you take matters into your own hands, which is sin, then people get injured
2. The old way operated in violence and vengeance, but the new Way is vigilance and virtue
3. God's healing power is not just for believers... but for all mankind, including our enemies and those who persecute us even unto death
4. When Jesus tells you to take a sword, then take one sword... not two, then wait upon Him to tell you the reason for having it

More than two swords could have resulted in a bloody battle and loss of life among His disciples, which fulfills the scripture, "I have not lost any that you gave to Me" (John 17:12; paraphrased).

So, why did any disciples have swords on hand? Well, there was a militant Zealot mindset among several disciples (like Judas and his father, Simon; Luke 6:14-16) that expected the Messiah to overthrow Roman occupation and liberate Israel, and it appears Peter also leaned in this direction. My personal opinion (not supported by the word in scripture) is that Peter was very much influenced by these rebellion-minded Zealots and Jesus was telling him "Enough!" as a minor rebuke. Nonetheless, when the moment came to make a stand for Jesus, Peter drew his sword, thinking he was acting boldly in righteousness, but instead... by his impetuous and impulsive act of defiance he created an opportunity for the Lord to restore a severed ear.

> "But Jesus said to him, "Put your sword in its place, for all who take the sword will perish by the sword" (Matt. 26:52).

And this, then, becomes an important message for new earth residents; understand the word... and resist the temptation to "take" the sword. If you live by the sword, you will die by the sword; yet if you live by the Spirit, you will take love that produces peace.

Jesus said we can take a sword (long knife) with us, but if you take it... you will likely suffer because of it. Over and over and over yet again, Jesus is teaching us how to operate and live according to the heavenly pattern through the Spirit. If we host love and grace in our heart, then we will release love and grace into the world; likewise, if we host feelings or theologies of hate or fear in our heart, then we will influence the world around us by what comes out of our heart. The worldly pattern is obvious – get mad and get even; the spiritual pattern is... righteousness, peace and joy in the Holy Spirit.

> "For those who live according to the flesh set their minds on the things of the flesh, but those who live according to the Spirit, the things of the Spirit" (Rom. 8:5).

When you take the sword, you will produce the fruit of the sword; however, when we take the Spirit, we will produce the fruit of the Spirit.

For many days I wrestled with the contrasting messages of Matt: 10:9-10 (take nothing with you for the journey to cast out demons and heal the sick) versus Luke 22:35-37 (now take these things and also get a sword), so I waited on the Lord for understanding. Having studied the scriptures very carefully, whenever Jesus uses a specific term, I have learned to take His word literally. We may want to rationalize the term "sword" as being metaphorical of His word, which I did, but then I received understanding from the

Spirit... there are two types of training in righteousness for disciples: basic and advanced. Suddenly, the rules of engagement for His disciples changed!

Once our basic training in righteousness and truth is complete, we will be tested by the Lord according to righteousness and truth... by application of the truth... for advanced training in righteousness. Step number one: never act impulsively or independently. Wait upon the Lord to see what He wants you to do. If you hear nothing, then do nothing... and trust in the Lord... for He is our righteous Right Hand, our Deliverer, our Strong Tower, and the Defender of the weak!

When the Lord tells us to go out and minister to people, we are to go out and rely completely on the Lord for His power, provision and protection; yet, when the Lord trains us for war and sends us into spiritual battle against principalities and powers, then we must be armed and fully prepared for conflict, but not armed with material weapons.

While it seems Jesus is teaching us to be armed with a sword, it is important to note Jesus never told His disciples the reason for taking the sword. Most importantly, the sword (*machaira*-G3162) is "an instrument for ordinary violence (or dissensions) that destroy peace (Matt. 10:34)."[50] Swords can be used for defensive and offensive purposes; however, as is always the case with Jesus, He is teaching us to operate according to the heavenly pattern of vigilance, rather than violence, and to rely on the Spirit of God to engage the enemy – as we partner with the Spirit in this heavenly warfare for earthly dominion – armed with the sword of truth.

> "And war broke out in heaven: Michael and his angels fought with the dragon; and the dragon and his angels fought, [8] but they did not prevail, nor was a place found for them in heaven any longer. [9] So the great dragon was cast out, that serpent of old,

---

[50] Strong's Concordance.

> called the Devil and Satan, who deceives the whole world; he was cast to the earth, and his angels were cast out with him" (Rev. 12:7-9).

On earth as it "was" in heaven, the warfare for earthly dominion continues…

> "And from the days of John the Baptist until now the kingdom of heaven suffers violence, and the violent take it by force" (Matt. 11:12).

We are at war!!!

The cataclysm in heaven spilled over from heaven to earth; heaven was restored by the host of heaven and now earth is in the process of being restored by the host of earth (men). Mankind has been at war since the great rebellion broke out in heaven – and now the sons of men have been commanded by the Lord to take back and redeem what the enemy has taken captive, including the earth and creation itself.

> "For the earnest expectation of the creation eagerly waits for the revealing of the sons of God" (Rom. 8:19).

We are not being trained for worldly combat to fight battles and wars with swords (or guns); we are being trained to engage in spiritual warfare – with the sword of the Spirit. We are fighting an invisible war against a largely invisible enemy that can only be defeated with the sword of truth.

Man has been at war against demonic forces in the heavenly realm since we were sent to earth, and they will do anything to prevent us from establishing the kingdom of heaven here. Israel was always at war with some nation, and this is true even today, and the reason for this is rooted in our dominion mandate – to stand for the Lord and come against evil, which is why the Lord always kept some rogue nation around "so that the generations of the children of Israel might be taught to know war" (Judges 3:2).

Does this conflict with your "peace on earth" theology? Then keep reading...

There are five Greek words translated "peace" and each of them are very specific in regard to the type of peace mentioned:

- *Eirene* (1515) harmonious relationships between persons and with God (most common)
- *Siopao* (4623) to be silent or still, keep silence; a holding back, to hold thy peace; to be calm as quiet water (Mark 4:39)
- *Pimoo* (5392) put to silence, to close the mouth with a muzzle; be speechless (Luke 4:35)
- *Hesuchazo* (2270) to refrain from (labor, speech or meddlesomeness) (Luke 14:4)
- *Sigao* (4601) to be silent, hold one's peace (Luke 20:26); to be kept secret (Rom. 16:25)

'*Eirene*' is the peace we most often think of between persons and nations. This is the type of peace that Jesus gives His followers, and it is a perfect and permanent peace that only He can give within a divine relationship with Him (Luke 24:36; John 14:27; 16:33; 20:19, 21, 26).

You cannot have '*eirene*' peace on earth... if you are in the middle of a conflict or war. Any attempt at "peace at any cost" without conflict resolution is a compromised temporal peace that lacks the substance of true peace which cost you nothing.

There is a time in our discipleship training when Jesus teaches us to surrender our tendency to fight back, as servant stewards, and there comes a time when Jesus will teach us and train us for war as servant soldiers, hence basic and advanced training. A basic training servant knows basic doctrine, yet the advanced training servant comprehends we are at war against an evil empire that hates God, rejects Jesus and seeks to obliterate mankind from the earth. "This world" is their dominion and we were sent to take it back in the name of the Lord. Jesus said…

> "Do not think that I came to bring peace on earth. I did not come to bring peace but a sword" (Matt. 10:34).
>
> "Do you suppose that I came to give peace on earth? I tell you, not at all, but rather division" (Luke 12:51).
>
> "So there was a division among the people because of Him…" (John 7:43).

Bingo! Jesus came to teach us the truth so that we may live according to righteousness in order to create a division between sheep and goats… between those who desire to live obediently to Jesus, the Lord of heaven and earth, versus those who live according to the worldly pattern of wickedness and desire to do evil. In this worldwide conflict between good and evil, we have been commanded to align ourselves with Jesus and be obedient by hearing His voice to oppose this worldly dominion, or by default, we remain captives of the enemy.

> "For he who is not against us is on our side" (Mark 9:40).

Our primary mission on earth is to have dominion which involves several components: save other souls alive through faith in Jesus, and come against the enemy of God in the name of Jesus. We must be trained in the basic principles as ministers of the gospel to be gentle as doves, as sheep being sent to ravenous wolves, fully armed with little more than the truth of God, to operate under His authority, and to speak the truth in love… and then there will be times when we must stand and give account of the truth abiding within us, like watchmen and intercessors, to come against the enemy's lies with the truth of God in holy boldness with manifested *dunamis* and *kratos* Holy Spirit power.
Basic and advanced – authority and power – for servants and soldiers of Christ.

When you are a disciple of Jesus, He will impart His peace to you "My peace is My gift to you." When you are a mature disciple and are willing to do all that He commands, then you will also experience a spiritual shift (or change) in the rules of engagement by the way and manner in which the Spirit of Christ teaches you about the kingdom and His dominion. There will be times when you get the sense to muzzle it and other times to speak boldly under the Spirit's anointing… yet always as the Spirit leads. Basic principle disciples must also understand – and be willing to undergo – advanced training in spiritual warfare in order to become a soldier for Christ. Jesus is the Lord, as the scripture says…

> "The Lord is a man of war; The Lord is His name"
> (Ex. 15:3).

As an intercessor, I have come to regard worship as a form of spiritual warfare. When I sense the presence of the enemy coming against me, I will sing a spiritual song and enter into worship because the enemy cannot stand three things: prayer, worship and uttering the name of Jesus. If I feel anxious, fearful, negative, doubtful, confused or (fill in the blank), I sing songs of rejoicing with praise and thanksgiving… and those feelings dissipate quickly.

During one particular Sunday worship service, the Spirit of the Lord manifested Himself upon me and I began interceding in a most remarkable way; I, and others who were interceding as well, could feel chains of bondage being shattered off people by the Spirit of deliverance whereby multitudes of saints were being set free. Several days later, as we recounted this experience, many people experienced a spiritual shift in the room… and the sound of worship was magnified in such a way that we concluded was angelic participation joining us in worship.

Spirit normal!!! As you can imagine, we were all under spiritual attack by the enemy the next day, including me. When I awoke that Monday, a song was playing in my mind which is very typical of the Holy Spirit, but when I listened to the message… the words did not align with the Spirit; and indeed, the enemy counterfeited the Spirit's method to produce a counterfeit message. Over and over again, the message was: "Beat it. Don't you ever come around here. Don't wanna see your face. You better disappear!" "Beat it" by Michael Jackson is a song about intimidation which became a weapon the enemy used against me.

We must be alert and vigilant to spiritually discern previous worship methods that may have worked once before but now may be a counterfeit message produced by the enemy unbeknownst to us... that does not focus our heart's affection and attention – on Jesus! Within this context, hype and sensationalism are being used by many churches as a counterfeit presence of the Holy Spirit… and the Spirit grieves.

And the church would do well to consider the implications of the warfare happening within their congregation as well. Most importantly – intercession must never cease, nor must intercession be disregarded as inconvenient or irrelevant. A battle is being waged in the heavenly realm for any place where worship occurs, and is being manifested, especially within His church. I have witnessed a trend for many years, but I was not spiritually mature enough to discern what was happening – until now. Intercessors need to meet regularly, but when intercession stops… that, then, is when the spirit of control oftentimes takes over church operation… including (and especially) worship. More battles within churches are fought as a direct result of people trying to control worship music rather than allowing the Spirit to govern worship… in which "we" become instruments of worship under His guidance and administration!

When we fight over worship… could anything be more diabolically sinister by the enemy to cripple the Lord's church… or more egregious to the Holy Spirit??? Saints, this must cease!
We are at war… and now it's time to take the fight to the enemy!!! Our weapons are truth and fervent prayer through intercession and worship.

> Jesus said, "But the hour is coming, and now is, when the true worshipers will worship the Father in spirit and truth; for the Father is seeking such to worship Him. ^{24} God is Spirit, and those who worship Him must worship in spirit and truth" (John 4:23, 24).

Over the years, I have encountered the enemy's presence in palpable ways, including many attacks during the night when I felt a tangible heavy demonic presence upon my chest that prevented me from taking in breath. When I utter the Lord's name, Jesus, three times... the enemy leaves and the peace of Christ comes over me. Saints of God... if you are valuable, then you are vulnerable!

David, whom God called "A man after My own heart, who will do all My will" (Acts 13:22) was a worshipper and also a man of war whom Saul employed to worship in song in order to drive away evil spirits that were tormenting him.

> "Then one of the servants answered and said, "Look, I have seen a son of Jesse the Bethlehemite, who is skillful in playing, a mighty man of valor, a man of war, prudent in speech, and a handsome person; and the Lord is with him." (1 Sam. 16:18).

The Lord was with David – in Presence and Spirit! Worship was a weapon David used against spiritual enemies *and* he also used the sword to "slay his tens of thousands" (1 Sam. 18:7). That was the way of Israel according to the Old Covenant; however, when Jesus came, He established a New Covenant and we must do as we are instructed by Him if we call Jesus our Lord and Master to establish the kingdom of heaven in the midst of our enemies. Study the teachings of Jesus and you will see a very small yet exceedingly significant three-letter word that Jesus uses to designate a compare-and-contrast between the old way and the new earth way. "You have said before... **BUT**... now I say unto you." Jesus is teaching us the new way by comparing and contrasting with the old way... that He rendered obsolete. And yet, there are multitudes of teachers and prophets in the church today that mimic the pattern of the old way which didn't work because – they refused to listen to the Voice of Truth and live according to the Spirit!

New Earth warfare is different... very different indeed! It is manifested from a heart that desires to worship the Lord... in spirit and in truth!

Blessed Are The Peacemakers

> "Blessed are the peacemakers, for they shall be called sons of God" (Matt. 5:9).

The word peacemaker (*eirenopoios*-G1518), said by Jesus, appears only once in scripture and is a combination of two words: (*eirene*-G1515) peace and (*poieo*-G4160) "to make, to do... and is used of the bringing forth of fruit."[51] As servant stewards, servant ministers and servant soldiers, the fruit of peace is produced by living according to the Spirit to produce the fruit of the Spirit, which is "love, joy, peace....." (Gal 5:22).

When we live according to the Spirit, in faithful obedience and righteousness with Jesus, we will walk in the way of love and grace with one another. The peace we produce is not our peace – it is the Lord's peace produced within us by Him; it is not the type of peace that the world gives (which is a cheap peace without any cost). The Lord's peace comes at a significant cost to "self" as a total yielding and "dying to self" to do the Lord's will regardless of what may happen to you. For some of us, this peace is manifested as "power under restraint" which is humility, and for others, this peace is made manifest by coming against the enemy by tearing down strongholds through prayer and intercession. What you do must be according to God's plan for you, who made you according to His purpose, yet not according to someone else's plan. What you hold in your hand is determined by the Lord alone ... and by

---

[51] Strong's Concordance.

the word of His Spirit dwelling within you.

> "You have heard that it was said, 'An eye for an eye and a tooth for a tooth.' [39] ***But I tell you*** not to resist an evil person. ***But*** whoever slaps you on your right cheek, turn the other to him also. [40] If anyone wants to sue you and take away your tunic, let him have your cloak also. [41] And whoever compels you to go one mile, go with him two. [42] Give to him who asks you, and from him who wants to borrow from you do not turn away. [43] "You have heard that it was said, 'You shall love your neighbor and hate your enemy.' [44] ***But I say to you, love your enemies, bless those who curse you, do good to those who hate you***, and pray for those who spitefully use you and persecute you, [45] that you may be sons of your Father in heaven; for He makes His sun rise on the evil and on the good, and sends rain on the just and on the unjust" (Matt. 5:38-45).

"***BUT***" is the transitional word between things old and new things, between the old way and the new way according to the kingdom of heaven upon the earth. This is the new expression of righteousness in God's kingdom according to the new earth operating system for the New Covenant by new earth men… "by the Spirit, with the Spirit and through the Spirit" that is rightside-up versus a worldly pattern that is upside-down. It is not pacifistic by any means, nor does a person become a doormat for abuse; the Lord will give us a way of escape one way or another when we trust in the Lord implicitly – and without doubt. Believe… and do not doubt!

All men were created in God's image according to His likeness as a seed with His glory in them; we may erringly disparage some persons as less-than or subhuman or even expendable because they do not know the truth wherein they may be walking along an evil wayside path and some, even, doing violence against the people of God… but these are still God's children who need to come to the truth, even at the expense of our life, because the Lord cares for them and does not want them to perish. Why should we be concerned if we perish in service to Christ, if we already know Christ... since, through martyrdom, we have been guaranteed a better resurrection?

> "Women received their dead raised to life again. Others were tortured, not accepting deliverance, that they might obtain a better resurrection (Heb. 11:35; see Rev. 20:4-6)

We are the church militant, but we are not militant with carnal weapons! Our primary weapon is the truth of God which alone is capable of tearing down strongholds. And we enter this battle on our knees in prayer in oneness with the Spirit!!!

> "For the weapons of our warfare are not carnal but mighty in God for pulling down strongholds,
> ^{5} casting down arguments and every high thing that exalts itself against the knowledge of God, bringing every thought into captivity to the obedience of Christ, ^{6} and being ready to punish all disobedience when your obedience is fulfilled" (2 Cor. 10:4-6).

Jesus came as the Truth, to testify to the truth, into a world of lies, as a witness against the lies. Once we know the truth, by completely assembling truth with understanding in our mind – and then cultivating this truth within our heart to produce the fruit of truth in righteousness – then we can also come against the enemy just like Jesus did!

> "***But if I cast out demons by the Spirit of God***, surely the kingdom of God has come upon you.
> ^{29} Or how can one enter a strong man's house and plunder his goods, unless he first binds the strong man? And then he will plunder his house. ^{30} He who is not with Me is against Me, and he who does not gather with Me scatters abroad" (Matt. 12:28, 29).

Jesus accomplished many tasks associated with His Kingship,

including binding the strong man (Satan). Jesus also restored God's divine authority to man that we surrendered to Satan in the Garden – which we can reclaim by establishing a divine personal relationship with Him. And thus, by binding the strongman, we are now able to plunder Satan's house – in the name of Jesus. "The kingdom of God has come UPON YOU" when you exercise the Lord's authority and power over the enemy. Jesus exercised His authority and power over Satan's temptation to deceive Him and enter into sin through doubt, and this, then, becomes our heavenly example: submit your life to God, resist Satan's temptation and declare the truth in holy boldness.

> "Therefore submit to God. Resist the devil and he will flee from you" (James 4:7).

What need do we have for swords, guns or whatever? Jesus said we can "take" a sword, which I assume is for defensive purposes, so it is not against the Lord's teaching or doctrine to have ordinary weapons; however, there is a more excellent way for those saints who have become thoroughly armed according to basic principles to walk according to advanced training.

> "Above all, taking the shield of faith with which you will be able to quench all the fiery darts of the wicked one. [17] And take the helmet of salvation, and ***the sword of the Spirit***, which is the word of God" (Eph. 6: 16, 17).

Along our sojourn, we can "take" whatever instruments we want with us; if we chose to take a sword, then some unintended consequences may occur because the sword is an instrument of violence. However, if we take love, joy, peace and happiness as instruments of God's grace and mercy dwelling within us that we generously share with others, then truly… we have been converted by the Spirit to live according to the operating system of heaven… and "the kingdom of God has come upon you." When we walk in the way of love, it becomes impossible to produce the fruit of violence. In contrast… the kingdom of heaven suffers violence, and the violent take it by force" (Matt. 11:12). Take defensive measures, if necessary, when violent people come against you, but know this… if you are a follower and disciple of Jesus, you will suffer violence by worldly people.

Our adversaries who stand in rebellious opposition to Jesus Christ and His kingdom and His dominion will wage war against the faithful by violent vitriolic means because they have been deceived by the lie and are slaves to sin to live according to hatred in unbelief, and they will take the weapons of this world to come against the kingdom of God. Saints, however, must not succumb to this worldly manner because our primary weapon is truth – according to the Spirit – and we are to walk according to love as we have been commanded by Jesus our Lord and Savior.

> "This is My commandment, that you love one another as I have loved you" (John 15:12).
>
> "Beloved, let us love one another, for love is of God; and everyone who loves is born of God and knows God" (1 John 4:7).
>
> "What then shall we say to these things? If God is for us, who can be against us? (Rom. 8:31).

The kingdom that Jesus established is born out of a love doctrine. The dominion that we are to establish upon the earth in the name of Jesus, and for His glory, is a dominion firmly rooted and established in love; however, everything in "this world" that is not in alignment with Jesus Christ, our Lord, will come against you because it hates Jesus and this is the way of the world because it is rooted in hate. The Kingdom of Love is what the saints have been called to establish… "and His dominion is an everlasting dominion without end!"

It don't come easy. Now, go ye therefore…

> "Love never fails" (1 Cor. 13:8)

12. End Times

There has been much speculation regarding end times predictions throughout history. When the calendar was turning over from the year 999 to 1000, there was much speculation the end was near, and this was also the case one thousand years later with Y2K computer malfunctions... and yet, we are still here another sixteen years later.

Why are so many of us inordinately focused on end time theology? This is a question that prompts serious consideration because it involves everyone living on planet earth; however, the multitude of theories and doctrines based upon a plethora of Biblical interpretations of various prophetic messages has caused an unintended consequence: much spiritual complacency and apathy regarding the Lord's command for man to have dominion over the earth. Why care about something... or anything for that matter, if it is going to melt in the judgment fire? As is typically the case... when confusion abounds, we need to perceive the enemy's hand working to influence the faithful to take their eyes off of Jesus to focus on something else... including prophetic Biblical interpretation of scripture.

By distracting us with various end times interpretations resulting in doctrinal disagreements, the enemy has taken our focus off what we are supposed to be doing.

After searching the scriptures many years and seeking the Lord's guidance through prayer and meditation, I have come to a conclusion: end times don't matter much if you are already living eternally right now. If Christ is in you and you are in Christ, and you are living in oneness with God and His Spirit, then it really doesn't matter what happens... or when it happens... as you "continue" to live eternally right now. Regardless if Jesus comes back tomorrow or in a thousand years, your salvation in Christ has already been sealed by the Holy Spirit. In this respect, end times are irrelevant to those who live and operate within the eternal dimension of the Spirit. In this respect, even time is irrelevant within the eternal dimension!

> "For He is not the God of the dead but of the living, for all live to Him" (Luke 20:38).

Jesus knew exactly what He meant when He used the terms "living" and "dead," but somehow man, in an effort to understand spiritual things from an earthly or human perspective, is oftentimes confused by words that convey a different meaning from a heavenly perspective. In the front end of all books that I write, I include a glossary of terms (keys to understanding the kingdom) so readers can navigate the scriptures with clarity of understanding from a spiritual perspective.

Take, for example, the words "life, living, alive, dead and death." From a worldly perspective, these terms seem self explanatory in regard to our human body; however, from a spiritual perspective, these earth suits are merely a temporary vessel that we are using during this season (or phase) of eternity on earth. We are a soul – and our soul has always been in a state of existence from God's perspective, as being alive with life, even before the foundation of the world; yet when we were born upon the earth… our soul became manifest in an earthly body and we became a living *being* (*nephesh*, a *soul* dwelling within a created living being; Gen. 2:7) that became animated (alive) by the breath of life.

Your soul is alive with life eternal… and the ultimate goal of man is: to "continue" to live eternally (Psa. 49:9); however, this life can be *forfeited by us* at any time when we chose to live in rebellion against Jesus… and thus, it is "we" who blot out our names from the Book of Life.

Consider, now, these spiritual definitions:

- Life – the source from which all creation exists, and is made alive, as coming from God through Christ Jesus, who is "the Life" and the "author and finisher" of life (John 14:6; Heb. 12:2)

- Living – those persons spiritually alive with life, that no longer operate in the shadow of Death while sojourning in earthen vessels that will eventually perish for lack of life
- Alive – the spiritual state of being in existence from God's perspective, even apart from the body, and abiding eternally in communion with God's Presence and Spirit
- Dead – the spiritual state of being in existence from God's perspective, but temporarily separated from Him; the eventual disposition of the earthen body without life
- Death - the spiritual state of being permanently and eternally separated from God; the temporary holding place of the dead for those awaiting the resurrection of judgment

"As life never means mere existence, so "death," the opposite of life, never means nonexistence, but separation always." [52] "As spiritual life is conscious existence in communion with God, so spiritual death is conscious existence in separation from God." [53] Even in death, the soul of man is consciously aware of his existence either in communion with – or in separation from – God.

"Do you have the conscious awareness of God's presence in your life? Do you live your life with the conscious awareness that Jesus, the Lord of the universe, is dwelling within you? Are you aware that, because Christ is in you, your heavenly Father is also abiding in oneness within you and knows your thoughts, sees what you look at and hears every word and utterance you make? Are you taking your spiritual relationship with Jesus Christ for granted – that is, on your terms or are you living as His disciple on His terms?"[54]

What, then, does it matter what happens along the earthly timeline in regard to end times, the rapture, the great tribulation or any number of other prophetic events as yet unfulfilled – if you or

---

[52] Word study on "die" (*apothnesko*-G599). Strong's Concordance.
[53] Word study on "death" (*thanatos*-G2288). Strong's Concordance
[54] Excerpt from "Here: The Kingdom of Heaven Is" Chapter 6: "Where Do We Go From Here?"

anyone is living life apart from God's presence here and now? These events are subject to dynamic fluidity which are constant – and are constantly changing – all the time. If you are alive in Christ, then you are already living in life eternal while a resident on earth within a human body; what happens to your body is inconsequential and immaterial to the "life" of your soul as it abides in communion with the Lord your God, Jesus Christ.

Why, then, do we have need to understand timelines? Actually, we don't – and perhaps it is better this way rather than letting the enemy distract us from our earthly mission mandate to have dominion over him... as we keep our eyes upon Jesus. These prophetic events have created enormous schisms within the body of Christ, and the enemy is all too delighted with our high-minded theological distractions because we spend more time and energy focusing on the wrong thing while we tear one another down to embrace divisiveness within denominational camps of woe... rather than pulling down Satan's spiritual strongholds and having dominion over him.

How many prophetic messages have we heard since the dawn of the modern age? Perhaps thousands! Does anyone remember "Jesus is coming in 1988" and then "in 1989" due to an arithmetic error?

How many people are trying to predict end times and future events based upon prophetic utterances within an old covenant which Jesus fulfilled and then rendered obsolete?

How many end times theologies erringly suppose heaven as man's eternal destination? This one factor in itself is enough to cast a shadow over the manner in which we have tried to interpret prophetic scripture! They don't even know where they are going when their body dies, or what they will be doing in eternity, so how can they correctly interpret end times, seasons and signs associated with them?

It is infinitely more important to maintain your personal relationship with Jesus – by hearing His voice and doing all that

He commands – rather than speculate on rumors!!! The enemy is creating these rumors as a distraction technique so that the Lord's sheep sidestep their primary mission and, thus, focus on speculation, theories and fables.

If you believe in the Rapture… are you doing everything in your power by living up to your heavenly potential to tear down Satan's strongholds and save other souls alive? Will your wealth benefit the unsaved after you go? What good comes from believing in the rapture… if you are forfeiting your heavenly responsibility to have dominion over his kingdom here and now? If you believe in pre-millennial rapture, then you will be waiting in the clouds for a long time (since the scriptures are silent on continuing into heaven) while the first resurrection of martyrs under the altar of God is made alive again to rule and reign with Jesus a thousand years. Do you have any desire whatsoever to participate in the greatest demonstration of glory, grace and greater works upon the earth ever imagined… or do you want heaven more than being obedient to Jesus?

Consider all the distraction techniques the enemy is throwing at us: a multitude of many voices, more noise, faster lifestyles, stress about the present, anxiety about the future, worry about wars and rumors of wars, wickedness among the nations, natural disasters, inordinate busyness, fearful diseases, financial uncertainty, declining health, and a cacophony of hyperactive living to go faster and faster to produce more money and possess more stuff – all which prevents us from desiring "the one thing:" hearing the Voice of Truth.

We need to start destroying all speculation and every lofty thought that is raised up against the knowledge of God – beginning with Rapture doctrine and a whole host of wacky end times predictions that has already caused much anxiety and fear among already timid sheep. The church needs to focus on teaching believers about Jesus so that they desire to become His disciple, and then… and only then, we might possibly shift the heavenly timeline that is "in the Father's authority" known only by Him.

Consider this: if Jesus told us when the end would happen, we would focus on that rather than being obedient to do all that He has commanded us – here and now!

Even if the Rapture is a legitimate doctrine… so what! It doesn't change who you are or what you are supposed to be doing ***right now***; however, by believing in the Rapture, many saints have become complacent and apathetic disciples that yearn more for sweet-by-and-by heaven rather than faithfully walking in the authority and power given us by Jesus through our divine nature (spirit) to come against the enemy in the name of our Lord, Jesus Christ. Do I have an opinion one way or another if the Rapture is a truthful doctrine or not? Again, I say… ***so what!*** It does not change or influence my faithful obedience in doing the will of God as I have been instructed by Jesus Christ – in the least. It will happen… when it happens!

Have dominion – in the name of Jesus – is all anyone should really care about!

> "And He commanded us to preach to the people, and to testify that it is He who was ordained by God *to be* Judge of the living and the dead. [43] To Him all the prophets witness that, through His name, whoever believes in Him will receive remission of sins" (Acts 10:42, 43).

What will we receive… pie-in-the-sky or remission of sins? Focus on Jesus!

> "I charge you therefore before God and the Lord Jesus Christ, who will judge the living and the dead at His appearing and His kingdom: [2] Preach the word! Be ready in season and out of season. Convince, rebuke, exhort, with all long-suffering and teaching. [3] For the time will come when they will not endure sound doctrine, but according to their own desires, because they have itching ears,

they will heap up for themselves teachers; ⁴ and they
will turn their ears away from the truth, and be
turned aside to fables. ⁵ But you be watchful in all
things, endure afflictions, do the work of an
evangelist, fulfill your ministry" (1 Tim. 4:1-5).

We are in the last days... and yet... we are merely in transition between the church age (who forgot who they are and turned aside to believe in fables and superstition) and the kingdom age when we remember and become mighty servant warriors and servant stewards, as men and women of goodwill, who delight themselves in the Lord and are joyfully doing all that the Lord commands, having dominion in His name... even if it results in the death of their mortal body.

"Most assuredly, I say to you, he who hears My
word and believes in Him who sent Me has
everlasting life, ***and shall not come into judgment,
but has passed from death into life***. ²⁵ Most
assuredly, I say to you, the hour is coming, and now
is, when the dead will hear the voice of the Son of
God; and those who hear will live. ²⁶ *For as the
Father has life in Himself, so He has granted the
Son to have life in Himself,* ²⁷ and has given Him
authority to execute judgment also, because He is
the Son of Man. ²⁸ Do not marvel at this; for the
hour is coming in which all who are in the graves
will hear His voice ²⁹ and come forth—those who
have done good, to the resurrection of life, and
those who have done evil, to the resurrection of
condemnation" (John 5:24-29).

A day is coming after the millennium (when those saints under the altar have reigned with Christ) when the dead will rise and come forth (in the second resurrection) – ***on the last day***.

"But I do not want you to be ignorant, brethren,
concerning those who have fallen asleep, lest you

> sorrow as others who have no hope. [14] For if we believe that Jesus died and rose again, even so God will bring with Him those who sleep in Jesus. [15] For this we say to you by the word of the Lord, that we who are alive *and* remain until the coming of the Lord will by no means precede those who are asleep. [16] For the Lord Himself will descend from heaven with a shout, with the voice of an archangel, ***and with the trumpet of God***. And the dead in Christ will rise first. [17] Then we who are alive *and* remain shall be caught up together with them in the clouds to meet the Lord in the air. And thus we shall always be with the Lord. [18] Therefore comfort one another with these words" (1 Thess. 4:13-18).

One final comment about being caught up to meet the Lord in the air (or clouds): how many times will this occur? Only once, you say, in the rapture – and that would be correct. Ok, when will the rapture occur? Think about this logically for a moment. Consider what happens at the end of all ages, on the last day – and I mean the very last day – after the millennial reign of Christ and after Satan is loosed from the bottomless pit for a little while (Rev. 20:3, 4)… what is going to happen to those saints on the earth that are "alive" and are worthy of salvation who have *not* experienced death (to satisfy the human requirement that all men must die once (Heb. 9:27)? These people are still physically alive and need to be raptured, so how can they be raptured on the last day… if our doctrines teach the rapture happens before the tribulation? There is only one rapture – not two! A new earth in regeneration is going to happen, and in that instantaneous moment when the trumpet blast is heard, what would you do "if you were Jesus" with all the people that are still alive on earth with the Spirit of Christ abiding in them that have not tasted death? 'If' you were the Lord, would you not put them in a safe and secure temporary place? Perhaps an intermediate cloud, for example?

…now consider…

How can the rapture occur (to raise up the living) before the millennial reign of Christ "ahead of" the first resurrection of those saints that were martyred and have been waiting patiently under the altar who have already been counted worthy in the Lamb's Book of Life without need of judgment and have a more noble right to resurrection than cowards afraid of death? Consider it!

Have Dominion and focus on what you should be doing today!

In conclusion: **DO NOT** be obsessed with seasons and times that are in the Father's authority!

13. The Father's Kingdom

One morning while in prayer, I asked the Father, "What does the dominion of your kingdom look like?" (And then I smelled overcooked toast)

"The dominion of My kingdom reflects My glory. It does not appear in a manner as you would understand. It becomes life and motion and stillness in a moment. It enables the highest good to prevail. It loves unconditionally, it rejoices exuberantly, it forgives generously, it keeps no record of offense, it delights in everything good that was made according to My glory.

"The enemy will entice multitudes with many attractive looking life-way offers to see if they can rob Me of My children. Indeed, some will be lost, but those who are Mine will always be Mine. I know who are Mine; I know the thoughts of their heart.

"What can I tell you that you have not already read, but do not yet comprehend, or understand. Consider all the parables by Jesus and consider all His lessons: the kingdom of heaven is like…

"Think about things above, and not about things on earth, and your perspective will change."

The message of the kingdom is all about glory and becoming who we were intended to be.

- We were sent to produce a harvest in ourselves – and through others – to produce an increase of glory in us and through us
- We are called to yield all that we produce – and surrender the thing produced to God because everything belongs to God; none of it is ours, not even us
- Unless a seed dies… it remains just a seed, but when the seed yields itself and the right-of-way to another, the

> increase and abundance produced continues throughout generations… to the glory of God

Jesus taught us this lesson by living the perfect example of a yielded life. He did not surrender His Divine nature or His glory, but He laid them aside for one season, in yielded submission because He knew He was able to lay His life down and pick it up again (John 10:17, 18). And, likewise, so are we! When we lay down our life to magnify the Lord's glory that resides within us, the Lord Jesus then is able to use us completely and perfectly to perform that which we were originally intended and ordained to accomplish, as predestined disciples to perform preordained works, as His workmanship… created in Christ Jesus for good works. You are… because He is… I AM!

And even if we die, we have the guarantee of resurrection by the Spirit Himself, as the seal of approval, Who authenticates Whose we are… in Whom we have salvation.

The kingdom of God is full of polar opposites in dynamic tension:

- To have life, we must be born and die to self
- To live, we must yield this life – to live and be born anew
- To do well, we must give our glory to Another
- To strive, we must learn to wait
- To lead, we must follow
- To be full, we must be emptied
- To be perfect, we must be broken
- To become mighty, we are given weakness
- To attain greatness, we are given humility to serve
- To become rich, we must become poor
- To ascend, we must become meek and humble
- To attain salvation, we must believe and trust like that of a small child
- To be esteemed, we must become as nothing of any consequence and esteem others ahead of ourselves
- To have everything, we must give it all away to possess nothing

- To receive an inheritance, we must surrender all earthly treasure
- The beatitudes are the keys to living within the kingdom of God for New Earth residents
- All it costs – is all you've got!

We need to get out of the box we are thinking in to escape the familiar so as to enter in to the unfamiliar realm of the Spirit's heavenly dimension.

If someone has to die – then let it begin with me. I am a disciple of Jesus. I have surrendered all to follow Jesus and imitate His life for the good of many so that many may come to understand – and believe – in Him who was sent. And you, also, are one of many others – just like me.

14. The Lord's Dominion

Three days later, on October 27, 2014, I was awakened by the Lord in the early morning before sunrise, and, as I meditated upon His dominion and the magnificence of His glory, the Lord began to reveal many things to me. I have never considered myself a prophet, nor do I even now; I am a prophetic teacher and revivalist, and the Lord teaches me according to His ways because I desire to know His ways by listening to His voice.

As I began to worship the Lord in His beauty and majesty, I had a personal encounter with the Lord that has never happened before, and then – this understanding came to me: "The times are upon us. The restoration of all things has begun. The world as we know is it about to change – it is in transition." And then Lord began to speak to me with the hand of a ready writer...

"My kingdom is being restored and My dominion is being revealed. My dominion is not as the world sees or interprets dominion, but because you have asked to know, I will tell you the keys to understand and unlock the mystery."

"Everything is Mine, says the Lord. The illusion of having is merely an illusion. There are only two ways: My way – and the way that leads to death. I do not want you to be unaware. I have come willingly on My own accord. I desire to present to you the keys of the kingdom because you earnestly desired to know about My dominion. I have sought after someone like you. I am coming soon – and My dominion I will share with no other. My kingdom of My accord, My purpose and My plans which I have laid; My glory I will not give to another. You, O man, humble yourself, and be ready with the words I speak to you.

"What is My dominion like, O man? It is like streams of living waters, it beholds the highest good, and rewards itself with abundance. It cannot overtake any man unless they surrender all.

It is like a strong tower that one builds for defense, to see the enemy from afar and rejoices when it sees no one.

"What can I liken My dominion to? It is like the way of a donkey lost in the wilderness that searches for a home but finding none goes back from whence it came." And I asked, "Lord, do you speak of Yourself in this manner?" "No, He said, I speak of the sons of men, for they are like baying donkeys always searching and seeking out personal pleasure and significance, but they do not know the glory that already resides within them. They are lost and without hope because they forgot who I was and who I am to them. Write these words carefully…

"Behold, I bring today before you a fresh word, one that you may not believe, but My words are true and just and dependable. They alone are mighty for the pulling down of strongholds. Everything that has raised itself up against Me will be torn down. I am the Lord – and I do all things. I do all things for My glory – and you are My glory as well as them, but they would not listen to Me. You have turned an attentive ear toward Me, so I will speak plainly with you, but in mysteries to them." "So I asked, what is the mystery you are revealing to me?"

"My dominion. My dominion has no end. It is greater than the number of stars you can count." And I said, "Lord, I am just a man who is standing in the presence of the One who created everything. I am humbled." And He said, "That's what I wanted. I am majesty and glory. I created all things for My glory. Wrap your mind around that for a moment." And as I considered this, I thought: the Lord created the heavens and the universe to reflect His glory. All things consist to reflect His glory. Everything is a reflection of His glory. Everything – including you and me. It is far greater than my feeble mind can fathom. Everything exists to reflect His glory. They were not made for His glory; they were made to show us the magnitude of His glory and splendor, and how marvelous He truly is. For as high are the heavens above me, so also is the glory of His majesty. Truly, I sit in humbleness when I ponder this truth.

"I created everything for My glory. It is marvelous splendor and majesty. Out of creation My glory is revealed. Out of everything My glory is revealed – and I am revealed in My glory. When you see a light shining, this is merely a reflection of My glory. When you hear a sound, this is merely a reflection of My glory. Everything is bouncing off Me – and carries with it – My glory. The things you see are because of Me; they exist having come from Me and nothing is that was – that wasn't formed out of My existence. It is, therefore I AM. It is wonderful and glorious, therefore I am wonderful and glorious. Look to the heaven and behold the stars… do they not behold My glory? But they behold the same glory as you! Different glories, but the same glory." Then I said, "How can I comprehend the enormity of your ways, O Lord? My head feels pain from the knowledge of this truth – and who you really are." The Lord said, "That is of no consequence and to be expected."

"I am higher than you could imagine – and you are really good at that. (And I said thank you). Can you imagine the times ahead? "No, Lord, I cannot. I thought I could, but now I stand in Your presence I am no longer sure about the things I thought I knew, including you."

So I got up and repositioned myself, and as I moved about, I asked the Lord, "Are you going to teach me about Your dominion?" And His voice said, "I just did."

This is the understanding that I received from the Lord. Everything is His, belongs to Him, and everything that was-is will reflect His glory. The creation does not exist to reflect His glory, but rather, the creation itself manifests His glory because He exists as the One who created it – and His glory is in it. Everything the Lord created is glorious and was created to reflect His glory. There is nothing that is anything unless it was created by Him, and for Him, and part of Him… in His glory. To see the Lord is like looking into the center of an exploding star or fireworks. From the instant is begins, it goes through millions of instantaneous changes that all reflect the light of His glory. Billions of rainbow colors that all reflect one thing: His Glory! Nothing that is – cannot exist without His glory attached to it. If the Lord removes His glory from anything, then it is damned to the fire as a worthless work. And then, the Lord began to speak again…

"I have baptized the universe with My Spirit and fire. I have come to restore all things, as well as burn away everything that no longer reflects My glory. My dominion will be an everlasting kingdom that reflects My glory, abides in My glory, flourishes abundantly in My glory, and this… for the sake of My glory. How can I tell you in words other than this? What I created good, I created for My glory. If I do not call it good, then this is because it no longer reflects My glory. I call those things 'evil' that do not reflect My glory. Cain was evil; he brought to me an offering that reflected his glory, not mine. Cain grew an abundantly beautiful and glorious harvest, but it reflected his glory, not mine. The people of Babel built an incredibly awesome and wonderful city, but it did not reflect My glory. Even though they tried to build a strong tower to reach into the heavens, they failed to capture My glory and My presence, so I confused them, that is, they were already misguided and confused about who they were, so I simply confounded their speech – and scattered them abroad. That is all I have to do with My enemies… I just scatter them and let them alone and they come to an end all by themselves. I do not have to do it; I allow them to do it unto themselves. I allow the riches of My glory to accomplish all that it was created to accomplish. Everything else simply falls by the wayside and perishes. Consider the parable of the sower. Is it not Me who is doing it? Is it not for the sake of My glory and My name; is it not for the sake of My glorious name that I accomplish all things? How is it that My children still do not know or understand that all things exist for My glory. I sent you to My dominion in order to have My dominion and to have a share in My dominion, but some would not partner with Me. They robbed Me of My glory and claimed it as their precious works according to the efforts of their hands and intellect. But, I ask you this: who gave you your hands and where did you find your intellect? Were not all things given to you from the beginning? Were not the glories of My creation placed all around you for your benefit? I expected an abundant return from the dominion that I leased to you, but when I came back, all I found were kingdoms upon kingdoms and dominions of ordinary men, but none of these things reflected My glory. Nothing that man creates can even reflect his glory. Everything that man creates will reflect My glory because all things exist on account of My glory. I cannot tell you how disappointed I am that no one regards Me in the manner to which I am entitled. I am the Lord, all in all, and yet My creation (man) no longer acknowledges Me. Look and see, they say, the wonderful things we have made and done, but in all this marvelous awesome wondrous moment, the fire will burn it away like chaff because of – and for one reason only: it did not reflect My glory!"

"Consider, O man, that I created Adam – and from Adam, I constructed Eve. My glory resided within man (them) and I created within them the ability to create glory within themselves. This is My glory that I shared with man, but man has diminished My glory to a mere choice – and this abomination will receive My harshest reckoning. My glory I have given them – and they choose to kill My glory abiding within them. Never did I imagine such an abomination as this, not since Abimelech[55]. I will repay all according to their deeds" (and my heart melted within me.)

"I am sending My fire, My refining fire, and My winnowing fork is in My hand. I am thoroughly cleaning My threshing floor to remove the chaff from My saints, and they will worship Me in spirit and in truth. I will burn away all the heaviness that burdens them – the heaviness that does not reflect My glory. Only My glory will remain. My Spirit, My Glory, again and again, and

---

[55] This is the sound I heard, but the understanding I received was of the days when Judah/Israel sacrificed their children in the fire to the false god Molech (Jer. 32:34, 35).

nothing else – by My Spirit and for My Glory. See, I have told you beforehand.

"My glory. I am coming back for My dominion. It is Mine, not yours, it is Mine. I am coming back for My glory. If My glory does not reside in a man, then they are no longer Mine. I do not come to marvel at the glorious works of men; I am coming to admire My glorious work *within* man. For I created you and crowned you with glory and honor; indeed, I even placed My glory within you, as a small seed, hoping for it to bear much fruit. But the fruit that some servants grew was for their glory, not Mine. It reflected their glory, not Mine; this chaff will be burned away and only My glory will remain. See, I have told you beforehand.

"The tribulation that you fear is the burning away of man-made glory. This chaff was tolerated for a time in season, but no longer. My time and My coming are now upon the earth. I will shake as a winnower sifts wheat, and only wheat will remain. Some will be shaken, others crushed, but woe to whom the stone crushes altogether, when both wheat and chaff are to be thrown out, thrown away – into the unquenchable fire. I am coming soon. I am not coming back for your works; I am coming back for My works that I asked you to do. Your works are nothing; they are covered in the chaff of your glory. I am coming back for My glory. I am the Lord who does it. If I have not done it, then it is not Mine and it will be washed away in the fire.

"You are My workmanship, that I created in Me for good works. The works done in the flesh for the glory of the flesh will be burned in the fire. I am not coming back to see how well you did; I am coming back to see how well you did with My things and to see if you will give Me the glory for it. If My glory is attached to you, then I want you back again. For this reason I sent you – and for this reason I went away; I wanted to see what you would do with My things when I left you alone. Would you remember Me? Would you acknowledge Me? Would you consider My handiwork and seek My face? Would you regard Me as Lord over My dominion and reverence Me – or would you forget Me, disregard Me, and disrespect Me *and* My creation – *and* your fellow brethren. Do you indeed love yourself more than My things which I created for My glory? How dare you think of My glory with such irreverent callous disregard? I, the Lord, am holy and righteous altogether. There is no one like Me. No one else can compare to My glory, but some of your brethren have tried. They glory in themselves, but they will glory only in their end.

"Do not think it otherwise. I am coming for the righteous and the wicked. The righteous reflect My glory, but the wicked claim My glory for themselves and wear it like a garment, like a royal robe. They strut around like peacocks in My royal robe and bay like donkeys in heat, ever chasing their own pleasures to satisfy their desires. But I am the only One who can satisfy the desires of your heart. I, only I, can provide, and there is no other besides Me. Your deepest longing is for the presence of My glory. I created you in My glory and you crave this glory; this is what your soul craves: My Glory. Everything else is a created thing that has no glory in itself. Now do you understand what the root is? The root is in itself; it becomes joined to the seed and life begins anew. See, I have placed glory all around, it is everywhere, and it is in all things, and all things were created to sustain My glory. For what is life itself… is it not My glory revealed in creation? I made it simple, but you made it complicated. The complexity of creation is revealed in simplicity; life and glory – and they are the same in My dominion. I am the Life and I am the Glory. I AM – and I am coming soon. If it were not so, then I would not have revealed My face to you today. Thus says the Lord."

Lord, I have been humbled by the glory of Your presence within Me. I have a pearl of great price, a hidden treasure, a living root – Your glory abiding within me. Dear Lord, I ask for only more grace *upon me* that I may know more about Your glory *within me*. I am Your vessel. I desire that You pour into me only those things that bring glory to your Name. Not my will, but Your Glory accomplished in me and through me. Amen

----

And then, the Lord began to reveal more understanding to me. When I began this journey, to come back into His presence about two years ago, it began with the understanding, "It's all for His glory." Little did I know then that this word would come full circle to know mysteries and revelations about His dominion and His kingdom.

And now, He chooses to reveal even greater things.

>It's all about Jesus – and God gets the glory!

"The era of greater works is about to begin. Glory revealed in men and through men, though not a glory unto themselves, by My glory, which I placed within them, and even greater glory will I pour through them. Grace upon grace was for a former time, but now even a greater grace is being released so that My glory may be manifested in yielded submission, though not as the world understands glory, but all things according to My glory. Not by might, nor by power, nor in the efforts of anything designed by man, but by My Spirit. My Spirit and My glory. And I will overshadow thee, and great grace will be upon thee."

And I amused myself in the thought, "Will I glow in the dark?" And the Lord said, "If that is what you want."

Lord, you already heard my prayer several weeks ago. Though, Your will only, not mine. Let it be done as You commission it. Amen

The small still voice of the Spirit said… "Continue in the study… "Let them have dominion."

----------------------[END [56]] ---------------------

My Glory Will I Give

> "The earth is the Lord's, and all its fullness, the world and those who dwell therein" (Psa. 24:1; 1 Cor. 10:26).

> "And one cried to another and said: "Holy, holy, holy is the Lord of hosts; the whole earth is full of His glory!" (Isa. 6:3).

> "My glory I will not give to another" (Isa. 42:8).

Glory is the fullness of all that God is – and glory is all that God is. We do not become more of what he has… we become more of who He is.

The primary thrust of the Lord's dominion is to manifest His glory. The Lord does not manifest His glory for the sake of any other, nor will He give His glory to any "other." The Lord wants to partner with us to have a share in His glory, which He accomplishes through communion with Him.

The word communion is "*koinonia*' (2842) "a having in common, partnership, fellowship" is very similar in meaning to '*koinoneo*' (2841), "communicate, partaker; to have a share in, to go shares with."[57] We are servants of the Lord Most High, Jesus Christ, and He created us to have a share in His inheritance. He gives us nothing on our own accord, but in all things, is willing to "partner" with us in order that we may have a share in it as partakers of the divine nature. We were already created in His likeness, but the

---

[56] This ends the initial journaling session while in the Lord's presence. After a brief intermission to eat lunch, the Spirit of the Lord continued to teach me… with the hand of a ready writer for several hours and another four pages.
[57] Strong's Concordance.

Lord is testing us to see if we desire Him more than ourselves… or any "other."

"Let them have dominion" may also be translated as, "Give them a grant to have dominion" or perhaps "Let a lease be agreed upon and covenanted between Us and man (them) in order to have a share in Our dominion." The Lord never gave us the dominion to do whatever we wanted; He let us have use of it to see what we would do with it. "The earth is the Lord's and the fullness thereof" which includes "the increase of abundance" thereof. Everything exists for the Lord's glory and the Lord alone is worthy to receive all glory and honor and praise and dominion – and increase. Jesus is Lord of the harvest! And Lord of all provision. All of it!!! It all belongs to King Jesus!!!

When we regard the dominion as *His* dominion, then any material increase that is produced by His creation (including man) belongs to Him. We are merely servants, stewards and sojourners who were sent from heaven to be partners and partakers in His creation, His dominion and His redemption. We are stewards and caretakers of His dominion, to earnestly manage the resources of His dominion for one purpose: to generate an increase in abundance for His glory. The Lord created life for the purpose of sustaining and creating more life, which is done through the multiplication of life according to the Spirit of life in Christ Jesus. We are not our own; our life is not our own; our life and our breath are a gift from the Lord that we must carefully tend and manage until He returns.

The Lord also gave us His "utterance of words" in order to keep His commands, as well as the commands of the Father. The word "keep" is '*tereo*' (5083) meaning, "to watch, to guard from loss or protect from injury by properly keeping the eye upon it").[58] These are the commands of the Lord: "have dominion and keep it according to the manner in which I exist."

When an owner hires a manager, he looks for someone who will govern and operate his affairs in the similitude of his manners and

---

[58] Strong's Concordance.

ways. If a manager begins to mistreat other servants, or compromises the integrity of the operation, or misuses capital resources, or diminishes the performance or quality of the product, or creates consecutive loss upon loss, or denigrates the owner, will not the owner dismiss the manager for conduct not befitting the mission parameters of the owner's intentions? And such is the case with all men, who were created in His likeness to manage His dominion. There is no difference between the least ones and those who are seemingly important; God does not show partiality. To each one is given a measure of faith and, to each one, all will be held accountable to the working of His will that was entrusted to them. There is no least or greatest in the kingdom… there is only faithful and wicked. If we are faithfully doing what the Lord wants us to do, then we are considered righteous, not based upon our own righteousness, but based upon the righteousness imparted to us according to His righteousness – whereby we give Him all the glory in it! We are not righteous – we are the righteousness of Christ –being made righteous *only* by being faithful according to His will which He purposed and planned for us. Not my will, but Thy will be done.

We are partners under agreement who were sent by the Lord to have a share in His dominion. We must thoroughly comprehend and understand that it is His creation, all of it, that He sent us to produce abundantly therein, and that we are *also* His creation – who have been commissioned to be fruitful and multiply. Creation exists to produce life – and we are living souls that were sent to continue in – and with – the creation story. Only then does it becomes very clear that the Lord is looking for fruitful vines and branches and grains and herbs of every sort for one reason: increased abundance for His glory! The Lord is looking for a fruitful harvest. We do not need to know why – but we must accept things as they are. The clay does not ask the Potter, "Why have you made me this way?" How irreverently silly! Doesn't that clay know the Potter can recast and remold the clay however and whenever He wants? And this comes by way of breaking it into little pieces – and sending back into the furnace!

Consider this: the Lord's dominion reflects His glory. When the Lord let us have His dominion, it was never ours to keep; He leased it out to us to see if we would faithfully execute His command: have dominion – and give Him the glory.

Consider now the lesson of Cain and Abel. Both were operating to fulfill the Lord's command to have dominion, and in the passing of time, both men gave an offering to the Lord, but only one man's offering was accepted, and it was credited to him as righteousness (1 John 3:12). Cain's offering was unacceptable to the Lord (not respected, nor regarded as done well[59]), and various reasons have been erringly suggested for this (i.e. the sacrifice did not include blood, it wasn't the best, or it was not the firstfruit). God did not regard Cain's gift as acceptable because, quite plainly, *Cain did not regard the Lord*, nor did he acknowledge the Lord as the source of everything that was given to Cain. Abel produced an increase and then gave his offering as a showing forth of his testimony to God with God's glory attached to the offering.

"Abel thoroughly understood and comprehended that it was the Lord's doing that allowed him to create abundance to begin with; he also recognized that it was the Lord's creation, and therefore it was the Lord's increase, not his. He was the created vessel that the Lord used to produce this increase – and thus – he gave God glory in all that he produced whereby… he returned to Him "a portion" with glory attached to it.[60] Cain, on the other hand, gave an

---

[59] *Yatab* (3190) meaning, to be well (causat.) make well, literally (sound, beautiful) or figuratively (happy, successful, right): - be accepted, use alright, benefit, find favor, do (be, make) good (-ness), please (+well). It does not mean amend or improve your ways but to make one's course line up with that which is pleasing to God and that which is well-pleasing in His sight" (as in, being delighted by a goodly work or responsibility done, i.e. giving God glory in it). Strong's Concordance; (comments in parenthesis by author).

[60] This portion is not the precursor to the tithe; this portion is the precursor to righteousness through faith. The tithe was just a legal instrument that was implemented by God to teach Israel to remember the Lord and acknowledge the Lord as the Creator, Provider, and the Source of all increase – and the tithe was merely the minimum return that acknowledges the Lord God is worthy to receive ALL increase! Not just a 10% return, but all of it – 100% belongs to the Lord! The tithe, in this respect, is not a form of worship… but ***an act of***

offering that gave himself the credit and the glory for the increase – and God called it wicked. ***Anything that robs God of His glory is wicked."***

The knowledge of good that comes from eating the fruit from upon the tree in the midst of the Garden is simply this – give God all the glory in whatever you do and produce. The knowledge of evil is simply this: robbing God of His glory by taking credit for what God did in you and through you.

Consider now the lesson of Noah and the people of that day. The Lord regarded their works as wicked and evil, though the scriptures do not indicate why. By now, the terms used by the Lord for evil and wicked are synonymous for "doing your own thing, taking all the credit for it, and robbing God of the glory He deserves." Noah was righteous in his generation because he listened to hear the voice of the Lord, he did what the Lord commanded him to do – and then he gave the Lord all the glory for the working of His will through him. Noah was a yielded servant… even at the expense of all his neighbors and friends. God loves all creation, but nowhere else on the planet does creation exalt itself to take credit for its own glory – except man. Nowhere, indeed, except in sinful, arrogant, pride-filled, smug, self-righteous, selfish man!

Consider now the lesson of Nimrod's kingdom. The city was named Babel by Nimrod because it was Nimrod's kingdom, but the Lord wanted Nimrod to build the Lord's kingdom and His cities according to the manner that gives ALL the glory to God. When the men of Babel began to build a tower, to "let us make a name for ourselves," the Lord came down, took notice – and took offense! "Surely, nothing that they do they will be unable to accomplish." So, the Lord confounded their speech, not because they couldn't communicate without words, but because they were not willing to listen to the voice of the Lord to accomplish His

---

obedience to return glory to God that rightfully belongs to Him! If you want to regard tithe as a ***voluntary act of worship***, then return 100%!

purpose and His plan upon the earth. They wanted to glory in their works – so the Lord brought an end to it. Do you see the sinfulness of their speech, "Let *us* make a name for *us*" (Gen. 11:4)? When the Lord made us and gave us the command, "Let them have dominion," this command was given to *us* on account of the Divine *US*…. for His purpose, not ours.

And so it is with mankind today. We are exactly where the people of Babel were nearly 6,000 years ago. We speak with one language, we are building strong tall towers up to heaven, and we are creating our own kingdoms yet giving no regard and no respect to the Lord for His glory, His creation, His dominion, or His capabilities that He freely and generously has given to man. Mankind is taking credit for everything, "And surely there is nothing that they cannot accomplish." Man has created an orbiting city in space, as well as submarines that can survive months within environments without oxygen, no less. You do not have to be a student of theology to see by the signs of the times that the Lord is going to come down again – and He isn't a happy camper! We have been robbing God of His glory – and the Lord is going to bring an end to it.

We have truly evolved, but I say this to our shame. We have evolved from a spiritual being created in His image according to His likeness into one that originates itself in the lineage of apes; we re-created ourselves according to our own desirable attributes and then we justify our continued existence upon the planet by killing our unborn children. This is not reality – this is madness, utter wickedness and thoroughly evil in all manner of thought and application. We are evil, we are robbing God of His glory – and we will be judged accordingly.

Learn from Lot's wife, who having put her hand to the plow – was saved initially, but turned back to Sodom with the attentive desire to return to a former glory, and her glory was exchanged for a pillar of salt. And learn from Job's wife, who told her husband to "just curse God and die," and was never heard from again. Consider Ananias and Sapphira and what happened to them, or King Herod when he did not give God the glory (Acts 12:22).

Do not try to rob God's glory from Him! It never ends well.

And consider Satan, who was the angel of worship who received God's worship, until one day, he decided to keep God's glory for himself "to become like the Most High" (Isa. 14:13, 14). We all know what happened to him, and the same thing will happen to us when we try to rob God's glory. Is this not the real message of his temptation to Eve? "For God knows that in the day you eat of it your eyes will be opened and *you will be like God*, knowing good from evil" (Gen. 3:5).

The phrase "be like God" is literally "be as Elohim." God already told us we are like gods (elohims), lacking little of God (Elohim) and Jesus confirmed this message (Psa. 82:6; John 10:34), so God doesn't have a problem sharing His divine attributes and character with us (2 Pet. 1:3, 4). In fact, God wants us to be exactly like Him, and He sent Jesus so we could copy His pattern and imitate His example in every regard; otherwise, He would not have created us as His image that also appropriates His likeness and goodness attributes in all manner of holiness, righteousness and perfection – *but* – when we try to rob God of the glory that belongs to Him, then we have just committed wickedness and have eaten from the tree that gives man the knowledge of evil. A line has just been crossed – and we have entered into our own "in the day" death sentence.

Tree of Knowledge

Many preachers have preached about two kinds of fruit upon this tree as being good and evil, and that we should avoid this tree altogether, as if Adam and Eve let the jinni out of the bottle, but now, isn't it clear, that the fruit on this tree is neither good fruit nor evil fruit – it is God's glory! Indeed, it is the fruit of His glory! Mankind was seeded with the Lord's glory residing within us to produce more glory in the earth; however, how we use it determines if we are using His glory according to the knowledge of good – or – the knowledge of evil. The tree of knowledge (whose fruit is glory) is supposed to teach us to gain wisdom and understanding to use glory for good – not evil.

> "And the LORD God commanded the man, saying,
> "Of every tree of the garden you may freely eat;
> ^{17} but of the tree of the knowledge of good and evil you shall not eat, for in the day that you eat of it you shall surely die." (Gen. 2:16, 17).

We were sent into His garden as caretakers to tend… not takers to offend!

The Lord commanded us *not* to take and eat. This next point is very important: God had already seeded man with His glory i.e. the fullness of God – and crowned him with glory and honor. There was no earthly reason for Adam and Eve to take of the tree! They were created "***as gods***," to "be as elohims" on earth in the likeness of Elohim, lacking little of God in any manner, but Satan was tempting them to become "***like God***" (by taking God's glory according to Satan's example with evil intent). There is great wisdom found in comprehending this message… that results in '*dianoia*' understanding!

You are a manifest expression of God's glory within creation – and God's glory dwells within you richly. You are a glory-bearer! What you do with this glory on earth determines your eternal outcome. The message of Christ's gospel is to surrender your will and your desire for self-acclaimed glory whereby you will receive greater glory in the resurrection.

A greater glory is promised to us, but this glory can be forfeited by us on account of disobedience.

Two trees are in the midst of the Garden: the Tree of Life and the Tree of Knowledge with Glory-fruit. Jesus is the Life – and He came in the light of His Glory (Isa. 60:19; Acts 22:11). So, then, what do you suppose is on the Tree of Life? Perhaps it is "eternity bread" that Christ provides as His body, much like the manna that came to us from heaven, so that we may live in communion with Him... eternally! Selah.

In all you do, do it to the glory of God.

In anything you do, give all the glory to Jesus– and in this, God alone is magnified and glorified.

> "See, I have set before you today life and good, death and evil" (Deut. 30:15).

The Root Of Understanding

> "Most assuredly, I say to you, unless a grain of wheat falls into the ground and dies, it remains alone; but if it dies, it produces much grain" (John 12:24).

A seed that falls to the earth remains as just a seed... unless a root becomes attached to the seed... and then it becomes alive (born again) to produce more of what it was created to produce: more seed. Apart from the root of understanding, the seed is worthless; however, once men begin to walk in the knowledge of the truth, then a root of understanding comes to us through the tutoring of the Holy Spirit, Who He reveals all truth to help us understand and comprehend... for the root is not in (the seed) itself. The root is the work of the Holy Spirit within us – to produce understanding – and increase.

The tree of knowledge (of good and of evil) has glory fruit. Satan was tempting Eve to take more of God's glory without consulting Him or considering His preeminence or, more importantly... to think about acquiring the benefits without considering the consequences. She was being enticed to act impulsively and to act independently of God so as to take of God's glory without considering Him as being first in Preeminence in Glory – and in all creation.

The tree of knowledge with glory fruit is governed by the Lord of Glory: Jesus Christ. This is His tree and you cannot take of His things and use them for your own glory and personal benefit without asking Him and, equally in importance, returning unto Him all the glory you produce through this glory which He gave you.

God has sown the seed of glory in all of us to see what we will do with it. Either we will acknowledge Him *in* all of it and give Him the glory *through* all of it… or we will take what belongs to Him and use it in an irreverent manner… which is evil.

Jesus said, "My glory I will not give to another" was said only two times, both recorded by Isaiah. And yet, the Lord Himself placed a seed of His glory within us to produce additional glory through our surrendered lives that yields unto Jesus more glory – and honor – and majesty – and praise – and thanksgiving – and worship – and adoration – and exultation. And yet, all this knowledge in the truth of God's word is completely worthless… apart from understanding.

> "And the glory which You gave Me I have given them, that they may be one just as We are one" (John 17:22).

Jesus taught us about the kingdom of God and how it operates; however, whatever we do with this knowledge will either puff us up to glory in ourselves… or it will humble us to consider ourselves rightly and, thus, to remain in proper servant-Sovereign relationship with God. The knowledge of good and evil should spur us on to gain wisdom – and understanding – and comprehension – and perception – to possess '*oida*' understanding within '*dianoia*' minds that thoroughly comprehends the reality of Christ and His kingdom – on earth – as it is in heaven. The kingdom of heaven was established upon the earth as a forward operating position in Israel, but they rejected His plan to walk in disobedience; **YET NOW** the keys to understanding God's kingdom are freely given to ALL disciples of Jesus, as many as are called and as many as are far off (not just to the original twelve), to establish His kingdom and His dominion upon the earth.

This is the big picture.

Walk humbly with your God!

We are seed sown upon the earth. We were predestined to die to self, to fall to the ground in complete surrender, to worship the Lord of glory in His holiness, whereby we gain understanding to produce the fruit of righteousness, through obedience, and give all glory unto Jesus.

"My glory I will not give to another," and yet Jesus gave us His glory (John 17:22) so that we should produce more glory upon the earth in discipleship obedience to Jesus Christ. All glory belongs to Jesus... and again, I say... all glory and honor and majesty belongs to the Lord of Glory, Jesus Christ.

Sadly, we have gotten so used to taking His glory and using it for our own glory that we do not even have the basic knowledge of glory anymore whereby we are unable to discern good from evil; and worse even... those things that are evil and wicked we call good – and those things that are good we call evil. Anathema! We have become completely deceived and perverted by the enemy to believe the irreverent lies of the enemy to disregard the goodness of God which they market as superstitious, benign, malevolent, old fashioned, unenlightened, stupid, foolish, unthinking and not progressive enough. The people of God are ridiculed daily for their faith... not because of what we believe, but because:

- We lack the simple basic knowledge to defend what we believe
- We lack the understanding needed to declare the Lord's glory (so we glory in ourselves)
- And we lack power (which is the proof of Christ's message and truth in the gospel)

My people perish for lack of wisdom (and also lack of vision, knowledge, and understanding).

Jesus is the Vine and we are the branches. Apart from the Vine, we can do nothing because all power flows through the Vine; it flows to us from Jesus, through His Spirit, when we remain in relationship with Him (John 15:1-5). Professing grace, yet lacking power, we are woefully unprepared as disciples to courageously press forward from basic training into advanced training in righteousness... and spiritual warfare.

This world under the sway of Satan and spirit of antichrist will continue to tear us to shreds as we attempt to stand upon "our own" righteousness as we declare our faithfulness in the word of God, through faith, without truly understanding what we believe... and why. Where is the glory in that, I ask you? How are we exalting Jesus without understanding why we were sent here? What a great show-forth we have made of this man-made Sunday charade! The sad thing is this... the enemy sees through our duplicity and our hypocrisy and this world mocks us because we lack the One Thing we need... Who teaches us in the knowledge of all things: the Holy Spirit!!! Apart from the Spirit, we know nothing and comprehend even less, and yet... through the Spirit "You know all things" (1 John 2:20), and you are able to accomplish "all things through Christ who strengthens you" (Phil. 4:13) because the power of God enables you to do the will of God and become who you were created to be: mighty warriors and kings and priests, and judges, rulers, magistrates, and potentates to have dominion over this world. Without the knowledge of glory, the Lord will not give us His power because we will use His glory *with* power for evil rather than good. We must give Jesus all the glory that is produced through our sacrificial lives to serve the Lord Jesus. If we attempt to do anything without acknowledging His glory in it, then I say this emphatically... STOP DOING IT!!! THERE IS NO GLORY IN IT!!!

How dare we disregard the Lord and His glory which was freely given to everyone! The Holy Spirit will hold us in contempt and the Lord Himself will manifest His indignation and fury toward us.

We need understanding... and we need it fast! To get a full grasp of glory, read "Understand" to comprehend what it is, why we were given glory and what we are to accomplish – for the praise of His glory.

The fruit on the tree is neither good nor evil; it is glory. How we use it determines whether we are using it for good – or for evil! Apart from knowledge, without understanding, and without the guidance and tutoring of the Holy Spirit, God's glory will be used by men for evil, not because we have a sinful nature, but rather – because we prefer the glory we get through sin *more than* the glory we receive through righteousness. Yet... we were not always this way. We were sent to earth as men of goodwill, created upright and very good, to live in rightness, having been crowned with glory and honor... to do the Lord's will. Yes, we were crowned with glory and sown as seed upon the earth to produce more glory – and more-so now in these last days – to produce even greater glory. When the greater glory happens... this world will not be able to comprehend what is happening... and neither will the institutional church. Jesus was rejected once before... and it appears it will happen again unless the church undergoes a major course correction with reformation realignment to seek Jesus only, follow Him, become His disciple and be led by the Spirit who guides us into all truth!

Quickly now... seek wisdom, gain understanding, knock vigorously upon the door of comprehension and give all glory to Jesus... before the last trumpet blows.

Glory Revealed In Man

Even though Jesus said, "My glory I will not give to another" (Isa. 42:8), mankind was given a measure of His glory, yet we, on account of sin, have all partaken of the tree of glory to possess greater glory, but this was done by "taking" without being granted permission. Herein lies the difference: receiving that which is freely given as a gift of grace to glorify God… is good – yet that which is taken with wicked intent to promote the impulsive, sinful, selfish works of the flesh… is sin.

> "Now we have received, not the spirit of the world, but the Spirit who is from God, *that we might know the things that have been freely given to us by God*" (1 Cor. 2:12; which is a working of the Spirit of God).

> "Heal the sick, cleanse the lepers, raise the dead, cast out demons. Freely you have received, freely give" (Matt. 10:8; which was done when Jesus sent out the disciples under His authority with His power).

> "He who did not spare His own Son, but delivered Him up for us all, how *shall He not with Him [Christ] also freely give us all things?*" (Rom. 8:32).

> "And He said to me, "It is done! I am the Alpha and the Omega, the Beginning and the End. I will give of the fountain of the water of life freely to him who thirsts" (Rev. 21:6).

Our heavenly Father shall "with Christ" also freely give us all things.

> "If you then, being evil, know how to give good gifts to your children, how much more will your Father who is in heaven give good things to those who ask Him!" (Matt. 7:11)

> "Every good gift and every perfect gift is from above, and comes down from the Father of lights, with whom there is no variation or shadow of turning" (James 1:17).

Do you now see your heavenly Father and the Lord Jesus in a new way, as generous givers of their things according to grace, who desire to freely give us all things when we ask – but – the giving is not done so that we can better ourselves or build our kingdom; Jesus will not share His dominion with "any other" whose intent is to rob Him of His glory to build their own kingdom and dominion. Anathema!

> "To Him be ***the glory and the dominion*** forever
> and ever. Amen" (1 Pet. 5:11).

Our heavenly Father has only good gifts and perfect gifts to offer to those who ask with a pure heart and a good conscience – whose only desire is to give glory to God. Are your prayers said in secret to glorify you – or to glorify God in accordance with His will (1 John 5:14). Selah. Meditate on this.

The way leading to the Tree of Life is heavily guarded and protected, and only Jesus – who knows the way – will lead us to this tree, but the way to the tree of glory wherein the knowledge of good and evil abide is freely open to all. The glory is already in you, but are you willingly surrendered so as to yield all your glory unto Jesus who will receive this glory as righteousness which He will return to us when Christ returns again in His glory? Are you willing to surrender everything you've got in order to receive the greater glory that shall be revealed in us – and through us? (Rom. 8:18)

> "And the glory which You gave Me I have given them, that they may be one just as We are one" (John 17:22).

> "as His divine power has given to us all things that pertain to life and godliness, through the knowledge of Him who called us by glory and virtue" (2 Pet. 1:3).

If you are not producing glory in oneness with Jesus, then it is chaff. If you desire to do anything and you cannot give God the glory in it for lack of virtue, then do not do it – this is sin. There is no glory in it. If you do anything but you decide to take the glory for yourself, then this is what the Lord calls wicked and evil – do not do it. If you do an extremely good and noble thing, and you are able to cast out demons and heal the sick and even raise the dead, and you even give away all your riches to the poor and needy, but you rob God of His glory, then these works are evil. God will simply say to you, "I never knew you." If you have been doing this, then…

Turn, repent, seek Jesus, ask forgiveness and give Jesus all the glory.

In doing so, you will be saved – and you will be known by God – and you will be rewarded according to your deeds.

Our deeds and our workmanship are to be done – with His power, by His Spirit, under His authority, for the praise of His glory. This is His dominion. Everything else is chaff.

The Pearl of Great Price is the Lord's glory that He placed within us – it is like a treasure hidden in our field of faith (the heart; Matt. 13:44, 45). Once we discover it, we must do all we can to possess it, honor and protect it, *'tereo'* guard it carefully, and reverence God – and give God glory in it and through it. It is not about us – it is about His glory residing within us.

Here is another example: the seed in us is the Lord's glory – and His alone! God's glory remains attached to the seed, and when a root with understanding attaches itself to the seed to bear much fruit… God is glorified in the increase! Otherwise, the seed without a root with understanding fails to produce glory for the Lord; it becomes a worthless work that will be cut down and thrown into the fire; it is like salt that has lost its saltiness; it is like a lamp that has lost its ability (oil) to give light. If the Lord's glory in us has lost its brilliance because we prefer darkness, or we have usurped our authority as men to claim this glory for ourselves to build our kingdom so as to reflect this glory we stole from the Lord, then I, for one, do not want to be standing next to that person the next time a storm passes overhead. See, I have warned you beforehand.

> "It [the soul] is sown in dishonor, it is raised in glory. It is sown in weakness, it is raised in power" (1 Cor. 15:43).

Glory with power is how we were predestined to live on earth. We were created within creation to bear the fruit of His glory. All glory belongs to God!!! We were seeded with His glory and we exist for His glory to be fruitful and bear much glory on account of His great name.

> "Do not boast against the branches. But if you do boast, remember that you do not support the root, but the root supports you" (Rom. 11:18).

We were all created for His glory as stewards, caretakers and partners of His dominion.

> "You have made him [man] to have dominion over the works of Your hands; You have put all things under his feet" (Psa. 82:6).

Give God all the glory, and through Christ Jesus, you will be glorified in the last day.

> "How great are His signs, and how mighty His wonders! His kingdom is an everlasting kingdom, *and His dominion is from generation to generation*" (Dan. 4:3; i.e. the many generations of man).

The glory of the Lord remains forever, but if the glory does not abide within us or in anything anymore, then the Lord will disregard it altogether. See, I have told you beforehand.

It's all about Jesus – and God gets the glory!

Consider who King Nebuchadnezzar was and how the Lord humbled him greatly when he took the Lord's glory for himself. May we remember this lesson – and come to the understanding that results in only one conclusion: we live in the Lord's dominion – for the praise of His glory!

> "And at the end of the time I, Nebuchadnezzar, lifted my eyes to heaven, and ***my understanding returned to me***; and I blessed the Most High and praised and honored Him who lives forever:
>
> ***For His dominion is an everlasting dominion***,
> And His kingdom is from *generation to generation*.
> ³⁵ All the inhabitants of the earth are reputed as nothing;
> *He does according to His will* in the army of heaven
> *And* among the inhabitants of the earth.
> No one can restrain His hand
> Or say to Him, "What have You done?" (Dan. 4:34, 35).

It's all about Jesus – and God gets the glory! All of it!!!

Amen.

15. Dominion of Goodness

The Father is good. The Father represents the highest good in His kingdom and His goodness is exalted above any and every other good. His goodness is supremely glorious and the glory of His goodness fills the heavens, the earth and the cosmos. There is simply not enough room within the created physical reality to express His goodness that dwells among us, nor words to express it. We cannot imagine how wonderful, awesome, majestic and glorious this goodness truly is, so God made a way, in the person of Jesus Christ, whereby Jesus could express – within Himself – and through His manifest works – the wondrous nature, loving character and Divine attributes of our Heavenly Father. Words will never be enough, so the Father started with one word being greater than all other words, as the name above all other names: Jesus.

There is no other good, nor any other goodness, whereby we may be saved: Jesus only! Any attempt to cling to anything other than the grace of Christ alone… is utter foolishness. The fullness of the Godhead abides tangibly, mightily and magnificently "in Christ" (Col. 2:9). There is no other name whereby goodness is supremely manifest, nor is there any other name whereby goodness can be conceived and understood. Jesus only!

Jesus responded, "Why do you call Me good? No one is good but One, that is, God" … that is, unless you are calling Me good – and you are also willing to call Me God (Luke 18:19).

God places His goodness and His glory on everything *and in* everything He makes! And the fullness of His glory was given only to the Holy One: Jesus Christ. Listen to Him, understand Him – and do what He tells you. This is the Lord's Dominion, so do whatever He tells you to do. If you do not yet have ears to hear, then: read the Bible, start listening to hear the Voice of Truth and start living according to what you have read and heard.

It was my sole intention to talk about the goodness of the Father, since I dedicated this chapter to Him and the glory of His greatness (Mark 10:18), His glory (John 11:4, 40), His power (Matt. 22:29), His majesty (Luke 9:43), and His gospel of grace revealed in the One (Acts 20:24), but every time I tried to talk about the Father, all He wanted to do is talk about His Son. The Father is so lovingly entwined with His beloved Son that He has no problem in giving all His glory and universe attention to His Son. That is exactly what proud fathers do when they love their sons that much; they shift the entire focus of their expectant praise and exuberant adoration toward their son because of the enormity of pride for them. And in this case… the glory in Jesus.

The Father gave Jesus His glory, as the only begotten Son (John 17:20-26). The Son was glorified in the Father and the Father is glorified in (and through) the Son. And this glory, that the Father gave the Son, the Son then gave to those who are willing to be called sons of God, by grace through faith, according to the testimony and gospel of Jesus Christ, the Holy One of God.

Jesus gave us His glory. Try to wrap your head around that thought for just a second… or a millennia!

Jesus created the heavens and the earth, as well as all created things, both visible and invisible. Jesus created you and me and gave us hands with fingers, and a mind with intellect, and He breathed into us the breath of life (our spirit) and then He sent the Holy Spirit to come alongside us, to guide us in the truth and to help us remember who we are. The Spirit also helps us to know this great love that has been poured out for us and revealed to us that we may thoroughly understand and comprehend this great and precious gift within us: the pearl of great price within us – which is God's glory – revealed "in" man! And yet, a greater glory is promised, through faith, to obedient disciples of Jesus. Christ in you – is the promise – and our hope of glory. Not just a little glory and grace, but we have received from Him glory and grace without measure so that we may attain our high calling in Christ Jesus, as His emissaries and ambassadors upon the earth to establish His dominion. Friends, I don't really know how we can wrap our mind around this concept, but if we could, our ability to change the world (not just fix it but change it) would be nothing less than supernatural.

Jesus sent us as His representatives, in His image, according to His likeness, to finish a job that was given to us (ordained) from the beginning. This plan has never changed, nor has it been completed. This is the will of Jesus, that we have dominion, in His name, to overcome the enemies of His kingdom with truth – and to overtake the darkness with His light.

We have no earthly idea just how incredibly awesome this mission is. Consider this: if you were sent as one person behind enemy lines to rescue a thousand, or if you were told to plant a garden that created a thousand meals a day, or if you were told to build a house that turned into an entire city for the homeless… would you do it? Now, honestly, would you do it? But for the glory to be revealed in us, that is exactly what we have been called to do. Some of us will succeed – and some of us may die in the process, but whoever remains faithful, regardless of how much we accomplish, will receive an inheritance of His glory in great abundance according to deeds of righteousness that gives glory to Jesus. It is not our glory to keep; it is His glory that was poured into us and through us, whereby a future glory will be given to us – and this shall be done at the wedding feast while seated at the table of conquest… in the presence of our enemies.

How can we grasp such a concept? Though it may seem difficult, it is not entirely impossible to comprehend, were it not for the anointing of the Spirit to enlighten our minds with understanding *Who birthed us into this spiritual paradigm to begin with.*

To us has been promised a kingdom without borders, a liberty without restrictions, and an inheritance that can never be taken away. If this sounds like pure science fiction, I can assure you that these concepts are all found within Holy Script. It may not be the gospel you've heard, but it is certainly a gospel you can read about for yourself. Trust me – it's all in the Bible. Read it for yourself, and let the Holy Spirit guide you into this truth. There is more to life than just getting up every day, going to school for 12 years, then working for 40 years, and then retiring in Florida or someplace sunny wearing Bermuda shorts living off retirement checks. There is far more going on than we have been taught, and you know this is true, because you know deep down – there is more – and you were created to be more. There is an "unlimited more" out there that you may be unaware of, but you sense it and it is available to those who ask, seek and knock upon the Door of the Divine who want to become who you were created to be: a manifest expression of Christ Jesus upon the earth. More upon more! Christian – what are you waiting for? Grace upon grace upon us so that we *grow* (*anabaino*-ascend) into our high calling in Christ: glory upon glory within us and through us. There is so much more to the heavenly dimension that we *must* awaken from our slumber, but sadly, we have been taught to settle for left-over circus peanuts that elephants dropped as the Sunday morning man-show passed through town.

God is so good. In His incredible goodness, the Father wants to share this goodness with His creation, so Jesus created man "upright" and "very good" according to His likeness, and crowned him with glory and honor, and made him a little lower than the angels, and keeps him as the apple of His eye. And all this is yours – if you will bow down, worship Jesus and serve Him!

Absolutely every last bit of what I have written here can be found in the scriptures and is entirely consistent with the Holy Scriptures. So why, then, do we continue to doubt? Look up every scripture to see this truth for yourself… and believe!

We have an open invitation by the most wonderful, loving, kind and generous Father in the universe. He wants to shower us with gifts, not like the kind of gifts an earthly father gives, but these good gifts and perfect gifts are amazingly wondrous gifts of glory and conquest. In order to experience all the wonderful things God has prepared for us, He sent His Son to show us how to live in this manner… and copy His example. Jesus did not come surrounded by angels to operate in His glory; He came in sublime simplicity, as an ordinary Man doing extraordinary things – in the fullness of the Holy Spirit! The signs and miracles and healings that Jesus performed were done with the empowerment gifts of the Spirit as an ordinary Man. Jesus operated in all the gifts – and so can you! Everything that Jesus did – you can also do.[61] There is no mystery and there is nothing miraculous or superstitious about it. Jesus did it – and you can do it also. "As He is, so are we in this world" (1 John 4:7). But there are two stipulations:

- When Jesus did it, He gave all glory to God. Likewise, when we continue in His mission to work His works, it is Jesus doing it in us and through us, and therefore, we must give all glory to God
- And… we must be willing to do greater works than Jesus did (John 14:12).

There is nothing that is separating us from this great adventure in Christ Jesus – except doubt. We have all been deceived, manipulated, lied to and told over and over again that we are worthless and this supernatural hogwash is simply impossible, but then… explain to me how Peter walked on water? Since Peter did it, so can you! How do you explain miraculous healings and supernatural events happening all around you? Do you think this is just some kind of fluke happenstance that is occurring without rhyme or reason? Do you really think the universe is so well ordered so as to allow all these things to be happening at the same time? Do you really think evolution has any explanation in this regard – that would ordinarily be considered upward academics, but now, has no earthly idea why these spiritual events are happening? Do you seriously want to know why this is happening – *or do you only want to know what you want to believe*?

---

[61] Read "Image" to understand Jesus as our heavenly example who taught us to do the same things He did.

Jesus came to teach us so we may understand – and believe; so I invite you to read "Understand"[62] and begin to live according to your high calling in Christ Jesus on earth.

There are answers coming that we will not even know the questions to; it will happen – and we will wonder why, but the answer is this: Jesus is coming back! How amazing is this going to be! But before He comes back, a season of greater grace and glory will be released into the earth.

We were sent as His servants on a mission to have dominion over the earth. We were not sent to fix the earth – nor were we were sent to bring order out of chaos. **We were sent to bring rightness and order to the chaos and confusion** – and usher in a regime change to change this world from darkness to light. This is our legacy in Christ. This is our legacy with the Holy Spirit in us, enabling us and empowering us to do exceedingly more than we can think or imagine (and God gave us a fantastic mind with incredible imagination).

Do you want to know why we can create science fiction movies that are so fantastic and incredible? Because there is an element of heavenly truth is them. Do you want to know why cults and other quasi-spiritual religions can see visions and experience paranormal behavior? Because the reality of this truth has been copied from out of a heavenly existence which has been hijacked by people with depraved, ungodly and occult minds! Do we have any idea why the cults do what they do? Because they are willing to copy and imitate what they see and hear; yet doing so in ignorance of Christ… having been blinded by the spirit of antichrist. Christian – this is the inheritance that was promised to the saints who follow Jesus Christ – but we would rather sit in doubt and disobedience as we cling to the TV remote to watch re-runs and sitcoms.

Wake up church!!!

---

[62] "Understand" is book #4 in the Image Bearer series by the author.

Train disciples in the truth!!! God *and* creation are waiting for the sons of God to be revealed!

If we cannot discern the times, then please just get out of the way, but stop telling your children and your children's children, as far off as they may be, that this spiritual reality that Jesus taught and demonstrated is fake, that is was for a former time in history only during the apostolic age to establish the church. Hello, read Acts 2:39; as many as the Lord Jesus calls, to them are afforded the promises of the Holy Spirit's anointing, and power, and manifested guarantee of sonship in obedience to the Son of God, Jesus Christ.

The time for play church is over, the time of pretend church is over, and the time for wimpy powerless church is over. A great awakening has already begun, and it is the Lord's good pleasure to pour enormous grace upon us and Christ's glory into us so that we can complete the dominion mission He gave us. Declare His Name! Decree His kingdom is at hand … and decree His dominion is near!

It's time to set captives free!!!

Believe – and trust Jesus. This is the gospel truth. What have you got to lose? So, let me put this another way… what are you willing to forfeit by default? Do you think you will be rewarded for hiding your denarius in the ground? Do you think Jesus is coming back after His horrific crucifixion and torturous death to retrieve His denarius with dirt on it? Come on. Get real. ***Is there any glory in this***? Is there any way you can scripturally justify passive mediocrity in the face of Him who died on the cross for your sins, to redeem you and purchase you back from the enemy, to reward you with heavenly bliss just because you flicked your wrist, said the sinners prayer, and then sat back down to count how many hairs are on the persons head sitting in the pew in front of you?

Lord Jesus, please forgive us, we know not what we do. Father, forgive us, we have forsaken the glory of your Son that He gave to us – and we hid it under a bushel basket. Forgive us, Holy Spirit, for blaspheming you by calling those things evil which are good, having been administered by You as those things, having come from the Lord Jesus, as every good and every perfect gift, which were to be used to establish the kingdom of heaven upon the earth – "through the church" (Eph. 3:10).

Wake up church!!!

We have been unfaithful servants who do not deserve to be called according to His Name. Help us, Jesus, I pray, to see You as You really are, in all Your glorious splendor and majesty, and to know deep in our heart that You are coming again, in the glory of the Father – and in Your glory with Your angels, to take it all back and to burn away everything that does not reflect Your glory.

The Raptured Church

Consider this: is there any glory in the current church's model for the rapture?

If the church really believes that saints will be raptured and taken into the third heaven, then the church should make decisions immediately for all church assets and provisions go somewhere or to someone that is being left behind – so that these storehouses may continue to benefit the unsaved and lost, and thus, guard from theft rather than reverting to the government or any other institution. None of it was ever ours to begin with, so why do you want to withhold good while there is still a blessing that remains (hidden) in our provision?

We cannot continue standing in between two ways. If Jesus is your Lord, then do what He would do. Blessed are the beatitude believers – who give God all the glory.

> "For I consider that the sufferings of this present time are not worthy to be compared with the glory which shall be revealed in us" (Rom. 8:18), "but rejoice to the extent that you partake of Christ's

sufferings, that when His glory is revealed, you may also be glad with exceeding joy" (1 Pet. 4:13).

"The glory of the Lord shall be revealed, *and all flesh shall see it together*; for the mouth of the Lord has spoken." (Isa. 40:5).

Are we willing to accept such a gracious gift of glory, which is freely given, without also partaking of Christ's sufferings? Do you, as one of His glory bearers, hold the cup of the Lord's suffering in contempt because "this is not part of your tradition?"

Stop standing on the wayside. Hear the Voice of Truth – and walk is the Way of Christ.

The Lord's kingdom, His glory and His dominion are already here in the earth, but is anyone willing to suffer on account of Christ for the sake of His glorious name? Two types of servants will be sent into the fields to help with the last day harvest… so… which one are you?

"For our light affliction, which is but for a moment, *is working for us a far more exceeding and eternal weight of glory*" (2 Cor. 4:17).

The tribulation era has already begun, but do we have ears to hear?

"Dominion and fear belong to Him; He makes peace in His high places" (Job 25:2).

"But even if our gospel is veiled, it is veiled to those who are perishing, [4] whose minds the god of this age has blinded, who do not believe, lest the light of the gospel of the **glory of Christ**, who is the image of God, should shine on them. [5] For we do not preach ourselves, but Christ Jesus the Lord, and ourselves your bondservants for Jesus' sake. [6] For it is the God who commanded light to shine out of darkness, who has shone in our hearts to *give* the light of the knowledge of the glory of God in the face of Jesus Christ." (2 Cor. 4:3-6).

It's all about Jesus – and God gets the glory!

16. The Lord's Victorious Dominion

The kingdom of God is all about showcasing His dominion, which He has put on display before all His enemies. The Lord has enemies on this earth and He has enemies in the heavenly realm, which is why we are suppose to engage in spiritual warfare against His enemies (which are also our enemies), because we wage war, not against flesh and blood, but against principalities and powers in the heavenly realm (Eph. 3:10; 6:12).

God is not intimidated by these, His enemies; He could smite them in the blink of an eye, but because of His great love and His eternal goodness, His enemies remain, not as a threat, but so He can show forth His great goodness "in the presence of His enemies" (Psalm 23:5). We see a type and shadow of this when the Lord kept enemies around Israel so that they may always have knowledge of war (Judges 3:1). Why the Lord keeps His enemies around so that they can watch and see if He can be accused of any wrongdoing is beyond my pay-grade; nonetheless, this is what He established – and the Lord is entitled to at least one mystery, isn't He?

Make no mistake about it – "The Lord is a man of war; The Lord is His name" (Ex. 15:3). He *WILL* vanquish all His enemies and we will all rule and reign with Him over His enemies, and we will sit as judges and magistrates in the city gates within His dominion and everlasting kingdom. When God acts to make war, we see one Person in the Godhead who was created to make and wage war: Jesus Christ. Jesus is a conquering King, a Deliverer, a Strong Tower, Mighty, and All Consuming Fire.

Many of us see Jesus returning in glory with pastoral hands and outstretched arms to lovingly embrace us, and this is true on one level – the invitation to enter through the Door of faith into salvation. When the Lord comes to each of us, this is how He appears, as one with all the loving promises of our loving heavenly Father, but when Jesus comes again "in His glory" in the clouds, He is returning first – with a winnowing fork in His hand, and then with a sickle in His hand and fire in His eyes. The Lord released the Holy Spirit upon the earth as the all consuming fire to burn away everything that does not acknowledge His lordship, and it is the Holy Spirit who sanctifies us to burn all chaff from the wheat that cannot give Him all the glory.

We see this dual-natured approach evidenced when Jesus walked upon the earth. When He was in the outlying areas, He appears pastoral, but when He gets closer to the temple of God, He creates a whip with three strands of chord whereby He begins to zealously overturn the money-changers tables. To sinners and the brokenhearted, He becomes meek just as they were meek, but when He came into the presence of His enemies, those institutionalized religious leaders who want to walk according to their doctrines and traditions, Jesus becomes a mighty force to be reckoned with; He came to pull down strongholds and to establish an everlasting dominion of truth and love in the kingdom of His Father –for His Father's glory.

Do we teach this on Sunday, or are we still trying to lead people into a mediocre salvation of greasy grace and sloppy agape by teaching a loose-goosey gospel, which is no gospel at all?

Jesus is the Victor and – through Him – the kingdom is victorious and He alone has attained the victory. Jesus only! Jesus is a Lord of conquest and victory; He was sent to earth to have dominion over the enemy and to have victory over the power of the enemy, whereby He vanquished the penalty of sin, which is death. Jesus came to take away the sin of the world, whereby the enemy is left powerless, and without the ability to have or get power, or the ability to lead people into death anymore – except by deception. Jesus came as one who was hidden, as a mystery known only to the Father, to accomplish all that He was sent to do in order to become the righteousness of God upon the earth – so that He may be revealed according to who He really is: the Resurrection and the Life!

If we choose to walk in sin or any unrighteousness that leads to death, then that is your choice, but this is not the nature of the Lord's dominion that He established in His Father's kingdom. We have been set free from the bondage of sin that results in death so that we can do one thing: return to our mission – and have dominion. The kingdom was delivered to Jesus – and Jesus returned it to us as He ascended into heaven.

When – are we going to realize that we have been given many great and wonderful promises – and to start walking these out (living) in faith? The reason we don't believe in all the encouragement and self-help books that tell us to walk in the promises of God is because we do not appropriate the power that has been made available to walk therein. We claim the promise and then declare it with our mouth, we put banners over our doorways and bumper stickers on our cars to help us get into the mood of walking in the promises, but these efforts fail because of one reason only: there was no power.

The promises of God are only as good as the power that is being made available to walk in these promises; otherwise, these become empty promises that are "mere hopes" filled with false expectations. But – when we have been completely sacrificed upon the alter of God by an act of our own self will, then and only then, is the Lord able to perform according to His promise. Why would He want to fill us up with so many great and wonderful promises, including the power that enables us to walk therein, if we are only going to be using them to build our kingdom? Why, indeed!

We need to adjust our thoughts and affections to embrace a new paradigm of thought that sees everything from His Divine perspective. Stop looking at your neighbor, yourself, your circumstances and situations, your nation, your courts and electorate… just stop looking around – and focus all your attention and affections upon Christ. Jesus only! In order to begin the journey of "in," we need to embrace the gospel of grace in its fullest sense. You were born into death and you lived life as a dead man walking in the midst of sin; the only way you are getting out of earth alive is if you reckon yourself fully dead in order to be crucified on the cross of Jesus by faith in Christ alone. And this faith is not a one-time profession with the mouth; it is a continual dying to self daily, to lay down all your agendas and to come to the Lord with empty hands, stretched outward toward Him, so that He can give you His promise: carry your cross.

What, you say? I was promised so many great and wonderful promises, and God does not want us to suffer – and God wants me to be happy. Yes, this is true at one level, for converts who initially come to faith in Christ because He promises to save us into a better way, but He also promises to deliver us from the pit of destruction as we walk in maturity in the deep things of Christ. Jesus does not want skim milk dependent or lactose-intolerant babies, He is looking for mighty men and women who know His will and will faithfully do all that He commands – and have dominion. Well, do you want the gospel you want – or the gospel that is?

Meat is for those who have grown weary of milk only.

Things are about to start heating up and speeding up; the kingdom is in the pre-birth phase when the pangs will be felt by all believers – and I mean all. We will have a choice to make; either we will go out to work in the field like we were asked to – or we won't. Jesus has invited us into His kingdom on His terms to do His will for the glory of the Father, but if you want to continue standing in between two ways, then that is your free-will choice. However, if you consider yourself a servant of the Most High God, then Jesus is going to expect you to hear Him, follow Him, obey Him and He will ask you to get ready – because the beginning of the end of this age is about to begin. This will be a time when we will not have time to drink milk and think. The Lord will tell us to act and we need to be prepared to act – in the moment He tells us to. If we are told to go here or there, or to do this or that, or to say this or that, then we must obey, because we are a faithful servant who trusts in the Lord – and His plan of dominion!

Our first act of preparation is to learn how to hear His voice. "***For who, having heard, rebelled?***" (Heb. 3:16). We accomplish this simply by removing two of the three voices we hear. First, silence the enemy. Second, silence your thoughts and imaginations. Third, get still and wait. Perceive this moment (for yourself) as someone who is standing in a very large crowd and you are looking forward, as is everyone else, to focus on "the One" who is calling names. Everyone is silent and motionless, and when you hear your name called, you take one step forward and immediately – you are in His presence. And your response is, "I am here to do Your will, Lord, what do you want me to do for You?"

Our second act is to hear – and understand. We must know this according to the fullness of '*oida*' understanding, having prepared our hearts and minds beforehand, to recognize His voice so that we can know His will and do it – in His name, in His power, and in His authority.

Our third act is to hear – and obey. No ifs, ands, maybes or buts. Let your yes be yes.

Some of us will be given wonderful jobs to do, and others will get dirty jobs to do. Some will stand before princes and kings, and some will hold the hands of lepers. Some will make peace, and others will wage war. Some will plant and build up, and others will tear down. The age of all things for the building up and the encouraging of the saints is fine inside the church, but when we are sent into the world, we will do as we are told. "We are in the world, but not of it" (John 17:16 paraphrased).

We are residents of a heavenly kingdom and our citizenship is in heaven, but we have been sent to earth to do the will of the Lord on this earth – as the sons of men – so that we may attain, once again, our rightful title as "sons of God." In this final determination, even the creation waits *also* for the glorious revealing of the sons of God. We are here to establish His everlasting dominion by invading earth with the atmosphere of heaven.

When we are done, what will this earthly dominion look like? Well, simply put, it will be heaven on earth. Yes, when we die, we are all going to heaven, but the new heaven and the new earth that we are going to – will be a unified heaven and earth, in glorious oneness, "as it was in the beginning, now and forever shall be, world without end. Amen."

Do you remember praying this creed before? Well, it is absolutely true. The world will end, and it will be regenerated into newness and untied once again in oneness with heaven. There will be no more division once Jesus comes again to restore the kingdom – in oneness of one – and only One. And we will be raised to newness according to the resurrection of Christ, into newness of life in Christ, so that we are no longer living as sheep in darkness without a Shepherd, and no one will say to his brother, "know the Lord, for all will understand the Lord" (Heb. 8:11).

So, by grace through faith in Jesus Christ, you will receive a glorified body in a glorified heaven and earth that have been united in oneness as "the new heaven in an everlasting kingdom of His dominion;" so where do you think the sons of men are going to reside for all eternity? If you can see the truth for what it is, then that's great! We will all be living as glorified sons of God "in the kingdom of heaven upon the earth" as His workmanship within Christ's dominion that resides within the kingdom of God.

The problem we have with understanding who we are and what we are to do is because we are more focused upon our concept of what heaven is instead of focusing all our attention and affections upon Christ alone.

Can you imagine just how wonderful it will be to walk in all the promises of God with Jesus by your side? How incredibly wonderful and marvelous and glorious! But – these promises are fulfilled only when we remain in His presence, both now *and* forever more.

We need to come into His presence daily, by prayer, and to meditate upon the Lord and to seek His kingdom come so that we also become His will being done. His will is being accomplished on earth as it is in heaven – and in us as well. We are living in a one bifurcated kingdom where Jesus is Lord of heaven and earth, currently now in division, but soon in unity – and thereafter in multiplication glory and magnificence.

"My soul does magnify the Lord, and my spirit rejoices in God my Savior (Jesus Christ)." This is the Magnificat of Mary, when it was revealed to her by an angel that she would be the servant who brings Christ into the world. And this same truth is our truth as well. With Christ in you, go *also* into the world, as an obedient servant, to do His will according to the miraculous '*dunamis*' power that is at work within you. Jesus has given us His authority to do it, and He has given us His *dunamis* power to do it, and He has commanded us to do it – so – what are we waiting for? A better offer? Christmas? The End Time? Rapture? The end time is already upon us, which is why I write so feverishly about the kingdom which has been revealed to me. I write what I am told to write about – and I do it for God's glory, not mine; otherwise, I would be writing for profit instead of languishing in abasement, but indeed, it is all for His glory – according to His dominion in His Father's kingdom.

We must no longer be standing in between two ways. If Jesus is Lord God, then do what He says. Listen – and understand. Listen – and obey. The days are quickly getting shorter.

It's all about Jesus – and God gets the glory!

Read the entire Image Bearer series!

Grace and peace be yours in abundance, paul.

Made in the USA
Middletown, DE
12 November 2018